Bloom's Modern Critical Interpretations

Bloom's Modern Critical Interpretations

Richard Wright's
Native Son
New Edition

Edited and with an introduction by
Harold Bloom
Sterling Professor of the Humanities
Yale University

BLOOM'S
LITERARY CRITICISM
An imprint of Infobase Publishing

Editorial Consultant, Brian Johnson

**Bloom's Modern Critical Interpretations: Richard Wright's *Native Son*—
New Edition**
Copyright ©2009 by Infobase Publishing

Introduction ©2009 by Harold Bloom

Bloom's Literary Criticism
An imprint of Infobase Publishing
132 West 31st Street
New York NY 10001

Library of Congress Cataloging-in-Publication Data

Richard Wright's *Native Son* / edited and with an introduction by Harold Bloom—
New ed.
p. cm.—(Bloom's Modern Critical Interpretations)
Includes bibliographical references and index.
ISBN 978-0-7910-9625-3 (alk. paper)
1. Wright, Richard, 1908–1960. *Native Son.* 2. Thomas, Bigger (Fictitious
character) 3. African American men in literature. 4. Trials (Murder) in literature. 5.
Murder in literature. 6. American literature—History and criticism. I. Bloom, Harold.
II. Title: *Native Son.*
PS3545.R815N3443 2008
813'.52—dc22

                                                 2008031372

Bloom's Literary Criticism books are available at special discounts when purchased in
bulk quantities for businesses, associations, institutions, or sales promotions. Please call
our Special Sales Department in New York at (212) 967-8800 or (800) 322-8755.

You can find Bloom's Literary Criticism on the World Wide Web at
http://www.chelseahouse.com.

Cover design by Ben Peterson

Printed in the United States of America
Bang BCL 10 9 8 7 6 5 4 3 2 1

This book is printed on acid-free paper.

All links and Web addresses were checked and verified to be correct at the time of
publication. Because of the dynamic nature of the Web, some addresses and links may
have changed since publication and may no longer be valid.

Contents

Editor's Note

My Introduction is totally at variance with the essays reprinted here. I have no apologies for this, even if in old age I verge upon being the pariah of my profession. The pungency of my remarks stands, since they involve the primacy of the aesthetic in regard to what purports to be a novel.

Kathleen Gallagher sees Bigger as a metaphor, while Tony Magistrale ponders the influence of *Crime and Punishment* upon *Native Son*, and Alan W. France reflects upon Wright's misogyny.

Kimberly W. Benston uncovers African-American modernism while for Alessandro Portelli, *Native Son* benefits by being restored to its contemporary critical scene, after which Lale Demiturk considers Bigger an apt student of white society.

Desmond Harding studies the Spirit of Place, while Damon Marcel DeCoste gives us the politics of realism.

Spectacle engages Jonathan Elmer, and drama intrigues Hazel Rowley, in two gallant attempts to shift the grounds of judgment.

Mark Decker concludes this volume by contemplating the gap between legality and social justice.

HAROLD BLOOM

Introduction

RICHARD WRIGHT'S *NATIVE SON*

Bigger Thomas, the protagonist of *Native Son,* can be said to have become a myth without first having been a convincing representation of human character and personality. Richard Wright listed five "Biggers" he had encountered in actuality, five violent youths called "bad Niggers" by the whites. The most impressive, Bigger No. 5, was a knife-wielding, prideful figure "who always rode the Jim Crow streetcars without paying and sat wherever he pleased." For this group of precursors of his own protagonist in *Native Son,* Wright gave us a moving valediction:

> The Bigger Thomases were the only Negroes I know of who consistently violated the Jim Crow laws of the South and got away with it, at least for a sweet brief spell. Eventually, the whites who restricted their lives made them pay a terrible price. They were shot, hanged, maimed, lynched, and generally hounded until they were either dead or their spirits broken.

Wright concluded this same "Introduction" to *Native Son* with his own vision of the United States as of March 7, 1940:

> I feel that I'm lucky to be alive to write novels today, when the whole world is caught in the pangs of war and change. Early American writers, Henry James and Nathaniel Hawthorne, complained bitterly about the bleakness and flatness of the American scene. But I think that if they were alive, they'd feel at home in modern America. True, we have no great church in America; our national

1

traditions are still of such a sort that we are not wont to brag of them; and we have no army that's above the level of mercenary fighters; we have no group acceptable to the whole of our country upholding certain humane values; we have no rich symbols, no colorful rituals. We have only a money-grubbing, industrial civilization. But we do have in the Negro the embodiment of a past tragic enough to appease the spiritual hunger of even a James; and we have in the oppression of the Negro a shadow athwart our national life dense and heavy enough to satisfy even the gloomy broodings of a Hawthorne. And if Poe were alive, he would not have to invent horror; horror would invent him.

The citation of James, Hawthorne, and Poe is gratuitous, and the perspective upon the United States in the months preceding the fall of France lacks authority and precision, even in its diction. But the dense and heavy shadow athwart our national life indubitably was there, always had been there, and for many is there still. That shadow is Richard Wright's mythology, and his embryonic strength. He was not found by Henry James, or by Hawthorne, or by Poe, and scarcely would have benefited by such a finding. A legitimate son of Theodore Dreiser, he nevertheless failed to write in *Native Son* a *Sister Carrie* or a new version of *An American Tragedy*. The reality of being a gifted young black in the United States of the 1930s and 1940s proved too oppressive for the limited purposes of a narrative fiction. Rereading *Native Son* is an experience of renewing the dialectical awareness of history and society, but is not in itself an aesthetic experience.

And yet, I do not think that *Native Son,* and its reception, present us with a merely aesthetic dilemma. In the "afterword" to a paperback reprint of *Native Son,* one of Wright's followers, John Reilly, defends Bigger Thomas by asserting that: "The description of Mary's murder makes clear that the white world is the cause of the violent desires and reactions" that led Bigger to smother poor Mary. I would think that what the description makes clear enough is that Bigger is indeed somewhat overdetermined, but to ascribe the violence of his desires and reactions to any context whatsoever is to reduce him to the status of a replicant or of a psychopathic child. The critical defenders of *Native Son* must choose. Either Bigger Thomas is a responsible consciousness, and so profoundly culpable, or else only the white world is responsible and culpable, which means however that Bigger ceases to be of fictive interest and becomes an ideogram, rather than a persuasive representation of a possible human being. Wright, coming tragically early in what was only later to become his own tradition, was not able to choose, and so left us with something between an ideological image, and the mimesis of an actuality.

KATHLEEN GALLAGHER

Bigger's Great Leap to the Figurative

That in a racist society blacks become criminals by virtue of their very existence is a predominant theme of Richard Wright's fiction. His criminals run the gamut from Big Boy and Mann to Cross Damon—from the illiterate victim of oppression, who acts in explicit self-defense, to the intellectual "ethical criminal," who acts to reshape the world to meet a self-definition. Other criminals fall between the extremes. Silas, of "Long Black Song," kills a white man who has had sexual relations with his wife. Tyree Tucker, of *The Long Dream*, controls gambling and prostitution rings which exploit blacks for his own aggrandizement and that of corrupt whites.

Wright implies that whether his characters become convictable criminals or not is largely a question of luck, context, and semantics. In the eyes of the dominant society, they are guilty and not to be proved innocent. Some may avoid an actively criminal role, as Fishbelly does by fleeing to Paris, or as many characters do by observing society's rules and remaining inconspicuous. Some may embrace or flaunt the role, like Cross Damon, Tyree, or Fred Daniels of "The Man Who Lived Underground." But they all are finally in the position of Big Boy, who, simply by being black and being in the wrong place at the wrong time, finds the role of criminal thrust upon him and a lynch mob at his heels. Even Wright's autobiographical protagonist in *Black Boy* ultimately resorts to theft to finance his family's exodus from the South. As

College Language Association Journal, Volume 27, Number 3 (March 1984): pp. 293–314. Copyright © 1984 College Language Association.

Robert Bone has said, Wright, like his fictional heroes, knows that the crime for which he will be punished is "the crime of being black."[1]

In *Native Son*, Wright develops most explicitly the metaphor of potential criminality that haunts much of his work. The crime for which Bigger Thomas is condemned to death, the killing of a young white woman in her bed, is a metaphor that represents the meaning of Bigger's life. Lest the point be missed, Bigger's Communist lawyer, Boris Max, will say with emphasis at the trial: *"His very existence is a crime against the state!"*[2]

Although it has received a good deal of scholarly attention, the imagery of *Native Son*, in general, is less compelling than what the book has to say about images. *Native Son* might be said to be about Bigger's perception of images. It is about his struggle to understand and control the metaphor of his own life. Bigger, who begins by refusing to confront the terrible reality of his life, at the end glimpses the truth: "I didn't want to kill! . . . But what I killed for, I *am*!" (p. 358). He comes to a comprehension of the metaphor as a result of his growing understanding of the partial and false images that have defined his being. Images at first cloud the truth for Bigger, but his growing ability to understand and control them launches him toward a deeper understanding of reality. By the end of the book, he will make the great leap from the literal to the figurative.

In Book One of *Native Son*, Bigger is dominated by images that he cannot control. Because of the false images or stereotypes that govern whites' perceptions of blacks, he is offered no acceptable image of who he is or what he might become. Because of his own partial image of whites, he lives in continual hate and fear. He fragments the reality of both worlds, keeping the painful truth of his own world at bay and creating a fantasy white world which he peoples with his own cast of stereotyped characters.

In the opening pages of the book, Wrights portrays the conditions that have shaped Bigger and which make up reality as he knows it. His family's morning ritual of turning their backs so the others can dress in their one-room tenant apartment is abruptly interrupted by the appearance of a large, black rat. They take battle positions like well-trained troops, but the scene conveys the violence, shame, and fear that never become routine to the Thomases despite the frequency of their occurrence.

By the time we meet Bigger he is a full-blown juvenile delinquent of age twenty. He is surly and rebellious, alienated from his family and friends. He often carries a gun and a knife. His relationship with his girl friend, Bessie, is held together with little more than liquor and sex. He is as close as possible to being that unthinkable child that not even a mother can love. She says, "Bigger, sometimes I wonder why I birthed you" (p. 7). Because the reality of his world is too frightening to confront, Bigger filters it through a mental curtain: "He knew that the moment he allowed himself to feel to its fulness how they lived, the shame and misery of their lives, he would be swept out of himself with fear and despair. So he held toward them an attitude of iron reserve; he lived with them; but behind a wall, a curtain. And toward himself he was even more exacting" (p. 9).

It is, of course, the white world that has set the narrow limits of the black world and forced Bigger to retreat behind his self-protective curtain. Bigger's notions of the white world are derived primarily from the mass media and are the stuff of one of his sustaining modes of escape. White men, to Bigger, are presidents, generals, and corporate executives. When he and his friend Gus "play white," they mimic the voices and manners of men of power. White women are promiscuous "rich chicks," like the featured character in a movie Bigger sees, *The Gay Woman*, who floats between "scenes of cocktail drinking, dancing, golfing, swimming, and spinning roulette wheels" (p. 26). Bigger has a passing acquaintance with the notion of "poor whites," but he dismisses it: "Poor white people were stupid" (p. 29). Bigger has no class-consciousness at all, whites are the glamorous rich he sees in the movies, and he is fascinated by his glimpses into their lives.

By sending Bigger into the Dalton household as a live-in chauffeur, Wright plunges him swiftly and dramatically the heart of the white world. Here the stereotypes loom more menacingly. Bigger can "play white" with Gus and be entertained by the whites in the movies because he restricts the white world to a comfortable cast of well-defined stock characters. Since these stereotypes are images of his own creation, he can control them. His perception of the real white world, however, is more closely represented in the vague, gothic whiteness of the blind Mrs. Dalton and her ubiquitous, Poe-like cat.[3] Later, he perceives her as a white blur, a white blur that will terrify him throughout most of the book. For Bigger, the white world is a "looming mountain of white hate" (p. 246). At the trial, Max will describe the distortive barriers set up between races and classes by stereotypes and false images. Rather than people facing people, he says, "They feel that they are facing mountains, floods, seas: forces of nature . . ." (p. 327).

In their misguided attempt at improving race relations, Mary Dalton and her Communist boy friend, Jan Erlone, succeed only in magnifying the color-line for Bigger. Mary and Jan use Bigger to fill a role that they are defining for him: they simply change the role from black servant to black proletarian. Their presumption is little more than a variation on Mr. Dalton's refusal to rent housing to blacks in white neighborhoods because "Negroes are happier when they're together" (p. 278). In a scene Bigger will recall throughout the book, Jan insists that the two of them shake hands. They pose as if for a propaganda poster, while Mary laughs softly and says, "It's all right, Bigger . . . Jan *means* it." Bigger feels violated and painfully self-aware: "It was a shadowy region, a No Man's Land, the ground that separated the white world from the black that he stood upon. He felt naked, transparent; he felt that this white man, having helped to put him down, having helped to deform him, held him up now to look at him and be amused" (p. 58).

Mary and Jan force a further conjunction of the black and white worlds by insisting that Bigger accompany them to a black restaurant on the South Side. As Dan McCall has noted, Jan and Mary regress further into stereotypes as they become more drunk.[4] Mary becomes a self-parody as she coaxes Bigger to help her sing a spiritual and, after Jan has left, flirts with Bigger and puts her head on his shoulder. When Mary passes out trying to climb the stairs of the Dalton house, Bigger finds himself in a rather traditional servant's role after all; having had their fun, Mary and Jan have left Bigger to protect both them and himself by cleaning up the mess. Quietly he carries Mary upstairs and locates her room, thinking, "Well, all they could do was fire him. It wasn't his fault that she was drunk" (p. 72).

Bigger suddenly has been dragged further into the No Man's Land between the black and white worlds than he ever has been in his life. He smothers Mary on her "white bed" with a pillow in "hysterical terror" when he hears the door creak and turns to see Mrs. Dalton, like a "white blur . . . standing by the door, silent, ghostlike" (p. 73). Bigger has no thought of killing Mary; his intention is to keep her quiet so that Mrs. Dalton will not come over to the bed and discover him. He puts first his hand and then the edge of the pillow over Mary's mouth. The pity of it is that Bigger succeeds only in encouraging Mrs. Dalton to approach. Attracted by the muffled noises, she moves closer to the bed. When she smells the odor of whiskey on Mary, Mrs. Dalton first becomes angry, then kneels by Mary's bed to pray before leaving the room. In killing Mary, Bigger achieves no purpose at all.

Wherever one turns, it is ultimately because of the racism of the white world that Bigger kills Mary. Bigger does not for a moment consider his course of action rationally. He acts as Wright says he himself once acted in a childhood misadventure: "I did not think; I did not plan; I did not plot. Instinct told me what to do. There was painful danger and I had to avoid it."[5] Bigger is "intimidated to the core by the awesome white blur floating toward him" (p. 74). Although he knows that the white blur is Mrs. Dalton, it is not until Mary has stopped struggling that he can "see Mrs. Dalton plainly." Over three hundred years of conditioning tell him the implications of his being found in the unconscious Mary's room, and he acts in response to a racial prototype rather than to the specifics of the situations. Mrs. Dalton is a white blur; Mary is a white body to be silenced; Bigger himself is a quivering black mass of terror and taut nerves.

In terms of the essential, almost archetypal, conflict Bigger is a victim of his environment: the killing is an accident, and Bigger is innocent. Without denying the truth of this view of events, Wright shows that reality is considerably more complex and even ironic. Mrs. Dalton is not really a blur of white vengeance. In his terror, Bigger forgets his earlier opinion that she would always judge him fairly. He has no way of knowing that Mary has caused trouble for her parents before, that the Daltons dislike Jan, that there is a very reasonable possibility that Mrs. Dalton would believe the truth and that Mary herself probably would confirm it. With good historical reason, Bigger has feared all along that the Daltons somehow would hold him responsible for the entire evening. All along, he has known that because he is black he is guilty.

Bigger is further predisposed to act as if he is guilty, however, because his own actions have been less than praiseworthy. As he brings Mary upstairs, he becomes aware that despite his hatred for Mary he is physically attracted to her. When Mrs. Dalton comes in, he has kissed Mary twice and is leaning over the bed with his hands on her breasts. Wright supplies Bigger with specific grounds for his guilty response, but he again backs the situation into racism. Mary and Bigger both are victims of the mystique of the black man and the white woman: neither her flirtation nor his later response has much to do with anything but race. Wright thus twists together social and individual guilt in the circumstances of the crime itself. A racist stereotype is at the root of Bigger's fear, but he has acted in accord with the stereotype.

The crime has two effects on Bigger: it gives him an identity for the first time in his life, but it also drives him to such a frenzy of fear and guilt that he quickly brings on his own destruction. Not once does Bigger consider shirking responsibility for murder. As soon as he realizes that Mary is dead, he accepts the image of himself that he knows society will see: "The reality of the room fell away from him; the vast city of white people that sprawled outside took its place. She was dead and he had killed her. He was a murderer, a Negro murderer, a black murderer. He had killed a white woman" (p. 75).

As he accepts the role society has assigned him, he comes from behind his wall of indifference. He now has a way to act, an image with which to conform, and he acts like a murderer. He begins to think, plot, and plan: what to tell the Daltons, how to burn Mary's body in the furnace, how to cast the blame for Mary's disappearance on Jan and the Communists, how to go about acting normally so that no one will suspect. With a definite role to play, he feels that he can control himself and other people, even white people, for the first time. What actually has happened is that, without understanding fully, Bigger has sensed that the symbolic truth of the image is greater than the literal truth of what has occurred:

> And in a certain sense he knew that the girl's death had not been accidental. He had killed many times before, only on those other times there had been no handy victim or circumstance to make

visible or dramatic his will to kill. . . . The hidden meaning of his life—a meaning which others did not see and which he had always tried to hide—had spilled out. No; it was no accident, and he would never say that it was. (p. 90)

In Book Two, Bigger learns to manipulate the images. With his wall of indifference down, he is able to look directly at both the white and black worlds for the first time. At home with his family the morning after the crime, he begins to see things that he has never permitted himself to see before. He sees the shabbiness of their lives and the passivity of their response to it. He also begins to perceive another metaphor that permeates *Native Son* to the saturation point, that of blindness.[6] Mrs. Dalton's physical blindness, without benefit of which Bigger could not have killed Mary, is symptomatic of the mental blindness that handicaps everyone in the book. Bigger now sees that his family, like everyone else, "wanted and yearned to see life in a certain way; they needed a certain picture of the world . . . and they were blind to what did not fit" (p. 91). Later, Jan will realize that he has been blind; Max will cite the Daltons' blindness at the trial; Bessie will realize that she has been "just a blind dumb black drunk fool" (p. 195); Bigger eventually will wonder if he saw everyone's blindness but his own.

The practical implication of Bigger's awareness of everyone's blindness is that he can use it to make himself invisible as a criminal. He assumes that people will see what they want to see; whatever does not fit their preconceived image will be discarded. Bigger has always known what whites want to see. The role works in two directions, pleasing them and permitting him to disguise his real feelings. His entire manner changed when he first entered the Dalton household; the surly, sassy Bigger became obsequious and softspoken. His lack of practice with the role made him play it nervously, but he did it well enough to pass inspection: "There was an organic conviction in him that this was the way white folks wanted him to be when in their presence; none had ever told him that in so many words, but their manner had made him feel that they did" (p. 42).

Now Bigger is able to use the stereotype consciously. If he conforms well enough to the preconceived image, no one will suspect him of being anything else: "Now, who on earth would think that he, a black timid Negro boy, would murder and burn a rich white girl and would sit and wait for his breakfast like this? Elation filled him" (p. 91). Living has become a great game for Bigger, a game to which only he knows the rule: "[A]ct like other people thought you ought to act, yet do what you wanted" (p. 96). He has done that all his life, he thinks, but now he sees it "sharply and simply."

Bigger has become a conscious dealer in stereotypes. He has made rapid strides in his ability to perceive and analyze. But his vision is only partial. He does not see that while he is manipulating the "obsequious servant" stereotype, he is being manipulated by another stereotype which he has chosen to assume, that of the "bad nigger."[7] Although he has acted like a "bad nigger" for much of his life, even with his family and friends, now he seizes the role with a vengeance. In the supposed rape and murder of a white woman, the image is fully realized. Bigger thinks, in effect, that if that is what society thinks he is, then that is what he will be; if he has wished and felt these things, then he will do them; if he will be judged guilty anyway, then he will be guilty. He will be the quintessential "bad nigger," all the while acting the role of "timid Negro boy." Because he controls one stereotype, he thinks he controls the situation. It is only on an emotional level that he knows that he is still a victim, and it is his emotions that will do him in.

Reaction to Bigger's characterization, especially in earlier years, has sometimes been negative. In one of the most influential commentaries, James Baldwin said that in the story of Bigger, Wright through his own subconscious rage inadvertently created "a continuation, a complement of that monstrous legend it was written to destroy." In his dispute with Irving Howe over Wright's impact, Ralph Ellison said that *Native Son* begins "with the ideological proposition that what whites think of the Negro's reality is more important than what Negroes themselves know it to be." In a strongly worded objection to the Bigger stereotype, Nathan Scott said that the book offers "a depraved and inhuman beast as the comprehensive archetypal image of the American Negro."[8]

But Wright was consciously using the stereotype. McCall perhaps says it best when he notes that Wright is "exploring the empirical truths of the passions that sustain the stereotype" and that Wright provides within the book the "artistic and moral equipment" to perceive a reality beneath the superficial one.[9] Margolies is only partially correct in saying that the arguments about the Bigger stereotype fall outside of aesthetics.[10] Unlike many of the charges against Styron's *The Confessions of Nat Turner*, for example, which tend to challenge the validity of Styron's statement in the book, the charges against Bigger cloud Wright's statement altogether. Wright knew what he was doing: Bigger's assumption of, and victimization by, stereotypes lies at the heart of the action of *Native Son*.

The rape and murder of Bessie are a mirror image of what Bigger is thought to have done to Mary. He becomes as nearly the animal that the whites assume him to be as is possible: the rape is a completely irrational act, and he bashes Bessie's skull with a brick, much as he had killed the rat. These deeds are superfluous to the plot, since it is the supposed rape and murder of the white woman for which Bigger will be condemned, not the known rape and murder of the black woman. Bigger already has accepted responsibility for raping and murdering Mary because he sees in those acts an objective correlative for his violent mental response to the white world. Of the murder, he thought that he had killed many times before, even though there were no corpses to show for it. When Bessie first points out to him that because he has destroyed Mary's body, the whites will assume that he raped her, he at first reacts with shock but then embraces this crime too. Again he sees that the symbolic truth carries greater weight than the literal:

> Had he raped her? Yes, he had raped her. Every time he felt as he had felt that night, he raped. But rape was not what one did to women. Rape was what one felt when one's back was against a wall and one had to strike out, whether one wanted to or not, to keep the pack from killing one. He committed rape every time he looked into a white face. (p. 193)

But Wright seems not to have been content to let Bigger's acceptance of guilt stand on its own. He wants to be very clear that Bigger's calling himself a rapist and a murderer is neither a romantic gesture nor some sort of psychotic delusion. Just as the state's attorney delights in having a corpse to display ghoulishly at the inquest, Wright flourishes Bessie's body to keep us from becoming hung up on Bigger's literal innocence of the crime for which he will be condemned to death.

Book Three of *Native Son* in a sense comprises two stories. The public story, made up of the trial and its attendant crowds, speeches, and newspaper headlines, is for the most part a predictable elaboration on ideas that already have been presented more dramatically through the action of the book. The private story of Bigger's attempt to find out what his life has meant before he has to die is the continuation of the story told from his point of view in Books One and Two. Within Wright's framework, both stories must be told, but the major weakness of *Native Son* is that Wright handles the balance between his two stories clumsily and never establishes any compelling link between them. Moreover, the private story, which contains the conflict that continues to develop, tends to be overshadowed by the speechifying and is torpedoed by a subversion of Bigger's point of view in the last few pages of the book.

It is the private story with which we are concerned here. With his capture, at the close of Book Two, Bigger is temporarily thrown back into passivity. His brief reign as the King of No Man's Land having ended, he rejects reality once again and retreats further behind his mental curtain than he ever has before. In Book Three, as he awaits his trial and execution, he must start from scratch in defining the reality of his life. He begins to see that in embracing the false images he has succeeded only in playing himself further into the hands of the white world. As the stereotypes crumble, he sees that he has let himself be used as a piece in someone else's image pattern.

One set of images that Bigger has rejected steadily throughout the book is that offered by Christianity. His mother's singing of hymns and spirituals while she works had been a continual source of annoyance to him. While he was in flight in Book Two, he overheard singing from a black church. The music was full of "surrender, resignation" and the belief that "all life was a sorrow that had to be accepted" (p. 214). When he is visited in prison by his mother's minister, the Reverend Hammond, he is again briefly drawn toward this ordered view of reality. Although he loathes the preacher's message, he responds to the configuration of images which the preacher presents: "They were images which had once given him a reason for living, had explained the world. Now they sprawled before his eyes and seized his emotions in a spell of awe and wonder" (p. 241). But Bigger will not accept his mother's solution simply as a way to die. He permits the Reverend Hammond to hang a cross around his neck. Later, when he associates that cross with the burning cross of the Ku Klux Klan, he will throw the preacher, his Bible, and his cross forcibly out of his cell.

Jan Erlone visits Bigger next, and this encounter proves more significant. Because he had attempted to frame Jan for Mary's disappearance, Bigger is "galvanized by fear" at the sight of him. But what Jan has to say quickly startles Bigger out of his fear. Jan says that although he was angry at first, now he understands why Bigger killed. Now he wants to break the pattern of racial vengeance by helping rather than hating Bigger, and he has a friend, a lawyer, who wants to help Bigger, too.

Wright is quite explicit about the effect Jan has on Bigger. In several stories in *Uncle Tom's Cabin*, Wright uses "erlone" as a dialect spelling of "alone." The impact Jan has on Bigger is unique and irreversible: he offers Bigger an escape from No Man's Land through a transcendence of the boundaries of the black and white worlds. Wright describes Bigger's experience as an almost religious and mystical one:

> Suddenly, this white man had come up to him, flung aside the curtain and walked into the room of his life. Jan had spoken a declaration of friendship that would make other white men hate him: a particle of white rock had detached itself from that looming mountain of white hate and had rolled down the slope, stopping still at his feet. The word had become flesh. For the first time in his life a white man became a human being to him; and the reality of Jan's humanity came in a stab of remorse: he had killed what this man loved and had hurt him. He saw Jan as though someone had performed an operation upon his eyes, or as though someone had snatched a deforming mask from Jan's face. (p. 246)

Where religion has failed Bigger by its rejection of humanity for another world, humanity itself offers him redemption. That Jan's forgiving nobility is not entirely credible is less important than it might be because of the emphasis Wright places on Bigger's role in the experience. Bigger is not just the passive recipient of the white man's enlightenment. Wright describes a reciprocal process that gives responsibility and control to Bigger. Because Jan sees that Bigger is human, Bigger is able to see that Jan is human. It is Bigger's recognition of Jan's humanity that breaks the color-line for him, that makes him feel remorse, and that offers him the chance to stop being a "No Man" and join the human race. Through Jan, Bigger begins to see through the image of the white mountain.

Despite its importance, what has occurred is only the beginning of an idea for Bigger, and he soon is confronted with other people and events that sweep him back into shame, despair, and hate. He is intimidated by Buckley, the swaggering, cigar-chewing state's attorney. He is terrified at the appearance of the Daltons and mortified by the behavior of his family and friends. While the public story marches to its foregone conclusion, Bigger continues his attempt to find a center of stability. The doings of the trial affect him emotionally at times, but his own conflicts are substantially independent of the arguments flying over his head. Bigger's confession to Buckley is born of a need to explain the overwhelming feelings that made him act as he did: "'the impulsion to try to tell was as deep as had been the urge to kill" (p. 262). But the literal synopsis of the action that Buckley seeks and gets is not what Bigger craves. Wright says that "the telling of it would have involved an explanation of his entire life" (p. 262) and that "there were no words for him" (p. 263) to explain how he felt.

The emotional fluctuation that has been part of Bigger since the beginning of the book has become a vortex that spins faster and faster. With his capture, he entered a new spiral between the hope suggested by his brief feelings of kinship with Jan and the despair engendered by Buckley and the whites who want to destroy him like a "black lizard." As he has become more aware, he also has become more susceptible to pain. Having decided that he will trust no one, he is dragged into this last major cycle through a conversation with Max.

Max comes to talk with Bigger in order to prepare his defense. Their talk is quite unremarkable, so unremarkable that Max later forgets that they had it at all, and the tremendous weight that it carries for Bigger can only be an index to his desperation for human contact. Max asks Bigger about the crime and about his life. Some of his questions and reactions seem insensitive; he says nothing brilliant or terribly perceptive. What is remarkable from Bigger's point of view is that for the first time someone has sat and listened to him talk about how he has felt about his life. The action is all Bigger's; Max provides the long-sought opportunity "to talk, to tell, to try to make his feelings known" (p. 295).

Bigger's reaction to this conversation may be a shade too much on the scale of Saul's on the road to Damascus, but Bigger is a creature of extremes who has waited a long time for his letter from the world. In Max's listening, he "felt a recognition of his life, of his feelings, of his person that he had never encountered before" (p. 305). He begins to wonder whether other people, even those who hate him, have the same kinds of feelings that he has. He senses the possibility of "a supporting oneness, a wholeness" (p. 307) to life that he had not perceived before. Relating this conversation to his earlier one with Jan, he sees the possibility of relationships "that he had never dreamed of": "If that white looming mountain of hate were not a mountain at all, but people, people like himself, and like Jan—then he was faced with a high hope the like of which he had never thought could be, and a despair the full depths of which he knew he could not stand to feel" (p. 306).

Bigger is unable to follow all these tantalizing new thoughts on his own. He is pressured into a frenzy by the shortness of the time he has left. Max, who is utterly unaware of what has been wrought, is too busy with the trial to talk with Bigger. When the judge hands down a death sentence, Bigger falls into a new despair, since "life was over without meaning, without anything being settled, without conflicting impulses being resolved" (p. 349). He longs to talk with Max, yet he has no idea what he will say when he has the opportunity: "He could not talk about this thing, so elusive it was; and yet he acted upon it every living second" (p. 351). He struggles to bring the words, the images, and his life together.

Max finally comes to the prison on the day Bigger is to be executed, having failed in his last appeal to the governor to save Bigger's life. Bigger has anticipated this meeting so much that at first he is unable to verbalize anything at all: "Then fear that he would not be able to talk about this consuming fever made him panicky. He struggled for self-control; he did not want to lose this driving impulse; it was all he had" (p. 352). In part, he has assigned Max such a godlike role that this last contact between them is his alone, that "any sure and firm knowledge . . . would have to come from himself" (p. 350). When at first he is unable to speak, he blames Max and is angry: Max does not understand, Max has left him, Max is no longer his friend. A shaft of sunlight then bathes his cell and his own body, and his physical situation suddenly becomes so "crushingly real" to him that he tries again: "He summoned his energies and lifted his head and struck out desperately, determined to rise from the grave, resolved to force upon Max the reality of his living" (p. 353).

After several false starts, Bigger does force Max onto his own wave-length, but the conversation that follows is a monument to human weakness. Bigger is still borderline-hysterical; he expresses himself shrilly and in fits and starts.

Although Max's concern for Bigger is genuine, his ability to make speeches does not qualify him as a master of intimate conversation. He reacts as the average person would when asked by a condemned man, "How can I die?"

What Bigger really wants to know is whether the insight that was born of his earlier conversation with Max is valid: is it true that despite their destructive isolation from one another, people all feel the same way and want the same things? With much stuttering, he tells Max that what he did was not reflective of what he had wanted, and he asks if that is also true of the people who want to kill him. This question is a weighty one for Bigger. It is his ticket into the human community; if he is right, his needs and longings will receive the validation of universal experience. If he is right, it also will mean that he understands the people who hate him, demolishing for good the image of the white mountain that began to shatter when he first recognized Jan's humanity. As much as the thought of a shared humanity elated Bigger, he is not unaware of the irony of his making the discovery in the face of death. When he first considered the idea, he thought, "Had he killed Mary and Bessie and brought sorrow to his mother and brother and sister and put himself in the shadow of the electric chair only to find out this? Had he been blind all along?" (p. 307).

Instead of answering Bigger's question directly, Max takes the opportunity to give a speech. His answer ultimately is "yes": he says that everyone wants the same things in life but that some men (capitalists), in their fear of losing what they own, force others (workers) to suffer. Their acts, like Bigger's killing, are wrong, but there are alternative ways for people to fulfill their needs without oppressing others. He says that Bigger should have faith in himself and in his own feelings.

It is at this point, mid-conversation in the last two pages of the book, that Wright abruptly and disturbingly abandons Bigger's point of view, giving the reader no more information than he gives Max and throwing the action into some confusion.[11] Bigger says that Max's words make him "kind of feel what I wanted. It makes me feel that I was kind of right" (p. 358). He goes on to say that he had not wanted to kill but that "when I think of why all the killing was, I begin to feel what I wanted, what I am." He says, "What I killed for must've been good!" and "I didn't want to kill! . . . But what I killed for I *am!*" Max is horrified. Staring with "eyes full of terror," he says, "Bigger, not that" (p. 358). He leaves the cell with his face averted and with tears in his eyes. Before Max leaves, Bigger asks him to tell his mother that he is all right and to tell Jan "hello." Bigger is last seen smiling "a faint, wry, bitter smile" (p. 359) and grasping his cell bars with both hands.

Throughout most of *Native Son*, Wright is quite straightforward about the meaning of the action; he provides his own gloss as the action occurs, and for anyone who misses it the first time around it is recapitulated in Max's speech to the court. In the last scene, however, Wright is willing to violate the point of view that he has maintained for Bigger's private story in order to effect a distance from the action that has not been part of the book before. Consequently, it is only this scene about which any substantive difference in interpretation has occurred.

One interpretation, represented most notably by Bone, Margolies, Kinnamon, Howe, and, to a lesser extent, McCall, assumes that Wright's primary intention is to make a pro-Communist statement in the book.[12] From this point of view, Max stands as Wright's spokesman, and Bigger is seen as lapsing into hatred. If one works from this assumption, the ending of the book inevitably is muddled: Communism has failed Bigger, Bigger has failed himself, and nothing much follows. The opposite interpretation assumes that Wright primarily is making an anti-Communist statement. From this point of view, Max must be discredited. Webb and Fabre both cite the failure of Marxism represented in Max's failing Bigger. Gibson emphasizes Max's failure to understand Bigger as an individual rather than as a representation of a class and race. Sadler perhaps goes furthest in saying that through Max Wright indicts the Communist party for its lack of understanding of the black experience.[13]

Both of these points of view require an assumption of great inconsistency on the teller's part, and neither suggests a particularly satisfactory ending to the book. Max is a good man. He has fought to the best of his ability to save Bigger. His anguish, both private and public, is real, and he is probably the only person in Bigger's life besides his mother ever to shed tears for him. It would be too perverse of Wright to assign him to some Red hell at the eleventh hour simply because he is not a saint and tends to overabstract. On the other hand, the idea that Bigger lapses into hatred flies in the face of the development of the entire third book of the novel. Bigger has crept closer and closer to communication and understanding. Moreover, we have seen Bigger in the grip of hate and, whatever he is now, he is not a Bigger we have seen before.

The problem lies in the false dichotomy presented in the assumption that Max must either speak for Wright or be condemned. The only clues that Wright plants in the scene itself do indeed suggest that Max has suffered a failure of insight. When he is about to leave the cell, Wright says that he "groped for his hat like a blind man; he found it and jammed it on his head. He felt for the door, keeping his face averted" (p. 358). Max is literally blinded by his own tears, but blindness has been such a consistent equivalent for lack of understanding that Wright hardly would have used the word carelessly in this important scene. Bigger's messages to Jan and his mother, his dropping of the title "Mr." at long last from Jan's name, and his solicitude for Max's distress also suggest that he has not become some despicable island of hatred.

In the last hours before his death, Bigger confronts reality directly. He sees what his life has meant and that he has no savior but himself. What Wright seems to have been trying to do in the last scene is to shift the action to a more abstract level. Bigger becomes for a moment the distillation of his own idea, and when he does he leaves Max behind. In "How 'Bigger' Was Born," Wright says that he intended to show Bigger "living dangerously, taking life into his hands, accepting what life had made him." That is precisely what Bigger does—no more, no less, no hate, and not even a value judgment except of his own being. He does exactly what Max told him to do. He separates his action, which he had not intended, from the feelings and desires that brought on the action. It is the feelings and ideas which are Bigger: he perceives what he is when he thinks of "why the killing was"; he says that it is "what he killed for" that must have been good and that it is what he killed for that he is. He shakes himself loose from the metaphor just long enough to perceive the relationship between who he is and what he has done, affirming himself but denying the senseless crime that society made of his life.

Bigger has moved in the novel from what Wright describes as "bare sensation" toward conscious thought. At first, he only responds to the stereotypes and vague images through which his reality is filtered. Then he assumes the stereotype and acts out the metaphor: the crime is his life, and he takes upon himself the "crime of being black." He uses the stereotype and the metaphor for his own ends, without understanding that it is still the image that is controlling him. Through Jan and Max he begins to see through the stereotype. The white mountain begins to crumble, and he catches a glimpse of a human community. At the end, he breaks through to a comprehension of the metaphor of his life. Max does not separate the figurative from the literal: all he sees is Bigger accepting the crime, but what Bigger accepts is the only life he has been given. As a white man, however sympathetic, Max cannot see Bigger's life as Bigger himself sees it. Nor can Bigger explain it to him; he can only reassure Max, saying "I'm all right. For real, I am."

Had Wright's primary purpose been propaganda rather than art, he would not have left Bigger standing alone on his pinnacle as he does. Bigger stands alone because, for Wright, that was the only way he could confront his life. As an individual, Bigger finds that he must answer his own questions and supply his own definitions—the kind of existential solution that Wright would use more consciously in his later work. As a black, Bigger stands alone as well. Despite the undeniable gifts that two white Communists have given him, he cannot depend on their vision unless he makes it his own. Bigger never believes it when Max tells him that society hates "Reds" and other working people as much as it hates blacks, and neither do we. Marxism cannot save Bigger any more than Jan could give him humanity; he must take responsibility for his own salvation.

Wright does not condemn the Communist vision in Max. His attitude is the more benign one he expressed in retrospect after he left the party: " ... they had missed the meaning of the lives of the masses, had conceived of people in too abstract a manner. . . . I would tell Communists how common people felt, and I would tell common people of the self-sacrifice of the Communists who strove for unity among them."[14] In *Native Son*, he goes one step further. In Jan he portrays a Communist who breaks through the abstraction to some understanding of Bigger's life. And in Bigger he demonstrates that for blacks a process of self-definition must precede specific political action. He tries to capture the pre-revolutionary Bigger at the moment of his first comprehension of the meaning of his oppression, an attempt more universal, more radical, and more ambitious than a propaganda statement. Max is deeply disturbed by the potential he sees in Bigger for two events that he dreads: a violent revolution or an irreconcilable split among the workers. But Wright freezes Bigger at the moment of comprehension, with a wry, bitter smile on his face. He leaves unanswered the question Max seems to answer: he asks what will happen when Bigger—a human being, a black, an oppressed proletarian—comprehends the metaphor and, in so doing, takes his life into his own hands.

Notes

1. Robert A. Bone, *Richard Wright*, Pamphlets on American Writers, No. 74 (Minneapolis: University of Minnesota Press, 1969), p. 17.

2. Richard Wright, *Native Son* (New York: Harper, 1940), p. 336. Subsequent references are given parenthetically in the text.

3. Dan McCall has discussed the influence on Wright of Poe's use of the Gothic and Hawthorne's use of the Romance: *The Example of Richard Wright* (New York: Harcourt, 1969), pp. 69–72, 76.

4. McCall, p. 86.

5. Richard Wright, *Black Boy* (Cleveland: World, 1950), p. 58.

6. Blindness and other visual imagery in the book have been discussed thoroughly. See especially Robert A. Bone, *The Negro Novel in America*, rev. ed. (New Haven: Yale University Press, 1965), p. 147; Thomas LeClair, "The Blind Leading the Blind: Wright's *Native Son* and a Brief Reference to Ellison's *Invisible Man*," *CLA Journal*, 13 (March 1970), 315–320; Edward Margolies, *The Art of Richard Wright* (Carbondale: Southern Illinois Press, 1969), 118–119; James A. Emanuel, "Fever and Feeling: Notes on the Imagery in *Native Son*," *Negro Digest*, 18 (December 1968), 20–21; James Nagel, "Images of 'Vision' in *Native Son*," *University Review*, 36 (Winter 1969), 109–115.

7. Bigger Thomas's very name has been read as a play on Uncle Tom or on "big or bad nigger." See Leslie A. Fiedler, *Waiting for the End* (New York: Stein and Day, 1964), pp. 106–107, 122; Keneth Kinnamon, *The Emergence of Richard Wright* (Urbana: University of Illinois Press, 1972), p. 130. See also McCall, pp. 63–102, whose discussion of the book is focused on Bigger as "the bad nigger."

8. James Baldwin, *Notes of a Native Son* (Boston: Beacon, 1955), p. 22; see also pp. 34–35. Ralph Ellison, *Shadow and Act* (New York: Random House, 1964),

p. 114; Nathan A. Scott, Jr., "The Dark and Haunted Tower of Richard Wright," in *Five Black Writers,* ed. Donald B. Gibson (New York: New York University Press, 1970), p. 16. See also Hugh M. Gloster, *Negro Voices in American Fiction* (Chapel Hill: University of North Carolina Press, 1948), p. 233.

  9. McCall, pp. 74, 79.

  10. Margolies, p. 10.

  11. Phyllis R. Klotman includes this shift in point of view in an argument that Wright makes consistent use, especially in Book Three, of what Booth would call moral distancing: "Moral Distancing as a Rhetorical Technique in *Native Son: A Note on 'Fate,'*" *CLA Journal,* 18 (December 1974), 284–291. The problem with this explanation is that in the other instances Klotman cites there is little doubt about what Bigger is thinking, so that the reader has a reference point for the "moral distance." Without Bigger's point of view, there is more confusion than distance.

  12. Bone, *Negro Novel,* p. 150; Margolies, pp. 106–107; Kinnamon, pp. 141–143; Irving Howe, *A World More Attractice: A View of Modern Literature and Politics* (New York: Horizon, 1963), p. 104; McCall, p. 72.

  13. Constance Webb, *Richard Wright* (New York: Putnam, 1968), pp. 174–175; Michel Fabre, *The Unfinished Quest of Richard Wright,* trans. Isabel Barzun (New York: Morrow, 1973), p. 183; Donald B. Gibson, "Wright's Invisible Native Son," *American Quarterly,* 21 (Winter 1969), 729–736; Jeffrey A. Sadler, "Split Consciousness in Richard Wright's *Native Son,*" *South Carolina Review,* 8 (April 1976), 19–23.

  14. Richard Wright, ["I Tried to Be a Communist"], in *The God That Failed,* ed. Richard Crossman (New York: Harper, 1949), p. 120; first published in the *Atlantic Monthly* in 1944.

TONY MAGISTRALE

From St. Petersburg to Chicago: *Wright's* Crime and Punishment

Michel Fabre and Constance Webb, in their separate biographies of Richard Wright, document their subject's attraction to the fiction of Fyodor Dostoevski. When Wright gave advice to aspiring young writers or discussed his own literary inspirations, Dostoevski's novels were frequently mentioned.[1] Wright read *Crime and Punishment* for the first time in 1928, when he was twenty years old. The novel impressed him tremendously and he returned to it often, but not until the writing of *Native Son*, nearly two decades later, is there evidence of its influence exerting a definite shape over Wright's fiction. This topic has been suggested by Kenneth Reed,[2] but his sketchy treatment is much too brief and requires supplementary material and distinctions.

Crime and Punishment and *Native Son* share obvious similarities: both revolve around the theme of an impoverished youth who commits a double homicide and is subsequently captured and imprisoned. The victims in both novels are women; each of the youths is the product of a maternally based family; and to some degree both are influenced by morally conservative sisters while neither knows his father. The comparison between the two novels, however, extends beyond plot and character parallels. Dostoevski heightened Wright's awareness of the psychological dimensions of physical space, the sense of the city or a bedroom in possession of certain traits which influence

Comparative Literature Studies, Volume 23, Number 1 (Spring 1986): pp. 59–70. Copyright © 1986 by Board of Trustees of the University of Illinois.

19

human behavior. But even more important than this, was Dostoevski's model of the criminal mind—the motivations and consequences of antisocial behavior—and the antithetical struggle toward moral advancement and spiritual growth. Wright's personal experiences would have sufficed to enable the construction of a story about Bigger Thomas without knowledge of *Crime and Punishment*, but *Native Son* would have been a far less complex and engaging book had its author never been aware of Dostoevski. As Edward Margolies suggests, Wright's work is a psychological as well as sociological novel, which not only shocks the reader's conscience, but also raises "questions regarding the ultimate nature of man."[3]

I

One of the most important aspects shared by *Crime and Punishment* and *Native Son* is an examination into the ways in which environmental conditions and society shape the individual personality. Dostoevski was strongly influenced by both the romantic and naturalistic schools of the eighteenth and nineteenth centuries. His vivid descriptions of room and city dwellings owe much to Poe, Balzac, Vidocq, and Dickens.[4] Unlike the fiction of his contemporaries in Russian Literature—Tolstoy, Turgenev, Chekhov—*Crime and Punishment* does not take place behind the expansive backdrop of nature or the countryside. *Crime and Punishment*, like the urban *Native Son*, has a distinctive sense of confinement throughout and the major events invariably take place in the crowded city, among the heat and press of buildings and people. As Raskolnikov haunts the suffocating streets of St. Petersburg before and after his crime, so too does the hunted Bigger Thomas move within the condemned and stinking buildings of the Chicago ghetto. James A. Emanuel argues persuasively that Bigger's entire perception of the city—and, by extension, reality—is presented through images of restriction: urban closure, walls, curtains, and blurred vision.[5] In both *Crime and Punishment* and *Native Son*, the individual characters are confined by small apartments, narrow streets, and each other's presence. Compare, for example, these two environmental descriptions, the first from *Native Son:*

> He stretched his arms above his head and yawned; his eyes moistened. The sharp precision of the world of steel and stone dissolved into blurred waves. He blinked and the world grew hard again, mechanical, distinct.[6]

Raskolnikov, likewise, inhabits a similar cityscape:

> A terrible heat had settled upon the street; and then there was the closeness, the bustle of the crowd, plaster all around, scaffolding,

bricks, dust, and that stench which is so peculiar to summer. The unbearable stench that was emitted from taverns, which were particularly numerous in that part of town, and the drunks, whom one encountered at every step, served to complete the picture's revolting and miserable tonality.[7]

Both Dostoevski and Wright lavish minute descriptions on the interiors of the living quarters occupied by their respective antiheroes. Raskolnikov's room in St. Petersburg is described as a "coffin," a "cupboard," a "tomb," where he sits "like a spider" in constant meditation. Similarly, Bigger's one room apartment must accommodate four people; their lack of privacy is a continual source of conflict and humiliation; and the family must cohabit this space with vermin the size of cats. The setting suffocates the characters by its tightness, noise, and filth; everything here, like Raskolnikov's garret, indicates a separation from nature. Both writers use the sordid cityscapes of *Crime and Punishment* and *Native Son* to create a world of chimera and illusion, where their antiheroes dissipate hours fluctuating between intense personal frustration and dreams of fantasy. Raskolnikov's gloomy room contributes to his depressed state and at one point he attributes to hunger his plan for murder. As the critic Konstantin Mochulsky points out, it would almost seem that the poisonous vapors that rise from the city's contaminated and feverish breath have penetrated the impoverished student's brain and there have helped give birth to his thoughts of murder.[8] Raskolnikov passes his life in thought; the exterior world, people, reality—these have ceased to exist.

Bigger Thomas's Chicago is as confining as Raskolnikov's St. Petersburg. Chicago's physical aspects—noisy, crowded, filled with a sense of power and fulfillment—make Bigger continually aware of the advantages available to whites, while simultaneously underscoring the impossibility of achievement for blacks. As Bigger acknowledges to his friend Gus early in the novel, "'They don't let us do nothing.... Everytime I think about it, I feel like somebody's poking a red-hot iron down my throat'" (p. 20). Consequently, Bigger seeks escape from the frustrations that accompany a black man living in a white milieu, by losing himself in the fantasies of motion pictures. As Raskolnikov escapes from his St. Petersburg reality through dreams of wealth and power, so Bigger escapes to the narrow confines of his ghetto realm in a world where wealth and power are commonplace and where desires are magically fulfilled: "He wanted to see a movie; his senses hungered for it. In a movie he could dream without effort; all he had to do was lean back in a seat and keep his eyes open" (p. 17).

Bigger's interest in movie fantasies and Raskolnikov's turgid daydreams find further extension in their similar thoughts regarding world historic figures. On one level of being, *Crime and Punishment* and *Native Son* are novels which illustrate, for uniquely different reasons, the lure of power, and both Raskolnikov and Bigger are attracted to leaders who translate this desire into worldly conquests. Related to Raskolnikov's belief that the death of one human is justified when it alleviates the suffering of others and brings humanity a "new word," is Bigger's dream of a powerful individual who will come to rescue the oppressed black populace. Bigger is acutely aware of the fear and shame experienced by black people stemming from their treatment by the white world. He anticipates his own version of Raskolnikov's "extraordinary man" who will free blacks from the white force that has kept them separate and despairing: "He liked to hear how Japan was conquering China; of how Mussolini was invading Spain. He was not concerned with whether these acts were right or wrong; they simply appealed to him as possible avenues of escape. He felt that someday there would be a black man who would whip the black people into a tight band and together they would act to end fear and shame" (p. 110). Raskolnikov's initial justification for the pawnbroker's death emerges from a similar logic; it is the quest to end the life of a pernicious and cruel usurer in order to bring happiness to those who otherwise might perish. Early in the novel he says to Sonya, "'By my very nature I cannot simply stand by and allow a miscreant to bring some poor defenseless being to ruin. I will interfere. Kill her, take her money and with the help of it devote oneself to the service of humanity and the good of all'"(p. 60).

Hegel's historic leaders—Alexander, Caesar, and Napoleon—become the basis for Raskolnikov's theory of the "extraordinary man" as an individual who possesses the right to circumvent conventional social ethics in order to become humanity's benefactor. While Bigger looks to contemporary political figures as illustrative of men who also exercised power to rise above the masses, it is important to note that he remains oblivious to Raskolnikov's larger issue of "the service of humanity and the good of all." This is less an indication of Bigger's insensitivity to the world or lack of a sophisticated intellect, than a reflection of the level of personal despair he must confront. Bigger simply does not share the comparative "leisure" of Raskolnikov's life; his awareness of power therefore exists only on the level of providing "possible avenues of escape."

While Bigger and Raskolnikov share similar environmental conditions and dreams of frustrated power, there exists an enormous difference between Raskolnikov's theoretical calculations and Bigger's existential bewilderment. In *Crime and Punishment* a good part of Raskolnikov's alienation proceeds from the interior sin of pride and deliberately cultivated speculation. In contrast, Bigger feels himself smothered by forces beyond his control. While environmental factors do play a major role in influencing Raskolnikov's personality, he, unlike Bigger, is able to exert his will upon circumstance. Raskolnikov *decides* to kill, he is not driven to do it.[9] Pinned between the grave of tomorrow and the racist barriers of yesterday, Bigger does not choose his choice; he lacks the initial freedom that allows Raskolnikov to construct his alternative superman theory: "He [Bigger] had been so conditioned in a cramped environment that hard words alone or kicks knocked him upright and made him capable of action—action that was futile because the world was too much for him" (p. 225).

The distinction between the two characters can also be extended to include their relationship to the crimes they commit. Raskolnikov's motives for the murders of the two women are as complex as the character himself. Dostoevski's notebooks are filled with various reasons, and at one point he has Raskolnikov murder in order to obtain money to aid his family. Bigger's crimes, by contrast, are nothing more than a desperate means of winning, through acts of spontaneous violence, the initial freedom denied him by the environment. Wright continually underscores the fact that Bigger is an impotent prisoner in a hostile land.[10] Since Mary Dalton is representative of all that the white world has traditionally held most sacred—aristocratic white womanhood—her murder brings Bigger his first real sense of power and identity. Consequently, a portion of the horror he experiences in committing the crime is alleviated by the knowledge that he, who is considered insignificant by whites, has actually killed a member of their race and outwitted them in their attempts to discover his identity. Essentially, Raskolnikov kills to test a self-will theory: the right of *l'homme superieur* to transgress the laws of morality.[11] Although *Native Son* does not attempt to condone the crime of murder, it does insist that only through that crime did Bigger manage to assert himself against those who had treated him as though he were merely a rat in a maze: "And, yet, out of it all, over and above all that had happened, impalpable but real, there remained to him a queer sense of power. He had done this. He had brought all this about. In all of his life these two murders were the most meaningful things that had ever happened to him" (pp. 224–225). Both Raskolnikov and Bigger kill out of the desire to attain freedom. However, the first understands freedom to mean the will to power; the second sees freedom as the legitimate claim of a human being.

In one sense, Bigger Thomas is a victim of his environment as Raskolnikov is a prisoner of his own self-willed theories. The crimes in both novels, then, stem directly from Raskolnikov's theory of a superior self and Bigger's contrasting inability to gain a satisfying concept of self. Neither Wright nor Dostoevski, however, draws a one-dimensional protagonist. Raskolnikov is more complex than merely another prefiguration of a Nietzschean *Übermensch*, while Bigger finally becomes a more complete character than most representatives of naturalist fiction. Although it may be argued that Raskolnikov and Bigger kill out of very different reasons, their crimes pave the way for similar moral awakenings. While Bigger and Raskolnikov experience a certain degree of "elation" in the commission of their respective murders, both men cannot escape the sense of guilt in reflecting upon their actions.

Despite Bigger's violent impulses and brutal reactions, there is in him none of the viceral delight in cruelty or perverse sexuality attributed by the Chicago newspapers and Buckley, the State's attorney. When he kills Bessie by hitting her with the brick, it is late at night, when she is asleep and the room is dark. Furthermore, the horror inherent in his disposal of Mary's corpse affects him so strongly that he has to force himself to go through each step of its dismemberment, fighting an omnipresent nausea and hallucinatory images. Indeed, Bigger is constantly beset by guilt and fear, from the haunting reappearance of the Dalton's white cat to the image of Mary's severed head, the dark curls wet with blood. He attempts to rationalize his actions by judging the white girl's behavior as foolish and conducive to a violent response, but eventually, as his dream subsequent to Mary's death effectively dramatizes, Bigger becomes aware that in performing the crime of murder he has also destroyed himself. In Bigger's dream, the streetlamp's light is the color of blood, and this "red glare of light" is associated with the fire from the furnace he has used to burn Mary's corpse. The dream forces a connection between the street (Bigger's life) and the Dalton furnace (Mary) and continues this affiliation until Bigger finally exchanges places with his female victim:

> . . . in a red glare of light like that which came from the furnace and he had a big package in his arms so wet and slippery and heavy that he could scarcely hold onto it and he wanted to know what was in the package and he stopped near an alley corner and unwrapped it and the paper fell away and he saw—it was his own head—his own head lying with black face and closed eyes and lips parted with white teeth showing and hair wet with blood. . . . (p. 156)

It is possible that Wright borrowed from Dostoevski the use of dream symbolism as a method for revealing the criminal's repressed guilt and unconscious identification with his victim's suffering.[12] It is through the language of dreams that Wright and Dostoevski represent their protagonists' early stages of remorse. Similar to Bigger's nightmare, wherein he exchanges identities with the murdered Mary, Raskolnikov's dreams of Mikolka and the mare (I, iv) and the pawnbroker (III, vi) are warnings to the student that the old woman's death cannot be separated from his own life. In the dream of the beaten mare, Raskolnikov identifies with the little boy witnessing the brutal act, Mikolka performing it, and the mare itself who receives it. The dream of the pawnbroker comes after he has re-examined his "extraordinary man" theory and the crime itself. In this dream Raskolnikov not only relinquishes his power in failing to kill the woman, but becomes the one tormented by her derisive gestures and "noiseless laughter":

> He stealthily took the axe from the noose and struck her one blow, then another on the skull. But strange to say she did not stir, as though she were made of wood. He was frightened, bent down nearer and tried to look at her; but she too bent her head lower. He bent right down to the ground and peeped up into her face from below, he peeped and turned cold with horror: the old woman was sitting and laughing, and shaking with noiseless laughter, doing her utmost that he should not hear it. (p. 250)

Both of these dreams reveal that Raskolnikov, like Bigger in his own dreamscape, is inextricably tied to the dual roles of the helpless victim and aggressive victimizer.

II

In relying on an axe as the instrument of murder in Raskolnikov's double homicide and Bigger's decapitation of Mary, the two men symbolically sever whatever bonds remain of their link to humanity as they split open the heads of their victims. The repulsive dreamscapes of *Crime and Punishment* and *Native Son* serve to introduce Bigger and Raskolnikov to the prison of self, incarcerating them both in spiritual isolation and torment. By themselves, neither man is capable of advancing beyond the acute awareness of his condition. Raskolnikov essentially acknowledges this after the death of the pawnbroker: "Did I murder the old woman? I murdered myself not her" (p. 297). In *Crime and Punishment* it is Sonya Marmeladov and Porfiry Petrovitch who lend relief to Raskolnikov by providing his suffering with moral direction. In *Native Son* the strength and concern of Jan Erlone and Boris Max convince Bigger that his life is important because it is linked to the fate of other people. Raskolnikov needs Sonya to forgive and love him and Porfiry to challenge his intellectual positions. Bigger's hostility is transformed into trust and love by the forgiveness of Jan and the sense of self-belief that Max helps him articulate at the end of the novel.

In Raskolnikov's acceptance of suffering as a way to salvation, Sonya becomes the only person capable of comforting him. She is the sainted whore whose abilities to express empathy give her the strength to accept Raskolnikov's cross. As is foreshadowed by the symbolic scene in which Raskolnikov and Sonya are united over the Biblical story of Lazarus (IV, iv), Raskolnikov, through the love of Sonya, comes to see and trust in the possibility of a "full resurrection to a new life, to a new and hitherto unknown future" (p. 492). Near the end of the book, when he leaves the police station unable to confess, it is Sonya's silent figure of suffering that makes Raskolnikov return and admit to the murders.

Just as Sonya comprehends and communicates her love to Raskolnikov, Jan Erlone forgives Bigger for killing the girl he loves and conveys to the black youth his first sense of a white man's humanity. When Jan first enters the room where Bigger is held after his capture, Bigger's initial thought is that Jan has come for revenge. Instead, Jan recounts his realization that if he were to kill Bigger, the dreadful cycle of violence would never stop, and asserts that his own suffering has led him to see deeper into Bigger's. By disassociating himself from hatred and revenge, Jan becomes the impetus to Bigger's change in perception:

> . . . a particle of white rock had detached itself from that looming mountain of white hate and had rolled down the slope, stopping still at his feet. The word had become flesh. For the first time in his life, a white man became a human being to him; and the reality of Jan's humanity came in a stab of remorse: he had killed what this man loved and had hurt him. He saw Jan as though someone had performed an operation upon his eyes, or as though someone had snatched a deforming mask from Jan's face. (p. 268)

Sonya and Jan serve as the embodiments of the deeply human qualities Bigger and Raskolnikov desperately need—acceptance of other people's differences, compassion, and selfless love. Sonya and Jan struggle not through ideas and sermons, but by deeds and example. They do not intellectualize and do not moralize, but trust and love. "'One can be great even in humility,'" says Sonya, and Jan's image in *Native Son* corresponds with few modifications.

In *Crime and Punishment* reasonings about life and about the meaning of spiritual suffering pass from Sonya to Porfiry Petrovitch. A corresponding movement can be traced in *Native Son* with the induction of Boris Max. Max, in his capacity as Bigger's lawyer, is able to elicit from his client a comprehension of his hopes and dreams, his frustrations and rages. In his courtroom arguments, Max shows a clear understanding of how Bigger's crimes were both destructive and liberating, in the sense that they furnished Bigger with is first real identity. Although it is too late for Bigger to join the others who, like Max, support principles of human worth and dignity, the lawyer continues to embellish Bigger's evolving commitment to other human beings: "He had lived outside the lives of men. Their modes of communication, their symbols and images, had been denied him. Yet Max had given him the faith that at bottom all men lived and felt as he felt. And of all the men he had met, surely Max knew what he was trying to say" (p. 386).

Like the version of Boris Max we find in *Native Son,* Porfiry Petrovitch in *Crime and Punishment* understands both the situation and context for Raskolnikov's crimes. Unlike Poe's Dupin or Hugo's Javert, the literary models Dostoevski initially may have had in mind in the development of his own magistrate, Porfiry is a new type of "super-cultured" administrator, straightforward and sympathetic; he is aware of the struggle for man's soul—for the inspector assumes he has one—the contest for the individual psyche as it is pulled between two abysses, good and evil. It is for this reason that he does not simply arrest Raskolnikov. Porfiry seeks more than merely the apprehension and punishment of a law breaker; he is interested in Raskolnikov's moral regeneration. Porfiry understands that the student's soul requires "fresh air, fresh air" (p. 412). Siberia is literally that fresh air, which Raskolnikov breathes after he is transplanted from the polluted depths of St. Petersburg. Thus, Porfiry's role is similar to Boris Max's: they exist to inspire Raskolnikov and Bigger to continue the process of self evaluation, and from this struggle to attain insight into moral development.

The influence of Sonya and Porfiry as well as the personal struggles of good and evil that tear at his soul, give Raskolnikov at least the possibility of a resurrection and a future life with Sonya. Dostoevski leaves his young student invested with the ability to distinguish good from evil and the capacity for exerting his moral will. Through the assistance of Porfiry and Sonya, Raskolnikov comes to acknowledge the principle of equipoise: that the evil in one's nature must be balanced through love, understanding, and suffering.[13]

In *Native Son* Bigger Thomas is not provided the chance for a new life in Siberia, and American society, as represented by a Chicago courtroom, once again forfeits the opportunity to liberate itself. But Bigger, like Raskolnikov, achieves his own freedom before his execution takes place. Although he is condemned to die as a violator of society's laws, his death is really a final triumph over forces that have controlled his life since birth. While society fails to change in its attitude toward Bigger, ironically his attitude toward society is transformed. His blind resentment toward the limitations of his family develops into a comprehension of the cause and compassion for their suffering; his violent outbursts against Gus, G. H., and Jack evolve into an awareness that they, too, are victims of prejudice and rejection; and his universal fear and distrust of white people are replaced by respect and love for Jan and Max.

Richard Wright's use of parallel characters, atmospheric effects, and a similar belief in the power of the human spirit to transform itself bear a marked resemblance to *Crime and Punishment.* The confluence between the two works, however, is never literal: it is not a matter of direct quotations or plagiarism,[14] but of a relationship in situations, motives, effects, and procedures. *Crime and Punishment* represented a reservoir from which Wright drew deeply—recasting characters and reshaping themes—in order to produce material relevant to his own purposes. It may be argued, for example, that Dostoevski's identification with a Christian vision of life finds a parallel in Wright's secular humanism. While Sonya guides Raskolnikov toward the philosophy of atonement as a method for counterbalancing evil, Bigger's life is given new priorities through contact with men who embody Marxist principles. Wright's interest is not in religion itself (although there are certainly a number of references to Bigger as a Christ-figure), but in its social excrescences: racism, ignorance, hypocrisy. Even as the central themes of *Crime and Punishment* and *Native Son* are filtered through each writer's personal affiliation with Christianity or radical politics, their protagonists are left invested with a similar commitment to other people and the capacity for moral growth. Unlike the naturalist tradition which influenced both novelists, *Native Son* and *Crime and Punishment* are not pessimistic evaluations of human destiny. In fact, quite the opposite is true, since both Bigger and Raskolnikov are finally victorious over the brutal facts of their personal histories. The differences between the two characters reveal much about cultural opportunities; their similarities address those elements universal to humankind: a deathless faith in the potential for self-improvement and the dream of a final reconciliation among all men.

NOTES

1. See especially Constance Webb, *Richard Wright: A Biography* (New York: Putnam, 1968), pp. 93, 145–146.

2. Kenneth Reed, *"Native Son: An American Crime and Punishment,"* *Studies in Literature,* 1 (Summer 1970), 33–34.

3. Edward Margolies, *Native Sons: A Critical Study of Twentieth-Century Negro American Authors* (Philadelphia: Lippincott, 1968), p. 82.

4. For a more complete discussion of Dostoevski's relationship to these earlier writers, the reader should consult the following sources: for Dostoevski's relationship to Poe, Alfred Kazin, *An American Progression* (Vintage, 1985); for Dostoevski's relationship to Balzac, Leonid Grossman, *Balzac and Dostoevski* (Ardis, 1973); and for Dostoevski's connection to Dickens, Albert Guerard, *The Triumph of the Novel: Dickens, Dostoevski, Faulkner* (Oxford, 1976).

5. James A. Emanuel, "Fever and Feeling: Notes on the Imagery in *Native Son,*" *Negro Digest,* 18 (Dec. 1968), 16–24.

6. Richard Wright, *Native Son* (New York: Harper and Row, 1966), p. 19. Further textual references will be cited parenthetically.

7. Fyodor Dostoevski, *Crime and Punishment,* trans. Constance Garnett (New York: Random House, 1950), p. 169. Further textual references will be cited parenthetically.

8. Konstantin Mochulsky, *Dostoevsky* (Princeton, New Jersey: Princeton University Press, 1967), pp. 290–291.

9. Dostoevski purposely creates the character of Razumihin so that the latter might provide a mirror to Raskolnikov and the subject of determinism: Razumihin faces almost the same problems as Raskolnikov; nevertheless, he solves them

differently. He gives lessons and translates articles to remain self-sufficient. Even Raskolnikov recognizes that he too could earn a living in the same manner. He says so to Sonya after the murder: "'Razumihin works! But I turned sulky and wouldn't'" (p. 375).

10. Wright further establishes his attitude toward the influence of environment on the individual in the essay "How Bigger Was Born": "I do say that I felt and still feel that environment supplies the instrumentalities through which the organism expresses itself, and if that environment is warped or tranquil, the mode and manner of behavior will be affected toward deadlocking tensions or orderly fulfillment and satisfaction" (p. xvi).

11. Raskolnikov provides illumination into the actual motive behind his decision to murder in a conversation with Sonya (V, iv): "'It wasn't to help my mother I did the murder—that's nonsense—I didn't do the murder to gain wealth and power and to become a benefactor of mankind. Nonsense! I did the murder for myself . . . I wanted to find out then and quickly whether I was a louse like everybody else or a man. Whether I can step over barriers or not . . .'" (p. 377).

12. As Andre Gide points out in his study *Dostoevsky* (New Directions, 1961), there is a fascinating narrative blend in Dostoevski's prose, combining both realistic and dream elements into a weave in which it is often impossible to distinguish one from the other: "Strange how Dostoevsky, when leading us through the strangest by-paths of psychology, ever must needs add the most precise and infinestimal of realistic details, in order to make more secure an edifice which otherwise would appear the extreme expression of phantasy and imagination" (p. 122).

13. The duality of Raskolnikov's personality, which presents a moral conflict throughout the novel, ultimately provides the reader with a final aesthetic question at the conclusion of *Crime and Punishment:* namely, how credible is Raskolnikov's spiritual and religious reawakening? Many critics, especially Edward Wasiolek in his book *Dostoevsky* (M.I.T. Press, 1964), have felt that the Epilogue is superimposed on the novel's overall structure and that Raskolnikov's rebirth is unjustified when examined in light of his prior behavior and strategies. Any conclusion about the novel must deal with the fact that there always two Raskolnikovs: the lover of life and humanity, and the murderer, who is "further than ever from seeing that what [he] did was a crime" (*CP*, p. 466). As Ernest J. Simmons argues in *Dostoevsky* (Vintage, 1940), it is impossible for Raskolnikov to accept either route as an absolute salvation: the path of blood and crime to power or the road of submission and suffering to a Christ-like salvation (p. 151). On the other hand, it must also be argued that in a final analysis the influence of the other characters mixed with the personal torment that Raskolnikov undergoes, provides at least the promise of resurrection and credibility toward a personal renascence.

14. Even in parallel passages such as the symbolic "soft and gentle eyes" of Raskolnikov's victim, Lizaveta (p. 249), reappearing in the piercing accusations of Bigger's victim, Bessie: "Suppose when he turned on the flashlight, he would see her lying there staring at him with those round large black eyes . . ." (p. 223).

ALAN W. FRANCE

Misogyny and Appropriation in Wright's Native Son

In his essay, "How 'Bigger' Was Born," Richard Wright reminds the reader of *Native Son* that the novel's point of view has been restricted to the horizon of its protagonist:

> because I had limited myself to rendering only what Bigger saw and felt, I gave no more reality to the other characters than that which Bigger himself saw. . . . Throughout there is but one point of view: Bigger's. (xxxii)

Poststructural literary criticism has at last rebelled against this kind of authorial control over texts and has endorsed a policy of expropriation: readings of literary works need no longer be synonymous with divination of authorial intention. Holding up the author's intention as the sole legitimate code for interpreting the work may be seen, therefore, as propaganda masking and muzzling an absent reality. The repressed absences are now empowered to challenge the inscribed, privileged interpretation of the work and to demand an equal voice in its dialogical world.

To change the figures, it is as if the maker had arranged an object of his art, half exposed, in wet plaster. With the fetish of ownership gone, we viewers are entitled, indeed required, to become participants in interpreting and

Modern Fiction Studies, Volume 34, Number 3 (1988): pp. 413–423. Copyright © Purdue Research Foundation, Johns Hopkins University Press.

31

evaluating the art of the work. This means that criticism must now break the work out of its authorial mold and examine the heretofore hidden impression made by its buried underside. In reading works of the patriarchal canon, this concealed impression can be conceived as a female mold that forms the work by its resistance but is absent from it.

The exposed presence of *Native Son* is the dialectical struggle between Bigger Thomas' desire for freedom and dignity, on the one hand, and the inhuman, oppressive degradation of racism used as a weapon of domination by the white propertied elite, on the other. This much of the meaning has been authorized by inscription into text; it has been exposed by the author to the study of critics and scholars for the past four and a half decades. It is now time to break open the author's cast and to examine the previously concealed contours, shaped by the absent Other.

When the text is read as one would read the black and white negative of a photograph, what immediately becomes apparent is a *second* dialectical struggle underlying the authorized one: the struggle to appropriate (and thus dehumanize) women by reducing them to objects of male status conflict, to what Hélène Cixous calls "The Realm of the Proper," which "functions by the appropriation articulated, set into play, by man's classic fear of seeing himself expropriated" (Moi 112). From underneath, *Native Son* is the story of a black man's rebellion against white male authority. The rebellion takes the form of the ultimate appropriation of human beings, the rape-slaying, which is also the ultimate expropriation of patriarchal property, the total consumption of the commodified woman.

Even feminist critics of Wright's work, while noting its strains of violence and misogyny, have not opened the text sufficiently to reveal its submerged underside. Sherley Anne Williams, for example, observes Wright's tendency to portray black women as treacherous and traitorous and to present their suffering as, primarily, "an affront to the masculinity of black men" (406). Williams, nevertheless, fails to challenge Wright's authority over the interpretation of female characters in *Native Son:* "We excuse these characterizations [of women]," she writes, "because of the power of Wright's psychological portrait of Bigger; this is Bigger's story" (397). It is time now to revoke these privileges accorded to Bigger and to recover the radical alterity in the text that reduces women to property, valuable only to the extent they serve as objects of phallocentric status conflicts. If read as the negative polarity of the text, this process of male deification and appropriation pervades the work.

In the initial episode of *Native Son*, Bigger kills a huge rat while his mother and sister, Vera, cower and scream on the bed in fear. This emblematic act occupies the surface of the novel's first six pages. The rat, an omnivorous, disease-bearing pest, fairly represents the socioeconomic system under which Mr. Dalton squeezes his fortune out of the ghetto. The killing of the rat represents, perhaps, Bigger's one chance to protect his mother and younger siblings as the patriarch of the Thomas family. The text urges us specifically to make this latter interpretation when its omniscient narrator tells us:

> He [Bigger] hated his family because he knew that they were suffering and that he was powerless to help them. He knew that the moment he allowed himself to feel to its fullness how they lived, the shame and misery of their lives, he would be swept out of himself with fear and despair. (13)

In this passage we are asked to privilege Bigger Thomas' feeling of power-lessness caused by the family's living conditions over the actual physical suffering that those conditions impose on the family. The text, that is, points to Bigger's status deprivation as the real significance of economic and social oppression.

In this initial episode, Bigger experiences his killing of the rat not with the pride of one who alleviates his family's distress, if only partially and temporarily, but with the giddy exultation of one glorying in the rare and momentary dominance that killing an adversary confers. Bigger uses the occasion of conquest to lord it over the dependent females of his family.

The phallocentricity of this scene is created first of all by Bigger's threatening his sister with the crushed and bloody carcass of the rat. The threat to Bigger (and the phallic suggestiveness can here be noted in his name) is indicated by a suggestively vaginal "three-inch rip" in his pantleg. Bigger crushes the rat's head with his shoe while "cursing hysterically: You sonofa-*bitch*!" The italics further suggest a reading of the episode as a struggle for phallic dominance with overtones of castration anxiety. In the economy of male aggression, Bigger's killing of the rat converts it into an object "over a foot long" that now becomes a weapon in his hands. As victor in a battle that the text compels us to see in overtly sexual terms, Bigger attempts to exact the maximum abasement of those whose subordination he has won by right of conquest. When Vera begs him to throw the rat out, "Bigger laughed and approached the bed with the dangling rat, swinging it to and fro like a pendulum, enjoying his sister's fear" (11). It is not the conquest over the rat, *qua* rat, in which Bigger most exults. Rather, he enjoys the dominance over the women that violent conquest has conferred on him.

Nor is it merely the physical destruction of the rat—its reduction to symbolic phallus—that allows him dominance over the women: it is their own contemptible weakness, that which denies them utterance of the words of the novel's epitaph from Job: "My stroke is heavier than my groaning" (6). From the very beginning of the text, narrative instructions make clear that the absent phallus is the source of shame as well as weakness. The mother calls to the sons as she stands in her nightgown in the single-room apartment, "Turn your heads so I can dress" (7). Bigger and his brother, Buddy, "kept their faces averted while their mother and sister put on enough clothes to keep them from feeling ashamed. . . ." And this aversion of the eyes is "a conspiracy against shame" (8). From the very outset of the novel, therefore, the text's psychodynamics are polarized sexually: Bigger and other male characters continue the violent struggle, presaged by the killing of the rat, for the appropriation or continued enjoyment of—the narcissistic desire for—status. Women, as characters in *Native Son*, are objects of this appropriation; they are at the same time desired as objects but contemptible in their weakness and passivity.

The woman, as displaced Other, is characterized as blind and weak. Mrs. Dalton is literally sightless; but to Bigger, all the characters who are not conscious of the predatory economy in which they are immersed are blind. It is, in fact, the killing of Mary Dalton that makes Bigger aware of the general blindness. After Mary's murder, he notices that those around him "did not want to see what others were doing if that doing did not feed their own desires." The corollary is that "if he could see while the others were blind, then he could get what he wanted and never be caught at it" (102). Mrs. Thomas' religion and Bessie's drinking blind and weaken these women, arousing Bigger's abhorrence: "He hated his mother for that way of hers which was like Bessie's. What his mother had was Bessie's whiskey, and Bessie's whiskey was his mother's religion" (226).

The text's denial of misogyny and appropriation of women most nearly bursts free from its self-authorized interpretation at three points of crisis that share to different degrees the ultimate patriarchal sentence on women, the rape-slaying. Although the negative polarity of female subjugation exists systematically throughout, it is most clearly visible at these cataclysms of phallic aggression and appropriation. We must look, therefore, in some detail at Bigger's symbolic rape-slaying of Gus, the partially effected rape and the murder of Mary Dalton, and the overt rape-killing of Bessie Mears.

The initial rape of the novel is a public act, performed in front of male peers. It presents the brutal subjugation of another male, Gus, by means of sexually symbolic violence. After Gus throws off his initial unprovoked attack, Bigger ("as graceful as an animal leaping") trips him and jumps "on top of him, with the knife open and ready"; Gus is completely in Bigger's power: he speaks "in surrender" and looks at his assailant "pleadingly" (40). The dominant male forces the subordinate to perform an act of ritualistic sodomy:

Bigger held the open blade an inch from Gus's lips.
"Lick it," Bigger said, his body tingling with elation.

Gus's eyes filled with tears.

"Lick it, I said! You think I'm playing?" (40–41)

This formulaic sodomy is aggravated by Bigger's threat to cut out Gus's navel, an act of disembowelment that, in addition to being murderous, seems clearly to have anal signification. Gus is able to escape before suffering any further violence, symbolic or otherwise, but Bigger is not finished with his knife. He challenges Doc's proprietary authority (signified by the gun) by slicing the felt of Doc's pool table.

The novel's narrative warrant attempts to control the interpretation of the foregoing events by making the assault on Gus a displacement of fear, Bigger's fear of holding up Blum's store: "He hoped the fight he had had with Gus covered up what he was trying to hide"; but the next sentence betrays the phallocentric struggle for domination going on beneath the text's narrative surface: "At least the fight made him feel the equal of them [fellow gang members]. And he felt the equal of Doc, too; had he not slashed his table and dared him to use his gun?" (43).

The underlying system of sexual terrorism breaks through both preceding interpretations, however, and casts Bigger's unprovoked assault of Gus (rendered "fight" in the narrative) in terms of phallic aggression. After it was over, we read that Bigger "stood for two whole minutes staring at the shadow of a telephone pole" and then "stumbled violently over a tiny crack in the pavement" (43). He has triumphed and humiliated the subordinate male; but instead of feeling elated, he feels remorseful and depressed. The symbolic rape-slaying of another male has disrupted the gang by reducing a member to the level of a woman. This process is analogous to the "ideology of rape" that Susan Brownmiller finds in male prison culture. It is "a product of the violent subculture's definition of masculinity through physical triumph, and [in prison] those who emerged as 'women' were those who were subjugated by real or threatened force" (Brownmiller 295). The symbolic "feminization" of Gus has rendered the gang ineffective as a unit for action (armed robbery here) and thereby further isolated Bigger. It is in this sense that Bigger may be said to have "stumbled over a tiny crack."

The struggle to establish dominance over another male by violent sexual aggression gives way in the second half of Book One to Bigger's appropriation of Mary Dalton, first attempted by rape and then accomplished by murder. The word "rape" is used here not merely in a figurative or approximate sense. In many jurisdictions, sexual penetration of a woman too intoxicated to be able to consent to the act constitutes a rape. But what happens to Mary Dalton in the minutes preceding her death suggests the term rape-slaying in a more direct way. In the course of the narrative, the text keeps its curtain of authority drawn over the events it relates. But later, when Bigger is telling Bessie about the fateful events, there is less certainty. "Had he raped her?" he ponders: "Yes, he had raped her. Every time he felt as he had that night, he raped" (213–214). This admission is quickly retracted by the broadening of the term into a metaphor for the struggle against white society ("Rape was what one felt when one's back was against the wall . . . "). Nevertheless, the narrative questions its own authorial interpretation here as it does elsewhere.

The circumstances surrounding Mary's death are further made problematic when Mrs. Dalton appears at Mary's bedroom door: we are assured that Bigger *"knew* that if Mary spoke she [Mrs. Dalton] would come to the side of the bed and discover him, touch him" (84, emphasis added). Yet Mary's failure to respond to her mother's call does indeed draw Mrs. Dalton to her daughter's bedside; and when she does enter the room, Bigger is able to match "each of her movements toward the bed" with a movement away from her. The silence of the text here, its refusal to explain why Bigger fails to discern one moment the very opportunity for escape that he in fact takes the next, is curious at the least. A more obvious subterfuge reveals itself when the narrative of Mary's suffocation is deconstructed. The text's authority for Mary's "accidental" death is the presence of Mrs. Dalton, "the white blur," that will catch Bigger in a situation prescripted for lynching. But the text itself calls into question the certainty of his being found out: he is not found out. If we remove the presence of Mrs. Dalton from the narrative of Mary's death and collapse the text, the following is what remains:

> She tossed and mumbled sleepily. He tightened his fingers on her breasts, kissing her again, feeling her move toward him. He was only aware of her body now. . . .
>
> He felt Mary trying to rise and quickly he pushed her head back to the pillow. . . . He held his hand over her mouth. . . . Mary mumbled and tried to rise again. Frantically, he caught a corner of the pillow and brought it to her lips. . . . [H]e grew tight and full, as though about to explode. Mary's fingernails tore at his hands and he caught the pillow and covered her entire face with it, firmly. Mary's body surged upward and he pushed downward upon the pillow with all of his weight. . . . Again Mary's body heaved and he held the pillow in a grip that took all his strength. For a long time he felt the sharp pain of her fingernails biting into his wrists. . . .
>
> He clenched his teeth and held his breath. . . . His muscles flexed taut as steel. . . . Then suddenly her fingernails did not bite into his wrists. . . . He did not feel her surging and heaving against him. Her body was still. (84–85)

This reading may be perceived as being too violent for credibility; yet Robert James Butler has used just such a technique recently to vindicate completely the authorial mandate, that is, the privileged dialectic, Bigger's struggle against a racist society. Butler concludes his restructuring of the passage above as follows:

> After her "surging and heaving" (74) body finally relaxes and Mrs. Dalton leaves the room, Bigger orgasmically utters "a long gasp" (75). In the afterglow of this strange experience, he is depicted as "weak and wet with sweat" (75), listening for some time to his heavy breathing filling the darkness. (14–15)

This reading, nevertheless, manages to go the text one better in its own repression of the sexual dialectic. Mention of Mary's drunkenness is completely suppressed; Bigger's exploitation of her condition is described as his giving in "to his warmer, more humane feelings" (15); the fatal episode is said to begin "romantically with Mary's encouraging Bigger's sexual attentions and his reciprocating, [but] Mrs. Dalton's entry into the room abruptly turns their lovemaking into deathmaking" (14). The "erotic images" of the killing are said to be "ironic," although the yawning absence of a possessive pronoun in front of "deathmaking" conceals perhaps still greater irony. And the final disposal.of Mary and Bessie is their reduction, in Butler's phrase, to "aspects of Bigger's radically divided self" (16).

In Book Two, the narrator will actually authorize an interpretation of Mary's death much like the one above, one inscribed by the removal of Mrs. Dalton from the text:

> Though he had killed by accident, not once did he feel the need to tell himself that it had been an accident. . . . And in a certain sense he knew that the girl's death had not been accidental. He had killed many times before, only on those other times there had been no handy victim. . . . (101)

Thinking back on his murder of Mary, Bigger reflects with satisfaction (but without conscious irony at the juxtaposition of these crimes) that whites "might think he would steal a dime, rape a woman, get drunk, or cut somebody; but to kill a millionaire's daughter and burn her body?" It is the appropriation of the woman's body that thrills Bigger, arousing in him a "tingling sensation enveloping all his body" (108).

The elation Bigger feels seems directly proportionate to Mary Dalton's value as a commodity, her status as the property of a millionaire. Thus, her life is fungible in dollars. In the economy of the novel, Bigger's use and destruction of the woman amounts to his expropriation of $10,000 worth of Mr. Dalton's property. Later, the narrative reveals exactly how Bigger perceives this transaction: "The knowledge that he had killed a white girl that they loved and regarded as their symbol of beauty made him feel the equal of them, like a man who had been somehow cheated, but had now evened the score" (155). Denied participation in capitalist commodity culture, the chance to "fly planes and run ships" (23), Bigger satisfies himself with the use (and destruction) of the Dalton's property in spite of his exclusion.

It is in Bigger's rape-murder of Bessie Mears, however, that the full misogynistic implications of the text are revealed. Before the discovery of Mary Dalton's remains, while the exaction of ransom is still possible, Bessie retains enough value for Bigger to risk the possibility that she might "snitch." After Bigger is found out, Bessie is of no further use to him; she has become disposable. Bigger's authorial apologist attempts to rationalize the inevitable disposal: "If she stayed . . . they would come to her and she would simply lie on the bed and sob out everything. . . . And what she would tell them about him, his habits, his life, would help them to track him down" (212). He must take her with him, "and then at some future time settle things with her, settle them in a way that would not leave him in any danger" (215). This final settlement takes place, appropriately, in an abandoned building which, like Bessie, has no further use nor value as property.

The rape and murder that follow are punctuated in the text by a veritable litany of narrative exculpations. Three times in two paragraphs: "He could not take her with him and he could not leave her behind. . . . He could not leave her here and he could not take her with him. . . . He could not take her and he could not leave her" (221–222). Yet he is on the run, has no idea himself where he is going, and so nothing Bessie could tell the police would help in his capture.

The identification of phallic aggression with death is completed by the rape and the murder that follow. Only the inscription of the text identifies the blunt instrument that "plunged downward . . . landed with a thud . . . lifted again and again . . . in falling . . . struck a sodden mass that gave softly but stoutly to each landing blow . . . seemed to be striking a wet wad of cotton . . . the jarring impact" (222) as the weapon of the murder and not the rape.

Before her death, Bessie comes to the realization that she has been used by Bigger, enjoyed as sexual property: "All you ever did since we been knowing each other was to get me drunk so's you could have me. That was all! I see it now" (215). In the context of their relationship, Bessie's rape-slaying comes to seem merely the last act in a long process of appropriation. During his conversation with Boris Max, Bigger admits the extent to which he perceives his proprietary interest to have gone: "I wasn't in love with Bessie. She was just my girl. . . . I killed Bessie to save myself. You have to have a girl, so I had Bessie. And I killed her" (326). Except for his knife and gun, Bessie is the only property Bigger has ever possessed. When her battered corpse is brought before the court as evidence in Bigger's murder trial, it is only textual authority that can maintain the reader's attention on the privileged theme, the black man's oppression by the white. Without that privilege, Bigger's "deeper sympathy" and his knowledge that Bessie "though dead, though killed by him, would resent her dead body being used in this way [to convict her murderer]" (307) are incredible.

The slippage of signification by which sexual penetration becomes confused with murder is nowhere more frighteningly out of narrative control than in the dialogue of the white men who are hunting Bigger:

"Say, did you see that brown gal in there?"
"The one that didn't have much on?"
"Yeah."
"Boy, she was a peach, wasn't she?"
"Yeah; I wonder what on earth a nigger wants to kill a white woman for when he has such good-looking women in his own race. . . . " (243–244)

The implied phallic violence in the equation of "killing" and "having" women has clearly leaked into the narrative while it points its readers toward the white man's hunt for Bigger Thomas.

An even more chilling possibility is suggested by the Derridean tactic of "double writing," a process of "erasure which allows what it obliterates to be read, violently inscribing within the text that which attempted to govern it from without" (6). If the text can suppress, can it deceive? If it can omit and apologize, can it lie? Given Bigger's insistence on the liberating power of killing women, it is only with difficulty that the text can absolve him of the rapes and murders that Buckley, the State's Attorney, accuses him of in the course of the interrogation. Once the external authority of the text is superceded, the assurance evaporates that another man, not Bigger, raped and choked to death the woman on University Avenue, climbed in Miss Ashton's bedroom window and attacked her, killed Mrs. Clinton, raped the woman in Englewood, and attacked the girl in Jackson Park last summer (283–284). The normality, the ubiquity of phallic violence, largely erased from the text, can be vaguely but unmistakably perceived in Buckley's question: "Listen, start at the beginning. Who was the first woman you ever killed?"

The final attempts of the text to cover the repressed phallocentricity and to achieve some sort of rapprochement between Bigger and the white male society that oppresses him are almost comic against this backdrop of violence against women. Jan forgives Bigger for Mary Dalton's murder:

> "Though this thing [Mary's murder] hurt me, I got something
> out of it," Jan said, sitting down and turning to Bigger. "It made
> me see deeper into men. . . . I—I lost something, but I got
> something, too. . . . I see now that you couldn't do anything else
> but that; it was all you had. . . . " (267)

Obviously, Mary Dalton has become an absence, a silence that Irigaray
believes patriarchal discourse always means when it inscribes "woman":
"Women are trapped in a system of meaning which serves the auto-affection
of the (masculine) subject" (122). Bessie, Mary, and the other victims that
appear like bubbles on the surface of the text are effectively silenced. The
last words are uttered by Bigger Thomas: "When a man kills, it's for something. . . . I didn't know I was really alive in this world until I felt things
hard enough to kill for 'em" (392).

Critics have only begun the process of "teasing out" (Johnson 140) this
textual silence that "serves the auto-affection" of men. One well-known reading maintains, for example, that *Native Son* "forces us to experience the truth
of what man does to man" (Reilly 397). Another concludes accurately, if with
what I hope can be recognized by now as unintentional irony: "Jan Erlone
forgives Bigger for killing the girl he loves and conveys to the black youth his
first sense of a white man's humanity" (Magistrale 66).

It must be stressed that the pathos of Bigger Thomas' diminishment,
the stunting and warping effects of racial oppression that form the text's
reigning dialectic, is in no way reduced by reading the repressed dialectic,
the violent and phallocentric appropriation of women. Both belong to a
system in which the Other is marginalized and dehumanized. This system
of ownership uses racism and sexism to reduce the Other to objects of
appropriation in the struggle over property relationships that determine
status. The centrality of these relations to the structure of *Native Son* is
suggested by the role inheritance plays. If the faithful family retainer, Peggy, can be trusted, the Dalton's wealth was inherited from Mrs. Dalton's
family. Mr. Dalton acquired it, along with Mrs. Dalton, in marriage. Mary
Dalton's earring, which becomes the only identifying trace of her existence,
was passed down to her according to the very same patrilineal property
arrangements by which her father inherited the slum properties that bred
her killer.

The misogynistic underside of the text, once exposed by wresting it
from authorial control, must become part of the critical reading of *Native
Son*. Only in this way can the interrelationship among patriarchical repression, racism, and capitalist culture be clearly understood. The novel grows out
of this suppressed interrelationship in which value is conferred according to

property arrangements, and status is a phallic prerogative assigned by access to and ownership of commodities, including women.

WORKS CITED

Brownmiller, Susan. *Against Our Will: Men, Women and Rape.* 1975. New York: Bantam, 1976.

Butler, Robert James. "The Function of Violence in Richard Wright's *Native Son.*" *Black American Literary Forum* 20 (1986): 9–25.

Derrida, Jacques. *Positions.* Chicago: University of Chicago Press, 1981.

Irigaray, Luce. *This Sex Which Is Not One.* Trans. Catherine Porter. Ithaca: Cornell University Press, 1985.

Johnson, Barbara. "Teaching Deconstructively." *Reading and Writing Differently: Deconstruction and the Teaching of Composition and Literature.* Eds. C. Douglas Atkins and Michael L. Johnson. Lawrence: University Press of Kansas, 1985. 140–148.

Magistrale, Tony. "From St. Petersburg to Chicago: Wright's *Crime and Punishment.*" *Comparative Literature Studies* 23 (1986): 59–70.

Moi, Toril. *Sexual/Textual Politics: Feminist Literary Theory.* New York: Methuen, 1985.

Reilly, John. "Afterword." *Native Son.* By Richard Wright. New York: Harper, 1966. 393–397.

Williams, Sherley Anne. "Papa Dick and Sister-Woman: Reflections on Women in the Fiction of Richard Wright." *American Novelists Revisited: Essays in Feminist Criticism.* Ed. Fritz Fleischmann. Boston: Hall, 1982. 394–415.

Wright, Richard. "How 'Bigger' Was Born." *Native Son.* 1940. New York: Harper, 1966. vii–xxxiv.

———. *Native Son.* 1940. New York: Harper, 1966.

KIMBERLY W. BENSTON

The Veil of Black:
(Un)Masking the Subject of African-American
Modernism's "Native Son"

1. Modernism without beginning

I used to spend the time in writing in the spaces left in Master Thomas's
copy-book, copying what he had written. I continued to do this until I
could write a hand very similar to that of Master Thomas. Thus, after a
long, tedious effort for years, I finally succeeded in learning how to write.
                    – Frederick Douglass, *Narrative* (1845/1968:58)

Entering the master's book: what logic or desire governs the slave's movement into the New World order's privileged site of meaning, power, and
presence? Does the slave's coming-into-language mark a moment of possession by anterior systems of signification or of self-apprehension? Does
he assume the master's position subversively (thereby preparing some larger
upheaval or displacement), or is he inexorably contained in a space already
overwritten by a discourse that denies him agency, subjectivity, voice?

Somewhere between repetition and irony, representation and parody, in-
corporation and appropriation, imitation and critique, the slave's writing begins
in specular relation to an antagonist that seeks his permanent enclosure. Like
the young Ben Franklin earnestly copying-out the cheerful pieties of Addison's

Human Studies: A Journal for Philosophy and the Social Sciences, Volume 16, Numbers 1–2
(April 1993): pp. 69–99. Copyright © 1993 Kluwer Academic Publishers. Printed in the
Netherlands.

Spectator in order to become a "tolerable English writer" (Franklin, 1950:19–20), Douglass might at first seem to accept at face value the master's book as the source and limit of self-understanding, as an exalted scene-of-instruction submission to which yields the signature of authenticity. But just as Franklin cagily inserts acknowledgment of his having altered and "improved" Addison's "method" even as he worked diligently to "correct" his own "faults" in replicating key passages, so Douglass's "hand"—the same hand that the master would force to work nigh-unto-death in the fields; to be bound in preparation for brutal whippings; to bear no arms in its defense; and indeed to lift no pen, even merely to reproduce the most powerful technology of power[1]—so Douglass's hand possibly seeks to usurp the authority of unconstrained expression by inscribing itself into the "spaces" of the very discursive apparatus that would silence him.

Franklin's "tinkering" with his elders' wisdom is, of course, only a mildly oedipal tweaking by a mischievous son seeking admittance to a comfortable, educated class concerned with customs and manners, collective temperance and self-advancement, not topical forms of institutional conflict. For Douglass, by contrast, the stakes of his ambiguous mimetism are much higher, much more immediate; theoretically, it involves a writing that enacts a rupture with the most cherished assumptions of received thinking. Notably, it is the technique, but not the sentiment, of the copybook which Douglass doubles as parasitical marginalia. Might this doubling's intent be masked, or even be the power of disguise itself? Might he only appear to conform to the master's text rather than produce his own meaning? Is difference really erased in repetition, affirming the master's insistence on his own hand as that which, as Truth's transcribing instrument, may remain visible? Or might the slave's very doubling spread over the master's page as a writing in excess of faithful imitation? Were we to examine the copy-book, could we discriminate the two hands there imprinted—or is the order of origin and supplement, and the idealization of revealed truth it would guarantee, rendered illegible by the very movement of mimesis that order claims to ensure?

Or more: is the master's book not itself already a site of improvised dissimulation and uncontrolled dissemination, an already disturbed scene of precepts, reinscription, errors, alternations, erasures?[2] Whose word might Master Thomas's writing itself double, displace, perplex? As the source-text of a black writing it fancies impossible because forbidden, this schoolboy's copy-book might well be thought the mimic offspring of America's "master Thomas," the paradoxical Jefferson of enlightenment and slavery, of liberty and limit. Let us then—anticipating the (ex)slave's revisionary movement toward non-specular spaces of self-representation—turn to *that* Master Thomas's book, which discloses mastery's imbrication with the "veil of black" it presumes to penetrate and discard.

2. The abject(ion) of blackness

Thomas Jefferson, writing fully in the spirit at once of Enlightenment idealism and colonialist ethnography, offers us a representative effort to establish the natural "distinction" between white and black which can ground their oppositional relations in the economy of modern (New World) political power:

> The first difference which strikes us is that of colour. Whether the black of the negro resides in the reticular membrane between the skin and scarf-skin, or in the scarf-skin itself; whether it proceeds from the colour of the blood, the colour of the bile, or from that of some other recreation, the difference is fixed in nature, and is as real as if its seat and cause were better known to us. And is this difference of no importance? Is it not the foundation of a greater or less share of beauty in the two races? Are not the fine mixtures of red and white, the expressions of every passion by greater or less suffusion of colour in the one, preferable to that eternal monotony, which reigns in the countenances, that immovable veil of black which covers all the emotions of the other race? . . . Besides those of colour, figure, and hair, there are other physical distinctions proving a difference of race. They have less hair on the face and body. They secrete less by the kidnies, and more by the glands of the skin, which gives them a very strong and disagreeable odour . . . Perhaps too a difference of structure in the pulmonary apparatus, which a late ingenious experimentalist has discovered to be the principal regulator of animal heat, may have disabled them from extricating, in the act of inspiration, so much of that fluid from the outer air . . . They are more ardent after their female: but love seems with them to be more an eager desire, than a tender delicate mixture of sentiment and sensation. Their griefs are transient . . . In general, their existence appears to participate more of sensation than reflection . . . Comparing them by their faculties of memory, reason, and imagination, it appears to me that in memory they are equal to whites; in reason much inferior . . . and that in imagination they are dull, tasteless, and anomalous . . . I advance it therefore . . . that the blacks, whether originally a distinct race, or made distinct by time and circumstances, are inferior to the whites . . . Will not a lover of natural history, then, one who gives the gradations in all the animals with the eye of philosophy, excuse an effort to keep those in the department of Man as distinct as nature has formed them? (Jefferson, 1787/1984: 264–266; 270).

Blackness, like the concept of "race" it is deployed to anchor, becomes in Jefferson's tortuous definitional performance the "striking" metonymic instance of an otherness which remains otherwise elusive, subject to a plethora of contradictory, if mutually generating, figures. If, on the one hand, Jefferson seeks to locate the "difference" between white and black within some pre-existent bodily space, it nevertheless remains an indeterminate trace of divergent subjectivities, inaccessible to any assignable origin or logic ("cause") and marked by the subjunctive apprehension of partially occluded "appearances." "Colour" is, in fact, the site of a constant formation and deformation of identities and meanings, as Jefferson's description proceeds in a dizzying spiral of self-affirming empiricism, rhetorical question, baroque scientism, and psycho-metaphysical speculation. Here ideology and fantasy intermingle and displace one another, propelling the peculiar self-legitimating narrative of (dis)enfranchisement by which the contingent process of affiliation, transgression, and exclusion seeks to naturalize itself as an objective, if bemused, account of the "Real."

And just where does this distinguishing feature of blackness "reside," and just what are its "distinguishing" features? Is it elemental to the blank (inertly full, or purely empty?) being of the other's *face* (the unimaginative "countenance"'s essential quality)? Or is it instead an extrinsic mark of otherness's very inscrutability as impenetrable, inexpressive (illegible?) *mask* (the ambiguously revelatory "cover" of vaguely acknowledged "emotions")? Whether natural imposition or supplementary surface, the "veil of black" provokes the desire to pierce, peel back, and explain that which, as natural ("fixed" and "immovable") fact, supposedly prohibits or suspends exegetical desire.

Jefferson's energetic compilation and dissection of "sentiments and, sensations" in itself, then, exposes the inescapable connections in his discourse among interpretation, projection, and possession. The Negro "founds" that discourse by its very existence as a *text to be read*, a text which must be at once transparent and overdetermined, its properties becoming indistinguishable from the reader's production of distinguishing signs. At once "eternally" the same and "anomalous" to the expectations it purportedly generates, Jefferson's blackness exposes the incoherence and perplexity of the self whose "comparative" language it also "proves."

Blackness, then, functions not simply as "fixed" other to a privileged order of white "reason"; indeed, the category of color itself cannot long sustain the simple binarism of self and other, "us" and "them," any more than it can be stabilized at any "known" intersection of body and affect. Rather, blackness serves as the writing subject's authorizing double, as its defining "shadow." In a sense, the language of mastery "covers" its conceptual tracks, making of blackness a locus of self-cancelling antinomies that "perhaps" translate its own unsettled "mixture" of "expression" and "reason" (asserting, for example, the Negro's emotional constitution to be at once "ardent" and "dull"). Indeed, the "negro"'s presence—and brutal containment, the underlying motivation of Jefferson's inquiry—must be simultaneously posited and annuled, as its constitutive relation to the master's own character hollows the very epistemology from which the master derives his "importance." Its shadowy ambiguity rhetorically mirrors the indeterminacies of "enlightened" mastery itself, as the cipher of absolute otherness blurs into the syntax of interwoven and mutually complicating differences.

In the grammar of white mythology, it "appears," blackness is not antithetical but integral to the narrative of mastery. Seeking closure where it hovers at the awful abyss hovers at the awful abyss of difference, this narrative nevertheless takes shape by employing a trope of blackness that is already divided and duplicitous, its articulation unavoidably enacting a slippage between the real and the seeming, between body and sign, condition and construction, face and mask. The more persistent the effort to focus the "nature" of blackness, the more evident its socially-bound composition; the more occult the "origin" of virtue's hierarchy, the clearer its "temporal and circumstantial" status as a projection, not observation, of the "philosophical eye." But this, after all, is intrinsic to the contradictory program of mastery: in order to signify itself, it must establish difference in a representation which is itself susceptible to further differentiating response, thus initiating an endless dynamic of contestatory mediations.

Here the curious passage concerning organic "secretion" (the body's mode of purification by self-othering, as it were) becomes more than just an unsavory detail in an elaborate image of demonization. As part of the larger project of ensuring "proper" social structure and securing unfragmented identity, the elimination of unclean and disorderly elements in the social body would clear a space for the speaking subject of power to declare its symbolic authority. Contrasting this sublimated, nearly decorporealized, hegemonic body (Jefferson's "delicate" white being seems nearly to have refined itself of odor and hair altogether, while it does not so much contain color as maintain it in reserve in order to strategically "suffuse" itself in carefully controlled "expressions" of rationally calibrated sentiment), the "other race" becomes an instance of what Kristeva (1982) terms the "abject," the unspoken but uncanny residue of the triumphant subject's claim to expressive force. As such it constitutes a liminal position in the emergent language of modern (American) subjectivity, neither fully outside nor inside the scene of speech—just as Jefferson's blackness is undecidably "between" or within various levels of interior integument and epidermis, mask layered upon mask! (The immediate context of Jefferson's meditation is the proposal to incorporate freedmen into the sovereignty of Virginia, a notion whose rebuttal requires extensive "coloring" of the larger discourse on cultural "laws" by the omnipresent awareness of white-and-black, and, moreover, does not prevent him from declaring slavery as such an indefensible crime [see Cash, 1941:61][3]).

In this sense, the "immovable veil of black[ness]" designates neither a factitious presence nor a fully repressed absence; rather, it describes an activity, a *movement,* of racial semiosis through which the American self alternately enters and is ejected from the space of privileged articulation, the "seat" of symbolic recognition. Threatening and yet also "inferior" by virtue of its alterity and autonomy, blackness, precisely in its resistance to the master's classifying gaze, testifies to the precariousness of the codes that seek its containment. But what language of the freed self, what alternative discrimination of figure ("colour") and genealogical datum ("race"), might escape or stand beyond this coercive apparatus of differentiation and nomination? Can any account of modern African-American being begin elsewhere as more than an oppositional (hence ironically replicatory) reversal of empowered and abject, proposing a speculative as well as structural reconception of the speaking subject? And might such an undetermined, subversive, and reconstructive discourse be the "language of blackness" *itself*?

Such possibilities entail further inquiry into relations among procedures of narrative, historical empowerment, racial othering, and self-validation in the prevailing discourse of Euro-American modernism. As James Snead (following the leads of Nietzsche and Raymond Williams) has outlined (1984:62–64), the linkage of narrative with subjectivity in Enlightenment accounts of history necessitated the abjection of blackness as the "mute" and unchanging threshold of legitimated culture. Origin, unity, teleology, causality, totality, ground, and, finally, fully realized consciousness itself attached themselves to a progressively revealed Western subject through the claim to narrative coherence, a logic of sequential (dis)closure which (to cite Hegel) the "natural spirit" of blackness, "a succession of accidents and surprises," definitively lacked [Hegel, 1955:215].[4] To exist in history was, necessarily if paradoxically, to stand beyond it in historiography. On this view, the event and its textual inscription become mutually determining; however partial and volatile, experience and writing reflect one another in an evolving structural unity. And it is this power of self-conscious narrativity which most precisely set the whiteness of history apart from the "eternal monotony" of blackness so abhorrent to the aesthetic politics of Jefferson and his Enlightenment heirs.[5]

Curiously, the status of history, considered either as event or writing, remains in Enlightenment historiography itself unexamined, even unthought; even when self-aware, the process of self-narration affirms experience in a circle of inevitability, never questioning the ideal congruity of the subject's intention and his complete self-articulation. Thus the most perplexing crux, the potential disabling paradox, of the black writer's challenge within and against "enlightened" modernism arises precisely in the moment when a liberated, dis-covered, or even invented blackness *sui gene-ris* is declared: understood as a process and exemplum of signification, any such self-presentational act stands in danger of recapitulating the ideology and rhetorical structure of reified self-disclosure upon which the master narrative of modernity bases its claim to a continuous, culturally readable, identity. Precisely by constituting an oppositional vector, and not merely functional absence, in modernism's fiction of enfranchised selfhood, any newly voiced language of blackness inherently runs the risk of revoicing that fiction's very specular tropology of identity and difference.

It is just here, as well, that the language of blackness might make its most profound intervention into the intersection of modernity and subjectivity: not as "another" autobiography of the recuperated, purified "other race," but as the interrogation of history's intersection with narration, of history and speech as problem and possibility. A search for a beginning that makes no claim to masterful origination, the language of blackness becomes audible in the exploration of its own possibilities of self-representation, in its emergence as a critical mediation of the self-interpretive apparatus which modernity's factitious blackness simultaneously enabled and fractured. But where is such a beginning to be found(ed), and, if it is indeed the point of departure *(post)* for a newly measured *(modern)* voice, in what voice can it be spoken?

3. The project(ion) of blackness

As my capacities and Condition of Life are very low, it cannot be expected that I should make those Remarks on the Sufferings I have met with, or the kind Providence of a good God for my Preservation, as one in a higher Station; but shall leave that to the Reader as he goes along, and so I shall only relate Matters of Fact as they occur to my Mind.

This is the beginning of Briton Hammon's *Narrative of Uncommon Sufferings, and Surprizing Deliverance,* the seminal work of the African-American narrative tradition, and as such the initiatory gesture of African-American modernism ("father" or "origin," as we shall see, would be a designation too ideologically burdened even if, in the present state of understanding, chronologically authentic). It is an opening that takes great pains to seem a merely presentational vehicle of zero-degree experience, effacing any pretensions to interpretive or even organizational authority. Its design will, it appears, be dictated by the "higher" narrational power of Providence, for whom the hero himself will serve as mere scribe. Its values, in turn, will be derived by a (presumably) white reader in nearly-direct communication with this transcendent compositional force, while Hammon, ever the passive ("suffering") reagent of the narrative's developmental process, will "meet with" those values as determined after and outside of his own tale. In a sense, Hammon presents himself as a kind of medium or mask through which another voice speaks, an instrumental effect rather than a willfull cause of a signifying power or system of meaning.

Yet the mask which operates as a mechanism of repression can also facilitate a strategic, even uncanny, repositioning of desire, specifically the desire for self-origination. Closer inspection of Hammon's prefatorial remarks, in fact, dislodges from the equable surface of self-effacement signs of subtle cracks in the structural divisions upon which his formal invocation of modesty is based. If the language of hierarchy, deferral, and submission seems at first glance to render Hammon the captive of his reader (even as the prefatory notice celebrates his return, at story's end, to "his good old Master") (Andrew, 1986:32–33, and Williams, 1970:33–34), certain peculiarities of diction and nuances of juxtaposition suggest a more complicated narrative stance. While the reader is enjoined to provide a commentary from some generalized exalted "station" as he "goes along," he can only do so at the pace and in the order that the story's data "occur to" and are thenceforth conveyed by the author himself. What announces itself as mere record, as an almost purified, unperspectival, realism, soon admits that it will come to us as the filtrate of a notably self-centering mental energy. It is, finally, the generalized activity of "mind," not the atomized "matter of fact" which will control both narrative's production and reception in equal measure.

Hammon's beginning, then, establishes a nexus of tensions between mimetic and expressive impulses which opens the *mise-en-scène* of African-American self-representation as a complex threshold of indeterminate possibilities. On the one hand, the writer is exposed to a supposedly unbounded critical gaze, stripped of all powers of aesthetic illusion and moral judgment. On the other hand, this very act of personal demystification, this artifice of humility by which the experiential persona becomes emptied of evident imaginative (or even decorative) invention (or even intention), precipitates simultaneously a remystification of authorial agency. By allowing us to see only that which he is *not*, thereby becoming, as it were, the very personification of providential design, Hammon shrouds himself in an illusion of unconditional self-lessness, productively confusing the ventriloquist with the medium, the re-veiled with the revealed.

Hammon's tale itself doubles the ambivalent dialectic of demystification and remystification that simultaneously energizes and destabilizes its moment of inscription. The narrator's adventures are initiated by an "intention" to undertake a sea-voyage from his master's residence in Boston to an unspecified destination. This impulse, like the master's permission which enables it, appears without recorded inspiration or motivation, suggesting already a dual and conflicted source of narrative movement: perhaps, alternatively, we have an initiating instance of providential design, providing material and formal cause for the story's consequent arrangement of event; perhaps we have an implied plot of escape, necessarily cloaked by the writer's present circumstances (he is, again, in Boston, under the sway of his "Master's House"). When his ship is wrecked along the Florida coast, Hammon is stranded on an island, apprehended by Indians, and thence thrust into a series of ransoms, failed efforts at escape, and fresh confinements throughout the Caribbean until, thirteen years later, he is "miraculously preserved" through an unexpected rediscovery by his "good old Master."

Once jolted from the brief safety of his leisurely travelogue into an iterative tale of entrapment and release, Hammon experiences the story of multiple fortuitous enslavements, (mis)recognitions, and deliverances—that is, documentary event, through patterned repetition, religious diction, and topographical imagery, is gradually transformed into figurative structure. In particular, the motifs of seafaring and return, captivity and rescue, and death and resurrection ("I was like one arose from the Dead," Hammon tells us in the final scene of recovery and *nostos*) mark the *Narrative* as a romance—so that the concluding evocation of David's deliverance from the lion's den is hardly the "plainly gratuitous" appendage of superficial piety critics have complained of,[6] but is instead the climactic appeal to a profoundly sanctioned mode of achieving cultural significance.

But the "intention" of that appeal, and thus of the narrative which generates it, remains unclear. The evocation of biblical liberational typology is possibly fashioned into a vehicle of continuing protestation and assertive struggle, as the character "freed from . . . Savages" and "return'd to my own Native Land" speaks again in a passive voice nonetheless capable of potentially subversive juxtaposition. The man who remains mastered in his own country, the man Jefferson would account a "Savage," would be the resurrected mediating voice between a "good God" and "all Men," an exemplary figure of that puritan narrative of salvation which will have such complex force in subsequent installments of the slave narrative genre (see, e.g., Stepto, 1979a; Smith, 1987; and Andrews, 1986). At the same time, the text he delivers is, modem editors generally surmise, "likely only dictated by Hammon"[7] to an unnamed amanuensis, a "servant" of the slave's own voice whose re-inscriptions must, in turn, open questions of mimetic fidelity. Being thus composed in an instructional scene permeated everywhere by a high-stakes play between representation and supplementation, Hammon's *Narrative* enacts a mimodrama of multiplied textual doublings proliferating from the inaugural division between naturalistic detail and fabulous contrivance, between "fact" and "Mind."

Where, then, does Hammon's text stand in relation to the differential struggle between revealed meaning and its figural disturbance which characterizes enlightened modernity's discursive codification and abjection of race? Is the framing co-implication of romance and rebellion a sign of the narrator's supreme naiveté or of his most trenchant irony? Is he fully absorbed by the exigencies of narrative, its obsessive detail and coercive/redemptive symmetry, or does he stand somehow beyond the tale as its shrewdly concealed critic and oblique final cause (speaking, for example, of unspecified omissions of "a great many Things," an authorial suppression which he nevertheless insists fails to imperil his assurance of ultimate persuasiveness)? Put differently, is the tale's continuous oscillation between documentary and romance modes encompassed by a closural ("providential") design or does it effect an opening to further revisionist engagement? Neither divorced from nor limited by its structuring archetypes, Hammon's *Narrative* is already enmeshed in the dynamic of an African-American tradition moving with nervous and disruptive energy within and against the structures of an equally labile, but antithetical, American modernist crisis. For in Hammon we find the mirror of Jefferson's liberal American racialism which, cut off from its "original," fully "manly," grace of European "nativity," reenacts the Western romance of return to the self-same as the movement toward purified whiteness, both physical and political.[8]

Specular rivals, Jefferson and Hammon jostle for sovereignty in the space between received language and self-authentication, as anxious master (himself a rebel) and illumined servant (himself a "native" claimant to the New World) alike seek to forge a new beginning through equivocal resistance to inherited circumstances. But the African-American, by doubling the enfranchised American's burden of belatedness, threatens also to become excessive to it, turning the desire for beginning into the very ground and telos of black literary tradition. Operating within a hermeneutical situation, within the data—the blood, the genealogy, the history—(s)he questions ("the opinion was also whispered that my master was my father," Douglass tells us), the African-American writer imbricates interpretation and invention so that the "language of blackness" is always, and always already, the language of the other, the disfigured language of mastery.

To the African American—so long denied the literary tools of a dominating logocentric culture, denied even the theoretical status of *homo faber* by which Western culture had established its own claim to civilized value (see West, 1982: ch. 12; and Gates, 1987: ch. 1)—the singular issue of his literature has been its very possibility. Hammon's *Narrative* already proffers an instructive instance of this modernist problematic, for in its bare fourteen pages we witness both the (un)masking of an imaginative critical intelligence and a characteristic response to what may be its culture's most pressing literary problem: the awareness that it has inherited from the past a world that is at once radically overdetermined with possible meanings (White Mythology) and at the verge of silence's blanched *tabula rasa* ("it cannot be expected that I should make those Remarks . . ."). Nearly a full century after the appearance of Hammon's *Narrative* the black critic "Dion" would write that "Colored American literature exists only, to too great an extent, in the vast realm of probability," while another century later Amiri Baraka would derisively lament "the myth of a 'Negro Literature.'"[9] The temporal chasm stretching between the ante-bellum milieu of "Dion" and the post-industrial context of Baraka—notwithstanding the tumultuous history of Emancipation, Reconstruction, migration, urbanization, various rights movements, and all their attendant discursive formations—is succinctly bridged by the shared perception of *dis*continuity, depotentiation, or sheer absence in the history of African-American expression. And yet this isn't a modernist expression of belatedness in blackface; the language of blackness is imagined taking shape in the "vast" arena of a future-perfect reopening of an apparent closure. Thus Dion proceeds to envision a return to the point of departure from the word of blackness, reversing the Jeffersonian dehistoricized and unnaming vision of the race's secondary relation to expressive power:

> The future may yet reveal to us—and in the feelings of hope, we dare predict, that the future *will* yet reveal to us the names of colored Americans so gloriously illustrated in the catalogue of literary excellence, as to remind the world of the days when dark-browed Egypt gave letters to Greece . . .

Writing-as-being is an act which involves the black modernist in what Heidegger (1961:32) serendipitously terms the "darkness . . . that attend[s] a true beginning"—but what the black literary modernist seeks is African-American literature itself.

In seeking the image of a specifically African-American modernism, we are thus compelled critically to begin, in imitation of the African-American writer, by calling the quest's object into question. African-American literature comes into being, much like the "American poetics" delineated by Joseph Riddel (1979:322–358), as an effort to restore an elemental plenitude, as unencumbered self. Yet as the bare fourteen pages of Hammon's narration discloses, the very effort to recover such power is enmeshed in the tensions of visionary temporality, claiming for the instruments of mediation the power to embody miracle. Situated in the provisional space between memory and possibility, becoming at once an extension and a repudiation of tradition, black modernism becomes a discourse on the idea of tradition per se, a self-distantiating and constitutive commentary on the interplay of expression and its negation.[10] Seeking linguistic freedom to image physical deliverance, while claiming typological significance for his circumstantial chain of incident, Hammon becomes in this sense the "surprising" but "providential" guide to the modernism of his literary successors. In his *Narrative* are discerned both the presence of a creative intelligence aware of its political positioning which it seeks to foreground as self-consciously as the freedman's *modesty topos* permits, and the dramatic presentation of an historically resonant challenge, here the plot and plight of the fugitive subject seeking refuge from the "savagery" of various competing "masters."

For African-American writers, such self-consciousness is, so to speak, primordial, their collective history cohering as a succession of modernisms turning on alternately enshrined and demystified realizations of a *new* black "Renaissance."[11] Nothing attests to the dialectical complexity of African-American literature so much, in fact, as the persistent attempt by its practitioners and critics to find within it the locus of pure black presence, its "Soul"-fullness. But were it ever forged or dis-covered, the long-desired "true" Revolutionary or Liberating Black Image (and its new "New Negro" author) would be, as Riddel says of the American quest for the Great Novel, in every sense the "end" of African-American literature—beyond the problematic of "mainstream"[12] expression, such a literature would no longer arise self-critically, putting itself into question, but would finally be, as it were, out of the question.

Having no pristine origin (the choice of Hammon is, after all, as perverse as it is pertinent), the history of that story could, in principle, itself begin in many places—with Jean Toomer's poetic of imagistic fragments; with the *New Negro*'s self-conscious explication of blackness as a trope as well as condition; with Zora Neale Hurston's embrace of the creative plasticity of imagination over the totalizing passivity of memory. Such "foundational" works of African-American modernism are in part driven by impulses general to Euro-American modernism, in part quickened by a desire for a position outside this informing condition of crisis: restless in the face of dissolving paradigms but wary of forming compensating structures, ever-suspicious of the insidious betrayals of *traditio* yet desirous of historically valid community, radically and destructively experimental but in search of a non-marginal power or authority. They engage change as an avenue to value, not as a mere mechanism for dismantling inherited hierarchy. They are therefore often organized around scenes vibrating with expectancy (either of consciousness or event), unfolding plural images of paradoxical significance: the northern city or southern church as a realm both of enabling freedom and anti-communal disruption; the instrument of musical or military technology (typically the horn or the handgun), a device of self-assertion and a sign of pyrrhic triumph; the sudden look in a mirror or familiar face providing a shock of familial recognition and a shudder of difference—images, like the blindingly illuminated hole of *Invisible Man* or the over-flowering home of Pilate in *Song of Solomon*, which seem to be at once celebratory and threatening, intense and diffuse, ethereally symbolic and suprarealistic. The profusion of these double images, these signs of possibility and impediment, gives black modernist expression its special and animating vitality, its tension between assertion and query—gives it the doubleness of what Robert Stepto (1979b) accurately described as the inner dialectic of call-and-response.

Our beginning lies elsewhere, however, with Richard Wright, whose formulation of the tradition's central metaphor of emergence and discovery continues to cast imposing shadows over those of our current explorers. For Wright's work, too, takes shape in the gap between abjection and recaptured identity which defines the peculiar terrain of the African-American modernist quest:

> What could I dream of that had the barest possibility of coming true? I could think of nothing. And, slowly, it was upon exactly that nothingness that my mind began to dwell, that constant sense of wanting without having, of being hated without reason. A dim notion of what life meant to a Negro in America was coming to consciousness in me, not in terms of external events, lynchings, Jim Crowism, and the endless brutalities, but in terms of crossed-up feeling, of psyche pain. I sensed that Negro life was a sprawling land of unconscious suffering, and that there were but few Negroes who knew the meaning of their lives, who could tell their story.
> — *American Hunger* (Wright, 1977:7)

Dream against possibility; consciousness against experience; psyche against fact; pain against reason; meaning against negation; suffering against expression—here are the antinomial hallmarks of the African-American writer's uneasy situation within modernity that we have been tracing. Reflecting here on his interior struggle between "desire" and "repression" that "the Chicago streets [of his youth] . . . were evoking in me," Wright could well be ventriloquizing his most volatile and influential creation, the desperately incendiary and hypnotically violent Bigger Thomas of *Native Son*. It is *Native Son*, with its eloquent but disturbing juxtaposition of brutal event, explanatory representation, and aching but unvoiced lyricism, that restages the slave narrator's drama of self-realization at a critical juncture of twentieth-century African-American cultural experience. At the threshold of Depression and war, suffused with the growing sophistication and limitation of "sprawling" urban life that was gradually erasing the political and psychic distance between southern and northern domains, black American culture in 1940 stood ready and in need of a fresh revision of its modal self-understanding. Such revision was provided with the shock of sudden illumination by *Native Son*, which accepted the challenge of reinscribing the slave narrative's psycho-political critique of blackness's presence in modernity through a reconception of its thematic and formal resources. And so it is to this most evocative instance of the "native"-born other's effort to revoice the story of enlightenment "once more" that this chapter of an impossible literary history now turns.

4. The subject(ion) of blackness

> I was born in North Carolina, in Caswell County, I am not able to tell in what year or month. What I shall now relate is what was told me . . . I was confined here in a dungeon . . .
> —Moses Roper, *A Narrative of the Adventures and Escape From American Slavery* (1837/1971) (beginning and conclusion, respectively)

It is possible that no work in the history of African-American literature has engendered more immediate or more passionate response than Richard Wright's *Native Son*. From the time of its publication in 1940, Wright's masterpiece excited heated interest in both black and white media. So striking was its story of grim urban violence within clearly delineated class structures that *Native Son* quickly became a template for all those aesthetic, political, and sociological debates typically swirling about the Negro Question, what Ralph Ellison was to term wryly "that oft-beaten boy." Commentators of all cultural positions seemed to find in *Native Son* an exemplum, whether negative or positive, of their peculiar visions of Afro-psycho-socio-political Man.[13]

Whatever its specific sociological import, *Native Son* clearly marked a new phase in African-American writing, for it successfully reinscribed the slave narrative's conventions of plight, alienation, and cultural violence in a representation of black life that departed radically from the quasi-lyrical nostalgia of his immediate predecessors. The "Wright School of Protest" (to risk Robert Bone's cunning phrase [1965:153–166]) which *Native Son* commenced might now be discerned as a revision of the narrative form announced by Hammon and focused by Douglass, but its exploitation of contemporary naturalism's methodology (the detail of Farrel, the stark structural clarity of Dos Passos, the occasional wry bitterness of Steinbeck) within the specific context of contemporary African-American experience gave it the appearance of an absolute break with black literary tradition. It seemed, as Addison Gayle (1975:xvii) asserts, that *Native Son* succeeded in "undoing the work of black novelists heretofore."[14]

Just what *Native Son* "undid" has been a matter of contention from the time of its first appearance, but the controversy has been conveniently organized around the novel's two central characters: Bigger—the (anti)hero whose acts of murder are seen by critics as somehow both "dehumanizing" and emblematic of black selfhood[15]—and his environment—the doubly oppressive world of white racism and black subservience against which Bigger is seen to rebel.[16] One mode of interpretation, what we might term the Boris Max School, views Bigger as the warped product of a hideously cruel culture, his murders the distasteful but inevitable conclusion of a long process of distortion and subjugation. The second approach to *Native Son*, what we might term the Jan Erlone School, contends that the deteriorating influence of a hostile world fails to annihilate, and actually helps produce, an essential "humanity" in Bigger. In the former case, culture is ethically castigated but given prominent authority within the novel's formal domain (Ellison (1964:114): "Here environment is all"); in the latter instance, the context of given urban existence which Wright's naturalism carefully constructs is reduced to a casually accepted donnée against which the protagonist's equally static but more weighty symbolic actions are set. Ironically, the critical Boris Maxes and Jan Erlones—much like their prototypes in *Native Son*—become estranged from their subject, finding it flawed by an imbalanced emphasis on what they themselves see as central (the world, the self). Yet what makes Wright's novel a signal text of African-American modernism is the dynamic interaction of character and milieu which is not only the work's continuous concern but, indeed, the hero's as well. What is needed in our readings of Wright's important book, perhaps, is a Bigger Thomas School.

The absence of such an approach is, finally, an ironic residuum of *Native Son*'s struggle for voice, but to grasp the novel's role in reshaping the continuing history of African-American modernism's quest for expressive freedom we must attempt a reading from within Bigger's encounter with culture. Interestingly, Wright himself provided the terms for this understanding in his own critique of *Native Son*, "How 'Bigger' Was Born."[17] Fiction, Wright avers, is a product of the "total" self's impact on "the blinding objectivity and tangibility" of the world; it occurs when mind and emotion are integral, collectively imposing their particular "design" on the difficult "facts" of social existence (the echo of Hammon's prefatory language is noteworthy). The implications of these remarks are profound for both thematic and formal concerns. The hero's search for identity appears to be neither a metaphysical gesture, divorced from the social context against which it is initially directed,[18] nor a mere existential revolt, thrusting the self into some utterly new domain in absolute contrast to material reality.[19] Rather, the self seeks a fusion of act and vision, his relation to culture ambivalently dialectical rather than uncompromisingly diametrical: "The most I could say of Bigger," Wright tells us, "was that he felt the *need* for a whole life and *acted* out of that need." His psychosocial territory became, therefore, neither the pristine arena of imagination nor the intractable world of what James called "brute fact," but instead a "No

Man's Land,"[20] what Ellison will rename in *Invisible Man* the "border area" of self-conception.

It follows that this doubleness in Bigger's presentation will occur in a narrative structurally more complex than that of the simple positivistic realism with which *Native Son* and the "Protest School" has traditionally been associated by its celebrants and detractors alike. Bigger, in fact, struggles to envision for himself a notion and language of value independent of external cause; he does not wish to be excused, pitied, or even apotheosized because his acts are determined by exogenous forces. And thus his final agony in Max's presence condenses every fragment of desire glimpsed heretofore into the climactic *"need"* of his life:

> Distractedly, he gazed about the cell, trying to remember where he had heard words that would help him. He could recall none. He had lived outside of the lives of men. Their modes of communication, their symbols and images, had been denied him . . . He summoned his energies and lifted his head and struck out desperately, determined to rise from the grave, resolved to force upon Max the reality of his living (Wright, 1966:386).

If Bigger is neither a helpless madman nor a calculating nationalist—neither fully Other nor oppositional to hegemonic power—why, we must ask, have his interpreters consistently sought to coerce his story into one or another of such formulations? The dilemma we face in understanding Bigger is, in fact, a key crux *within* the novel itself. "Frantically, [Bigger's] mind sought to fuse his feelings with the world about him, but he was no nearer to knowing than ever. Only his black body lay here on the cot . . ." (Wright, 1966:383). The scene is prison, the last in the novel, but it might well be the famous opening tableau which also finds the hero on a cold iron bed of procrustean terror and isolation. The climactic search for a beginning of meaning in Bigger's world returns us to the meaning of his beginning.

Foreshadowing the novel's plot (see Bone, 1965:147; Brignano, 1970:31), the powerful first scene in the Thomas family's cell-like, one-room apartment is also a symbolic microcosm of Bigger's condition. An anti-Eden of the cruelest sort, the room is the site of a "conspiracy against shame" as each dresses in a precarious solitude suddenly violated by the invasion of a rat. Escaped from its dark hold, the animal furiously seeks refuge as Bigger attacks with almost "hysterical" determination until the rat's "flat black body" falls dead, its head crushed mercilessly. An emblem of the unclean and forbidden, the rat has transgressed its "appropriate" place, unsettling whatever fragile propriety the family's impoverished habitat possesses. Its potential for contagion requires a violent containment, first rhetorical ("'Don't let that thing *bite* you

. . . Hit 'im, Bigger! . . . Kill 'im'" [Wright, 1966:8, 9]), then physical and ideological ("Bigger . . . pounded the rat's head . . . cursing hysterically . . . 'Take a
newspaper and spread it over that spot'" [Wright, 1966:10, 11]).

Clearly, the episode prefigures Bigger's futile flight from the terrifying
authorities he here ironically represents.[21] But the scene's symbolism is not
simply narrative and ironic, it is synecdochic as well: Bigger acts within a
situation that is emblematic of all that follows, and the pattern of uncanny
doubling enacted between him and the rat he expels structures his story as
a drama of repressed identifications and unrecognized reflections. His is a
world defined by enclosures (rooms, holes, metalic beds—later specifically
displaced as crowded car seats, furnaces, cells); by blinding light (the pathetic
echo of *Genesis*—"Turn on the light" (Wright, 1966:7)—metamorphosed
first in the furnace's horrid flames and then as the "fire of death" electric
bulb above Bigger's prison cot [Wright, 1966:384]); and by shattered icons
of consciousness (the rat's smashed head recapitulated not only in Mary's
decapitation and Bessie's "face of death and blood" but also in Bigger's crucial
dream of his own headless agony (Wright, 1966:223 f., 156). It is a world of
labyrinthine and hellish uncertainty, filled with images of severe privation
from which arise surrealistic distortions; the Thomas family's room, with its
circular maze in which the rat is lethally entrapped, is a metonymy of Bigger's
Chicago, an "icy black pit" (Wright, 1966:192) delineated by its Loop and
endless rows of enmeshing "cells":

> Sometimes, in his room or on the sidewalk, the world seemed to
> him a strange labyrinth even when the streets were straight and
> the walls were square; a chaos which made him feel that something
> in him should be able to understand it, divide it, focus it (Wright,
> 1966:176).
> Standing trembling in his cell, he saw . . . a black sprawling prison
> full of tiny black cells in which people lived; each cell had its stone
> jar of water and a crust of bread and no one could go from cell to cell
> and there were screams and curses and yells of suffering and nobody
> heard them, for the walls were thick and darkness was everywhere.
> Why were there so many cells in the world? (Wright, 1966:301)

Bigger acts inside a milieu, textual as well as mimetic, in which quest
becomes wandering *(error)*, a futile movement incapable of locating a principle of identity; where repetition does not define a useful sameness; where
the protagonist envisions representations of his dilemma which, in their
tortured distortion, remain identical to themselves only as disharmonious
parody of collective dissent. The imagined labyrinths, emblematic of black
Chicago's physical "reality," express the threat Bigger feels that his world

does not permit any principle of continuous selfhood which establishes a stable relation to the others, black or white, and where "suffering" never achieves the redemptive shape of story. In his family's sphere as much as in the Daltons', he is an "outsider";[22] the exasperated, accusatory cry with which his mother greets his mock-epic rat-slaying is the refrain of all his subsequent antagonists and critics: "Boy, sometimes I wonder what makes you act like you do" (Wright, 1966:11).

Ultimately, the hope of successful flight from this infernal Huis Clos dissolves, as Bigger is figured as the fugitive black animal whose plague is relentlessly quarantined:

> He could not leave Chicago; all roads were blocked . . . He looked at the paper and saw a black-and-white map of the South Side, around the borders of which was a shaded portion an inch deep. Under the map ran a line of small print:
> Shaded portion shows area already covered by police and vigilantes in search for Negro rapist and murderer. White portion shows area yet to be searched.
> He was trapped (Wright, 1966:230).

His frantic being, and the pollution it bears, is obscured by the blinding tools of official classification, the reductive mechanism of newsprint "covering" his inner reality as surely as it hid bloody traces of the rat's smashed head in the opening scene. Marshalling its most precise and compulsive technologies of de-limitation, a horrified society pursues the criminal victim to the very center of its rigorously graven—and excessively policed—cultural field. The abject black body thus serves to focus the structures of naming, differentiation, and delineation by which an imperiled authority can project its susceptibility to hysteria and maintain its hold on symbolic identity.

Pressured by such strategies of isolation and othering, Bigger is brought to a dizzying epiphany of *self*-dissociation:

> He was surprised that he was not afraid. Under it all some part of his mind was beginning to stand aside; he was going behind his curtain, his wall, looking out with sullen stares of contempt. He was outside himself now, looking on; he lay under a winter sky lit with tall gleams of whirling light, hearing thirsty screams and hungry shouts (Wright, 1966:250).

Bigger's universe has become a mass of chaotic indifferentiated centers in which he is lost and essentially unseen and which is *stricto sensu* unrepresentable. Neither the realism of his surroundings nor the fantasy projected against them (the minstrelsy of the pool-hall and the hypertrophied irreality of the darkened movie-house, equally false *loci amoeni* where people cannot *see* each other truly) suffice in Bigger's (or Wright's) effort to realize a vision of wholeness (cf. Wright, 1966:25ff; 32ff). As with the opening scene's tropological drama of contamination and expulsion, the doubling of Bigger into the object and agent of the controlling Look stages the potential reciprocity of mastery the potential reciprocity of mastery and the abject.[23] By thus suggesting that Bigger is a site of multiple positions of subjection and subjectivity, such passages disrupt the prevailing view of *Native Son* as the product of a single narrational perspective.

For we are certainly given to thinking of *Native Son* as a conventionally, if searingly, naturalistic narrative, where the relentless movement of plot—the unqualified display of interaction between man and place in time—is entirely the measure of the novel's design. Yet within *Native Son*, as within Bigger, is another novel struggling to take shape, one which might assume a unique form that masters the causal and temporal movement of determined events, a lyrically inward, yet aesthetically objective form. Neither the strict record of realism's unblinking gaze, nor the supreme fiction of an abstractive symbolic narrational consciousness, *Native Son* is a medium of rhetorical negotiation between an impassively observational and strategically encoded textual determination. And so Wright, the "designer" of facts, creates a hero who probes the meaning behind performed actions:

> . . . once more before he died he wanted to feel with as much keenness as possible what his living and dying meant . . . Though he lay on his cot, his hands were groping fumblingly through the city of men for something to match the feelings smoldering in him; his groping was a yearning to know (Wright, 1966:382 f.).

Writer and character, however, are symbolists *manque,* for in their story *mythos* and meaning must be sought without the prior assurance that any meaning can be confidently secured. Novel and hero, equally uncertain of voice, thus seek to evade the extrinsic limits of the genre by turning actions into scenes which embody recognitions,[24] but they find their dream *(vision* in the root sense) of the whole only in the fractured terror of nightmare:

> Out of the surrounding silence and darkness came the quiet ringing of a distant church bell, thin, faint, but clear . . . with each passing moment he felt an urgent need to run and hide as though the bell were sounding a warning . . . and he had a big package in his arms so wet and slippery and heavy that he could scarcely hold onto it and he stopped near an alley corner and unwrapped it and the paper fell away and he saw—it was his *own* head lying with

black face and half-closed eyes and lips parted with white teeth
showing and hair wet with blood and the red glare grew brighter
like light shining down from a red moon and red stars on a hot
summer night and he was sweating and breathless from running
and the bell clanged so loud that he could hear the iron tongue
clapping against the metal sides each time it swung to and fro . . .
and he . . . cursed the booming bell and the white people and felt
that he did not give a damn what happened to him and when the
people closed in he hurled the bloody head squarely into their faces
dongdongdong . . . (Wright, 1966:156).

As simple condensation of his entire life's waking fear into the concrete
imagery of unconscious articulation, Bigger's dream enacts a primal scene of
modernism's psychic economy—the recoil of the individual from a hostile
world into a private order of images which do not redress but instead reflect
the fragmented disorder of experience. The vision's aura of fire, desperation,
maimed speech, decapitation, and deception not only echo actual details of the
novel's own primal scene, the central furnace episode, but also cast a distort-
ing spell on that scene's gruesome reality, suggesting that Bigger's unresolved
sense of selfhood is in fact its inner content. The parataxis and surrealism of
Bigger's dream express his repudiation of naturalism's philosophical and cultural impulses—its suggestion that man exists by virtue of an environment in
which he rather gropingly reacts than boldly acts; that the self is a history of
separate experiences and disjunct concepts; that history and not imagination
is the custodian of value.

But in this way the dream also enacts the resistance of blackness to
any final absorption by modernist angst—or even to Euro-American culture's
understanding of blackness as the sacrificial abject of enlightened society's
resolution of its own spiritual and historical alienation. By projecting his psy-
chical interior into images of mutilated expression (evoking, in a strategic
fantasm reminiscent of Hammon's allegorical resurrection, an Orphic capacity for speech beyond death),[25] the dream suggests how Bigger's black presence in itself registers the disunity of "white" symbolic registration. Violently
traversing the border of Imaginary and Symbolic orders, the vision thereby
probes the social meaning of Bigger's fragmentation as the exile from or refusal of a stable, coherently coded position as speaking subject. As the object
of the objectifying Gaze, he suffers dismemberment, but as the subject of a
reversing Look, he threatens recognition of the master's incoherent claims to
supremacy. Corporeal boundaries are thus violated ambiguously in the scene,
effecting dispersal and assertion of the black subject. So, too, the black face
of Bigger's dream is undecidably inside and outside the bodies from and to
which it clamors to speak. The bloody head, like the apotropaic sight of a male

Medusa,[26] is severed and thrown both as an act of disavowal (through which the dreamer would acquire a provisional relief from sundering assault) and as a challenging reminder that the excessive residue of the sanctioned social body inevitably erupts to stain its illusory purity.

So the dream's vocabulary of disintegration is hurled at the narrative's face as if in defiance of its attempt to break him apart; its relation to nature, for all the parallel phenomena, is one of transgression, that is of interpretation, a deliberate deformation of objective circumstances that answers to their concerted effort to disfigure or caricature him. For whether or not Wright imagined Bigger to be, as Baldwin (1955:26–27) suggested, "a monster created by the American public," culture as represented *within* the narrative certainly portrays him in images of stereotypical defilement and distortion. What the dream suggests is that, while Wright deconstructs white imagination as a sleep of reason giving birth only to its *own* monstrosity,[27] Bigger's inner abnormality, his "smoldering" marginality, may itself be a sign of liberating ex-centricity. So the dream, like the first scene, takes us into the presence of unexpungeable difference where Bigger is a figure for the incomplete abjection of blackness from modem consciousness, its repression to the underground terrors beneath enlightened culture and its ghastly reappearance as the unsupressible, if unrepresentable, voice of revolutionary negation.[28]

It is toward redemption of this dream by the self's reconciliation with the violent otherness of imposed experience that Bigger gathers his energy in the final scene of his life:

> Why this black gulf between him and the world: warm red blood here and cold blue sky there, and never a wholeness, a oneness, a meeting of the two? Was *that* it? Was it simply fever, feeling without knowing, seeking without finding? Was this all, the meaning, the end? (Wright, 1966:383)

The final agon of Bigger's quest to "end" beyond mere realism in a coming together *(symballein)* of fulfilling significance turns, tragically, upon a double negativity: Max's blindness and Bigger's voicelessness. It is against Bigger's "lying voice" (Wright, 1966:376) that prosecutor Buckley thunders his most vicious accusations, but it is Max's voice that we hear throughout the novel's culminating section—even in the condemned hero's cell. The uneasiness Wright's critics have' felt in judging Max and his lengthy doctrinaire oration is apt,[29] but, as the final confrontation of the lawyer and his convicted charge makes clear, we should feel disturbed in *Bigger's* behalf. Indeed, Bigger's trial thus sustains narrative logic as the mirror-image of his central nightmare of suppressed meaning, as the effort of an official apparatus of repression to re-encode Bigger in terms of the motiveless malignity of any language of blackness. The very prolixity and laboriousness of this section, though courting imitative fallacy, appropriately echoes the lengths to which white culture must go in order to ventriloquize Bigger's acts as horrors it can name, contain, and finally cast out.

For Max, whose polemics and concluding visit establish him as the most sympathetic mediator of Bigger's "Fate," is only the final insidious barrier to the hero's self-creation. Throughout his tale, everyone wants to "tell" Bigger's story: Jan and Mary, barely camouflaging a preemptive insistence on the power to name, puzzle him with their blithe redefinitions of conventional social lexicons ("Don't say sir to me. I'll call you Bigger and you'll call me Jan. That's the way it'll be between us" [Wright, 1966:67]), reducing him to shamed inarticulateness ("Bigger did not answer"); his mother's despairing anger ("You shut your sassy mouth" [Wright, 1966:12]) elicits a singular rebuke from a son seeking some destiny beyond her room ("Stop prophesying about me" [Wright, 1966:13]); and the white world, not he, sings black songs of liberation while Bigger's "hunger" for freedom seethes in silence (Wright, 1966:77). It is no wonder that Bigger's lasting memory of Max's first visit to him in jail is that the white man "asked me to tell about myself" (Wright, 1966:387), and the result of their interview is the awakening of Bigger's consciousness-as-voice:

> . . . he had spoken to Max as he had never spoken to anyone in his life; not even to himself . . . in Max's asking of those questions he felt a recognition of his life, of his feelings, of his person that he had never encountered before . . . He had no right to feel that, no right to forget that he was to die, that he was black, a murderer; he had no right to forget that, not even for a second. Yet he had (Wright, 1966:333).

Death and consciousness are ironically reciprocal, corresponding yet emotionally inverted.[30] And so, when Max returns, redoubling and thus reopening the scene of their first prison interview, Bigger seizes a second chance to voice his tale, to exorcise the demon of meaningless as both symptom and subject of his recurrent *nihtmahr:* "How could he get into that man a sense of what he wanted? If he could only tell him! . . . He had to die and he had to talk" (Wright, 1966:386, 388).

Yet for some time it is, once again, Max's story that threatens to fill the scene. Bigger's assertion that his acts were "hard" and "blind" gestures against a harsh and "unseeing" world (Wright, 1966:388f.). So menaces Max's confidence in social advance, his readiness to believe that his heroic exposure of abuses would invite their annihilation, that the lawyer momentarily overwhelms Bigger with his *own* autobiography of "faith." The scene, which begins in mutuality, moves ineluctably to disjunction between Max and Bigger, between blindness and emergent voice:

> Max opened his mouth to say something and Bigger drowned out his voice ... Bigger saw Max back away from him with compressed lips. But he felt he had to make Max understand how he saw things now ... "I know what I'm saying real good and I know how it sounds." ... Max groped for his hat like a blind man; ... keeping his face averted ... He did not turn around (Wright, 1966:391 f.).

For Bigger, vision and language have always been logically correlative —"He felt in the quiet presence of his [family] a force, inarticulate and unconscious, making for living without thinking ... for a hope that blinded" (Wright, 1966:102)—but at this final epiphany of act as "meaning," seeing and speaking become mutually exclusive: "Bigger's eyes were wide and unseeing; his voice rushed on" (Wright, 1966:388). Bigger, through the grotesqueries and magic naturalism of this morbid dreamscape (the physiognomic markers of effacement and disfigurement are a final rewriting of the novel's "primal scene"), gropes toward a descriptive style adequate to the independent reality of perceived significance, even as Wright, through patterns of multiple repetition, seeks to craft a plot adequate to the vocabulary of both existential and political metaphors. For Bigger, this would mean that in obsessively returning to the "actual" acts leading to present condition, he would wrench from them a meaning that surpasses the boundaries of natural constraint. He would then be "free" in the order of imagination precisely by maintaining faith to the details of his experience: the "matters of fact" and the order of mind would interpenetrate one another in forging a definitive form of the hero's experience. For Wright, correspondingly, the success of the novel would depend on its ability to provide a definitive image of a reality anterior to but also commensurate with its representation. But in sharing this dream of a totalizing synthesis of imagination and being, Bigger and Wright also share in the anxiety of discontinuity and incompleteness. And so, as it was in the beginning, it is the metallic, distant world and not the self we hear last: "He heard the ring of steel against steel as a far door clanged shut" (Wright, 1966:392; cf. 7).

Thus the end of *Native Son* puts it on the threshold of an articulate realm it cannot see and voice at the same time, a kind of Pisgah moment it can image only as a performative desire—the telling of Bigger's tale not by some sympathetic, omniscient narrator (a kindly sort of rat-slayer), but by Bigger "himself." Indeed, I have suggested that various cultural discourses seek to inhabit Bigger's voice and body, making them speak and act in accordance with their preconceptions: but does the novel really offer access to the putatively *a priori* "self" which is being thus recoded by a colonizing cartographic force? Ellison suggested (1964:114) the crux in uncompromising terms: "Wright could imagine Bigger, but Bigger could not possibly imagine Richard Wright." Perhaps. But we do leave Bigger on the verge of the *Genesis* Reverend Hammond blindly announces (Wright, 1966:264 f.), the newly born *(native)* Son who is also his own father.[31] "Bigger, sometimes I wonder why I birthed you," snaps Mrs. Thomas (Wright, 1966:11); "What I killed for, I *am*! . . . What I killed for must've been good!" (Wright, 1966:391–392) comes the son's almost antiphonal reply, and if the echo of *Genesis* (1 :31) replaces God's "making" with a "black" unmaking, and the modernist *cogito* with a (de)creative *interficio*, is not this metaleptic subversion, this murderously ethical "dwelling on nothingness," the African-American quester's essential mode of beginning, again?

5. Post-modernism without end

> This time the shaded area [of the newspaper map] had deepened from both the north and south, leaving a small square of white in the middle of the oblong Black Belt . . . He was there on that map, in that white spot, standing in a room waiting for them to come (Wright, 1966:239–240).

In the same chapter of his *Narrative* in which the copy-book anecdote makes its appearance, Frederick Douglass writes of the horror and anger which began to consume him when, at the age of twelve, he realized he had been sentenced by a brutal system to the unimaginable fate "of being a *slave for life.*" Then, without further psychological or philosophical elaboration, striking instead that characteristic note of election which gives to every fortuity of Douglass's tale the Hammonesque quality of providential selection, as if his story might actually have been arranged in collaboration with divine narrative design, Douglass tells us that "just about that time I got hold of a book entitled 'The Columbian Orator.'"[32] Therein Douglass found a dialogue between a slave, newly recaptured after a third effort at escape, and his master. "In this dialogue, the whole argument in behalf of slavery was brought forward by the master, all of which was disposed of by the slave." The slave, we are told, spoke "smartly" and "impressively," which, Douglass observes with sly laconism, "had the desired though unexpected effect; for the conversation resulted in the voluntary emancipation of the slave on the part of the master."

The tale's curious combination of terseness and extravagance might lead us to pass over its remarkable significance: at a critical juncture in his story, "just" when, indeed, the narrative itself is theoretically threatened by its teller's condition to trail off into a repetitiveness or even silence mirroring the deprivation of perpetual slavery, Douglass and his tale are delivered, not by outrage or assertion alone, but by discovery of an exemplary act of liberating self-representation. "The Columbian Orator," at several levels of meaning, reflects the ideals and goals of the narrative which contains it. For Douglass, too, the end of his "argument" would be freedom; his *Narrative* aspires to be not merely a description but a demonstration of the emancipatory triumph of linguistic self-possession: to be free is to "get hold of" one's experience, one's history, and one's future through a persuasive expression of one's just desire in the world.

Such an ideal of performative power clearly imagines for itself a certain kind of audience. "The moral which I gained from the dialogue," Douglass tells us, "was the power of truth over the conscience of even a slaveholder." The effort to articulate and thereby enact the ends of justice implicitly creates its appropriately responsive community. The slave's rhetoric is efficacious in its appeal to an indwelling belief in a democratic vision which provides the common ground of an enlightened American identity.

Offering the fantasy of utterance as constitutive of the very aspirations it enunciates, Douglass's exemplum can also be taken as a model for a certain relation of writer and reader on the American scene: the slave's word, reduced neither to pure intention nor to absolute abstraction, becomes a force for change in the political economy of performer and audience, each party being permanently affected through dialogic exchange. Slave and master are equally revolutionized by this expressive interplay, the latter coming into possession of "conscience" just as surely as his black interlocutor finds himself materially transvalued by an "unexpected" didactic authority. In the vernacular terms to which Douglass covertly alludes (beneath a complex manipulation, by turns ironic and defiant, of Enlightenment norms of rational interchange), the master's conversion to "truth" is the self-liberating *response* to a *call* to "conscience" offered by the slave's discourse, a discourse which is itself already a response to the underlying call-to-freedom underlying Douglass's very American—very Jeffersonian "moral." In this sense, Douglass's tale may be taken not as fantasmic but as heuristic, as itself comprising a call, first to Douglass, and then, by way of his responsive *Narrative,* to his (primarily white) readership for participation in the ongoing, improvisatory, always surprising "conversation" about modem American identity and the principles it would affirm through ceaseless political action and communal interaction.

The "Columbian Orator" parable appears almost exactly in the middle of Douglass's *Narrative,* in a chapter introduced by his account of learning to read and brought to conclusion with the copy-book story of learning to write. Thus framed by the "tedious effort for years" of coming into possession of/through/as writing, the anecdote of liberation-by-persuasion can be seen as the imagined goal, if never the final resolution, of the revolutionary adventure begun by entering the master's book.

But what the dialogue of slave and master suggests is that such adventure, however endless and even labyrinthine it becomes in the play of the protagonists' differences, might also shatter the structure of determining Gaze and abjected object by resituating enlightenment in the voice of the Other. Enlightenment thus becomes an event that can emerge from any position, without positing the eradication or reification of a challenging alterity. (Post)modernism thus becomes a productively revisionary, if ever incomplete, mapping of darkened (but not necessarily unveiled) and unmarked (but not necessarily mystified) spaces. Indeed, it becomes the activity of spacing itself, the constant reshading of differences none of which assert any finality or fullness of presence: Bigger, signified as absence from the map he holds before him, decenters the white spot within the black ground[33] on the white page. *There on that map, in that white spot, standing in a room waiting for them to come.*

Notes

1. Following Derrida's (1976) explication of the hand as instrumental guarantee of existence within the ideologically privileged order of scriptive power, we can appreciate the *Narrative*'s obsessive attention to the hand as a mediating corporeal locus for the contest between enforced and self-authenticating modes of labor. At the same time, Douglass slyly sets a more Afrocentric notion of "hand" against this Eurocentric emphasis on self-as-signature when he inserts the tale of Sandy Jenkins's talismanic "root" (or *hand*, in black idiomatic usage) while narrating the climactic episode of his fight with Covey, the last master to "lay hold of him" (1845/1968:80–81). Cf. Roberts (1989:101–102). Sandy promises Douglass that the magical *hand* will prevent harm, and when Douglass does indeed defeat Covey in epical hand-to-hand combat the narrator openly struggles to reconcile the possible influences of Africanesque conjure, neo-Christian inspiration, and personal courage in accounting for the slave's extraordinary, and narratively pivotal, success. Rachel Kartch, in an unpublished essay on the *Narrative*, compares Douglass's "allegorical" use of the image with Miltonic depictions of earthly existence, a fascinating enterprise in view of Adrienne Rich's suggestion that Douglass "wrote a purer English than Milton" ("The Burning of Paper Instead of Children").

2. Franklin provides a typically suggestive, but unreflective, example of this dynamic of reinscription in a passage describing his habit of listing "Faults" on a paper which, due to constant erasure, "became full of Holes." This insouciant reversal of Puritan doctrines concerning original and unexpungeable sin is itself reinscribed and partially punctured by Douglass's inflection of the American autobiographical form, for the slave narrator, while sharing a similarly open view of self-invention, cannot look upon the sins of slaveholding with such comic detachment. Cf. Douglass's "Appendix" (1845/1968).

3. Throughout the late eighteenth century, Jefferson drafted bills and engaged in official correspondence designed to eliminate the black presence in America, including plans for deportation and absolute restriction on immigration. See, for example, the "Bill Concerning Slaves," no. 51 in "The Revisal of the Laws 1776–

1786," in Jefferson (1950–1982, 2:470–472). Cf. "Letter to George Washington," June 20, 1791, in Jefferson (1950–1982, 20:558).

4. I have slightly modified Snead's translation.

5. Not content to imagine blackness as inherently mute, slaveholding law ruthlessly silenced slave discourse, whether in the interdiction against literacy or in the delegitimizing of African-American speech as legal testimony. Jefferson provided one of the first and most authoritative warrants of this latter prohibition in the "Drafts of Bills Establishing Courts of Justice" (1776); see Jefferson (1950–1982, 1:633). Cf. "A Bill Concerning Slaves" (1950–1982, 1:471).

6. E. G. William Robinson, who complains that the "pious ending is plainly gratuitous" (Robinson, 1971:108).

7. As Robinson, following the analysis of Marion Wilson Starling (1946/1981), suggests in his introduction to Hammon's *Narrative* (1760/1971:108). The quest for the *pen*, as a quite literal image of authority and often violent power, animates the slave narrative and its derivatives from Douglass's famous measure of past wounds by present instrument of liberation ("My feet have been so cracked with the frost, that the pen with which I am writing might be laid in the gashes" [1845/1968:43]) to Wright's discovery, recalled in *Black Boy*, of a literally graphic means of defiance ("I pictured [Mencken] as a raging demon slashing with his pen, consumed with hate . . . laughing at the weaknesses of people, mocking God, authority" [1945/1966:271–272]).

8. Jefferson's *Notes* constantly registers this anxiety of American belatedness alongside hope for a freshly cultivated New World garden, its structural counterpart. European reactions to *Notes*, which was perhaps the best read American text of the late eighteenth century, often reflect the same hierarchizing and classifying motifs with respect to the relative value of European and American cultures as Jefferson employed in his discussion of the races. For a particularly apt instance of this intermingling of judgments, see David Ramsey's letter to Jefferson regarding *Notes* in Jefferson (1950–1982, 9:440–441).

9. "Glances at Our Condition: I–Our literature," *Frederick Douglass's Paper,* 23 September 1851, cited in Gates (1987:129–130); Baraka (1966:105–115).

10. Perhaps the most penetrating commentaries on the psychology, the paradoxical excitement, of the "modern" at any given "moment" of cultural history are those of Nietzsche (1968) and, following Nietzsche in a more contemporary context, de Man (1971:142–186). But cf. also Curtius (1963:251–255); and Freund (1957: ch. 1).

11. Cf. Gates's (1988) reading of the metaphor of "reconstruction" in early twentieth-century black letters.

12. The use of the term "mainstream," with its covert implications of central source and continuous con- and in-fluence, to designate Euro-American literary production and its authority can now perhaps be seen as one of the more effective ironies of African-American critical discourse. See, e.g., Baraka's riffs on the term in "The Myth of a 'Negro Literature'" (1966).

13. See Kinnamon's (forthcoming) fascinating study of the reception of *Native Son.*

14. Gayle goes on to set Wright against the supposed "descendants of Frederick Douglass" (1975:xvii f.), a most astonishing judgment in view of the fact that no writer exercised more insistent and profound influence over the shape and even content of Wright's fiction than did Douglass, as could be seen from even a

superficial reading of *Black Boy* (with its constant echoes of Douglass's *Narrative,*
from the correlation of ships and sudden mobility in early childhood, the acquisition
of language in the streets and through the fascinating terror of its prohibition, the
agitation of fights among slaves/blacks by masters/white businessmen, and other
specific scenic parallels, to the pervasive texture of hellish confinement from which
the hero is delivered only by discovery of the word-as-violence and literal escape
north by train).

15. For these views, see, respectively, Slochower (1942); Glicksberg (1950);
Ford (1954); Redding (1966); Cowley (1940); Bone (1965); Baldwin, "Everybody's
Protest Novel" (1955:17–28); and, most recently and most suggestively, Joyce
(1986).

16. For discussions of *Native Son* which center on culture as a major
protagonist see Gloster (1948:231ff.); Daiches (1940); Howe (1963); Brignano
(1970:28–39, 144–148).

17. "How 'Bigger' Was Born" first appeared in its entirety in the Harper and
Row publication of 1940. All quotations here are from the essay's reprinting in the
Perennial Classic edition of *Native Son* (1966:vii–xxxiv).

18. As argued, for example, by Slochower (1942:238) and in Baldwin's (1955)
"theological" reading of Bigger's "tragedy."

19. The case is forcefully argued, for example, by Cowley (1940) and Scott
(1956).

20. Wright's comments on the cultural "No Man's Land" Bigger inhabits
("How 'Bigger' Was Born," 1966:xxiv) echo a passage capturing the hero's social
uneasiness from the novel itself: "He felt that he should have been able to meet Max
halfway; but, as always, when a white man talked to him, he was caught out in No
Man's Land" (1966:321).

21. This association is subtly established later in the novel; first during his
frantic escape when, spying a rat, and looking rat-like himself from fatigue and fear,
he envies its mobility ("He reeled through the streets, his bloodshot eyes looking
for a place to hide. He paused at a corner and saw a big black rat leaping over the
snow . . ." [Wright, 1966:233]); and then in Buckley's grotesque call for revenge as
punishment ("Every decent white man in America ought to swoon with joy for the
opportunity to crush with his heel the woolly head of this black lizard, to keep him
from scuttling on his belly farther over the earth" [Wright, 1966:373]).

22. On Wright's use of the "outsider" motif, so prevalent in his later fiction,
in *Native Son,* see Scott (1956: esp. 132), and Kent (1972).

23. Cf. the scene that takes place between Bigger and the detective shortly
after Mary's murder: "The white man clicked on the light . . . In the very look of
the man's eyes Bigger saw his own personality reflected in narrow, restricted terms"
(Wright, 1966:146).

24. Cf. Joyce's (1986: esp. ch. 1) reading of the novel in terms of the dramaturgy
of tragic Greek theatre.

25. The imagery of the orphic sparagmos is prevalent throughout Wright's
early fiction and in *Black Boy.* See McDaniel (1954).

26. Cf. Garber's (1987:96-107) analysis of the male Medusa. The possible
influences of Shakespeare on Wright, though touched on briefly by Joyce (1986),
remain insufficiently probed.

27. Nowhere is this clearer, both ideologically and imagistically, than in the
white establishment's anxious effort to prove the "central crime" of *rape* against

Bigger (cf. Wright, 1966:377). Where the white authorities aossciate the "fact" of rape with Bigger's "monstrosity" (Wright, 1966:376), to the hero himself rape is a trope of anger and alienation, a dimension of "mind": "But rape was not what one did to women. Rape was what one felt when one's back was against a wall and one had to strike out . . ." (Wright, 1966:214). This figurative exploration of rape in relation to cultural, psychological, as well as sexual notions of "manhood" is the ancestor of such works as Cleaver's *Soul on Ice,* Bullins's *The Reluctant Rapist,* and Baraka's *Dutchman.*

28. It is in this sense that, as Gayle Wald argued in "Native Tongue," murder becomes a radical political gesture, not an irrational, illegible "scream."

29. See, e.g., Baldwin, "Many Thousands Gone" (1955:32); Bone (1965:151). An important exception is to be found in Stepto (1979c:201–203). Stepto relates this observation to the more daring assertion that Max embodies Wright's true voice in the novel.

30. One is reminded here of Foucault's observation that in the tropology surrounding execution of criminals in the eighteenth century an exchange of bodily existence and truthful speech took place (1977: ch. 2). But where, as Lennard J. Davis (1983: ch. 7) has observed, the traditional English novel takes over this relation of punished criminality and achieved discourse in the interests of the State—the accused's confession achieving the aura of redemption only by rewriting the cultural narrative of transgression and discipline which condemned him in the first place—, Wright precisely reverses this novelistic norm by making Bigger's potential speech a *refutation* of the discourse of criminality which would author his extinction.

31. Cf. Reilly (1966:393): "He is a character to shock everyone . . . The effect of acquaintance with Bigger is to be disabused of conventional attitudes." It is precisely this step beyond expectation and delineation that puts the hero into the No Man's Land of a self-making.

32. A 1797 anthology of fiercely abolitionist writings on themes of liberty and democratic zeal, *The Columbian Orator* (Bingham, 1797/1860) reads like a revolutionary response to the racialist republicanism and ethno-historiography of Jefferson.

33. "Black Belt" notably evokes the culturally resonant territory of southern African-American experience, as figured most prominently by DuBois in *The Souls of Black Folk.* See Stepto (1979a: ch. 3).

Works Cited

Andrews, W. L. (1986). *To tell a free story.* Urbana, IL: University of Illinois Press.

Baldwin, J. (1955). *Notes of a native son.* New York: Bantam.

Baraka, I. (L. Jones). (1966). *Home: Social essays.* New York: William Morrow.

Bingham, C. (Ed.). (1860/1979). *The Columbian orator.* Philadelphia: Lippincott.

Bone, R. (1965). *The negro novel in America.* 2nd ed. New Haven, CT: Yale University Press.

Brignano, R. C. (1970). *Richard Wright: An introduction to the man and his works.* Pittsburgh: University of Pittsburgh Press.

Cash, W. J. (1941). *The mind of the South.* London: Thames and Hudson.

Cowley, M. (1940). The case of Bigger Thomas. *The New Republic* (March): 382–383.

Curtius, E. R. (1963). *European literature and the Latin Middle Ages.* Trans. W. R. Trask. New York: Harper and Row.

Daiches, D. (1940). The American scene. *Partisan Review* 7:244–245.

Davis, L. J. (1983). *Factual fiction.* New York: Columbia University Press.

de Man, P. (1971). *Blindness and insight: Essays in the rhetoric of contemporary criticism*. New York: Oxford University Press.

Derrida, J. (1976). *Of grammatology*. Trans. G. C. Spivak. Baltimore: Johns Hopkins University Press.

Douglass, F. (1845–1968). *Narrative of the life of Frederick Douglass*. New York: Signet.

Ellison, R. (1964). *Shadow and act*. New York: Random House.

Ford, N. A. (1954). Four popular negro novelists. *Phylon* 15:29–39.

Foucault, M. (1977). *Discipline and punish: The birth of the prison*. Trans. A. Sheridan. New York: Pantheon.

Franklin, B. (1950). *The autobiography of Benjamin Franklin*. New York: Modem Library.

Freund, W. (1957). *Modernus und andere Zeitbegriffe des Mittelalters*. Köln: Böhlau Verlag.

Garber, M. (1987). *Shakespeare's ghostwriters*. New York: Methuen.

Gates, H. L., Jr. (1987). *Figures in black*. New York: Oxford University Press.

———. (1988). The trope of a new negro and the reconstruction of the image of the black. *Representations* 24:129–155.

Gayle, A. (1975). *The way of the new world*. Garden City, NY: Anchor.

Glicksberg, C. J. (1950). The alienation of negro literature. *Phylon* 1:49–58.

Gloster, H. M. (1948). *Negro voices in American fiction*. Chapel Hill, NC: University of North Carolina Press.

Hammon, B. (1760/1971). Narrative of uncommon sufferings, and surprising deliverance. In W. H. Robinson, Jr. (Ed.), *Early black American prose*. Dubuque, IA: W. C. Brown.

Hegel, G. W. F. (1955). *Die Vernunft in der Geschichte*. 5th rev. ed. Hamburg: Felix Meiner.

Heidegger, M. (1961). *An introduction to metaphysics*. Trans. R. Manheim. Garden City, NY: Anchor.

Howe, I. (1963). Black boys and native sons. *Dissent* 10:353–368.

Jefferson, T. (1950–1982). *The papers of Thomas Jefferson*. 20 vols. Ed. J. P. Boyd. Princeton, NJ: Princeton University Press.

———. (1787/1984). Notes on Virginia. In M. D. Peterson (Ed.), *Writings of Thomas Jefferson*. New York: Library of America.

Joyce, J. A. (1986). *Richard Wright's art of tragedy*. Iowa City, IA: University of Iowa Press.

Kartch, R. Douglass and Milton. Unpublished ms.

Kent, G. (1972). Richard Wright: Blackness and the adventure of Western culture. In *Blackness and the adventure of Western culture*, 76–97. Chicago: Third World Press.

Kinnamon, K. (forthcoming). The black response to *Native son*. In K. W. Benston and H. L. Gates, Jr. (Eds.), *The language of blackness*. Urbana, IL: University of Illinois Press.

Kristeva, J. (1982). *Powers of horror: An essay on abjection*. Trans. L. S. Roudiez. New York: Columbia University Press.

McDaniel, D. (1954). A study of the motif of flight in the fiction of Richard Wright. M. A. thesis. Fisk University.

Nietzsche, F. (1968). *The will to power*. Trans. W. Kaufman and R. J. Hollingdale. New York: Vintage.

Redding, J. S. (1966). The negro writer and American literature. In H. Hill (Ed.), *Anger and beyond*, 17–23 New York: Harper and Row.

Reilly, J. (1966). Afterword. In R. Wright, *Native son*, 393–397. New York: Perennial Library.

Riddel, J. (1979). The "project" of "American" poetics. In J. V. Harari (Ed.), *Textual strategies*, 322–358. Ithaca, NY: Cornell University Press.

Roberts, J. W., Jr. (1989). *From trickster to badman*. Philadelphia: University of Pennsylvania Press.

Robinson, W. H., Jr. (Ed.). (1971). *Early black American prose.* Dubuque, IA: W. C. Brown.

Roper, M. (1837/1971). A narrative of the adventures and escape from American slavery. In W. H. Robinson, Jr. (Ed.), *Early black American prose,* 115–121. Dubuque, IA: W. C. Brown.

Scott, N. A., Jr. (1956). Search for beliefs: Fiction of Richard Wright. *University of Kansas Review* 23:19–24,131–138.

Slochower, H. (1942). In the fascist styx, the fate of native sons: From Remarque, Zweig and Toller to Richard Wright. *The Negro Quarterly* 2:234–240.

Smith, V. (1987). *Self-discovery and authority in Afro-American narrative.* Cambridge, MA: Harvard University Press.

Snead, J. (1984). Repetition as a figure of black culture. In *Black literature and literary theory.* New York: Methuen.

Starling, M. W. (1946/1981). *The slave narrative: Its place in American history.* Boston: G. K. Hall.

Stepto, R. B. (1979a). *From behind the veil.* Urbana, IL: University of Illinois Press.

———. (1979b). After modernism, after hibernation: Michael Harper, Robert Hayden, and Jay Wright. In M. S. Harper and R. B. Stepto (Eds.), *Chant of saints,* 470–486. Urbana, IL: University of Illinois Press.

———. (1979c). I thought I knew these people: Richard Wright and the Afro-American literary tradition. In M. S. Harper and R. B. Stepto (Eds.), *Chant of saints.* Urbana, IL: University of Illinois Press.

Wald, G. Native tongue. Unpublished MS.

West, C. (1982). *Prophesy deliverance!* Philadelphia: Westminster Press.

Williams, K. (1970). *They also spoke.* Nashville: Townsend Press.

Wright, R. (1945/1966). *Black boy.* New York: Perennial Library.

———. (1966). *Native son.* New York: Perennial Library.

———. (1977). *American hunger.* New York: Harper and Row.

ALESSANDRO PORTELLI

Everybody's Healing Novel:
Native Son *and Its Contemporary Critical Context*

1. Freedom and Death

After *Native Son*'s enthusiastic initial reception, its critical fate began to
change when James Baldwin and Ralph Ellison attacked it in the context
of a broader assault on protest literature and the naturalistic tradition.[1]
According to Baldwin and Ellison, Bigger is so thoroughly trapped by his
circumstances and environment that he (and, inferentially, all black people)
is stripped of his humanity. Thus, when the time came to rescue the novel
for the burgeoning field of African-American studies, proving that it was no
protest novel at all was the only way to defend and rescue it. Rather than an
inarticulate victim of his environment, Bigger was now most often described
as a heroic self who achieves freedom and full humanity through psychological and linguistic mastery. By promoting less impressionistic readings of
the text, this approach allows us to perceive the artistry that went into the
making of the text. By recognizing the complexity and growth of Bigger's
humanity, it also rescues the humanity of his creator.

In order to take this approach, however, critics have felt it necessary to
play down the role of the social, economic, ethnic environment in Bigger's
life. The consequence is a degree of solipsistic optimism, in which Bigger's
spiritual recovery is described as complete and self-sufficient. History and

Mississippi Quarterly: The Journal of Southern Cultures, Volume 50, Number 2 (Spring 1997):
pp. 255–265. Copyright © 1999 Mississippi Quarterly.

society melt away like the walls of Mary's room, leaving Bigger not naked and vulnerable but powerful and free: "Bigger's *salvation* comes about through his own efforts, through his eventual ability to find *freedom* from the constraints of his past";[2] "Bigger, using sheer *will,* manages to *transcend* his world, to *accept* himself for what he is and to *accept* the consequences of what he has done";[3] he emerges from Book 3 as "the *articulate, pensive, tranquil* Bigger":[4] "learning to tell his own story gives him a measure of *control* over his life, and *releases* him from feelings of isolation."[5] Somehow, the fact that Bigger will die in the electric chair is either removed or reduced to the status of a secondary detail, mentioned in passing. "Although it does not save him," says Valerie Smith, language "provides him with an awareness of what life has meant" (p. 87). *Although it does not save him:* one whale of a qualifier.

According to Valerie Smith, both Bigger and Wright "rely on their ability to manipulate language and its assumptions—to tell their own story—as a means of liberating themselves from the plots others impose on them" (p. 70). Society's plot imposed on Bigger, however, is to kill him, and it fully succeeds; as for Richard Wright himself, his biographers have shown that he, too, was hounded by all kinds of "plots" unto his very death.[6]

These readings in fact share some of the assumptions of the Baldwin and Ellison criticism they correct. The basic premise remains that, in a work of art, the humanistic hero must always prevail over the "constraints" of the social and material world. Thus, Bigger can (or should) *will* or *narrate* himself to freedom, and there is nothing that society or environment can do about it. A further shared prejudice is the dualistic opposition between either victimization or total freedom, total inarticulation or consummate mastery of language. The imagery of liminality and fluidity, so dominant in *Native Son,* shows that nothing could be farther from its meaning than such a binary dichotomy. Though Bigger is never a passive and unidimensional victim, his growth is not a linear and unidirectional process, and is still in progress when it is interrupted by the clanging of the steel prison door.

Finally, the idealistic bias remains unshaken. Freedom is imagined to be a matter of the mind (more recently, of language), and material matters—biology, economics, politics do not impinge on it. Yet, whatever degree of psychological and linguistic mastery Bigger achieves is not enough to make him physically free, or to keep him alive. Indeed, Bigger's material powerlessness ultimately limits the horizons of his psychic liberation and growth. "We are left with conflicting feelings," aptly says Joyce Ann Joyce, "as we, like Bigger, understand that his spiritual awakening comes just at the point when he is condemned to die" (p. 51): one surmises that Bigger, who is the one who has to go through it, is at least as bewildered as we are.

"When I discover who I am, I'll be free," says Ellison's *Invisible Man.* Bigger Thomas complicates this aphorism by showing that the reverse is also true: "only when I am free," he seems to tell us, "will I know who I am." The same lesson had been taught, earlier, by Frederick Douglass's account of an encounter with the slave-breaker Covey: only after physically overpowering Covey, and after materially escaping from slavery, does Douglass master language and selfhood to the extent of being able to write his autobiography. On the other hand, Douglass fights Covey because "the few expiring embers of freedom" are still burning in his consciousness even at the lowest moment of his oppression: before facing Covey, he is in the same liminal situation as Bigger in the "dim, uncertain light" of many scenes in *Native Son:* not in total darkness, not in the light either.

Douglass defeats Covey and escapes from slavery; Bigger is murdered while his search is still an "ember." The dialectical implication between Bigger's incipient self-discovery and his brutal death tells us that, if physical freedom is meaningless without articulation and self-knowledge, self-knowledge and articulation in turn are limited and precarious without material freedom. In the "shadowy no man's land" between self-knowledge and freedom, liberation from material constraints and liberation from mental constraints cannot be legislated apart.

2. Spirit of the times

The Chippewa novelist and critic Gerald Vizenor has remarked that "Mostly younger Indians who are eager to present a more successful and 'healed' image are quite critical of me focusing too often on the tragic and the downtrodden and the victims."[7] More sympathetic and sophisticated readings allow us now to look at Bigger as a positive, self-affirming hero, rather than powerless victim; as active rather than merely re-active. But they do so at the cost of dismissing the meaning of his fate and removing the obstacles he faces. The ideology of our age has much more sympathy for (individual) winners than for (social) losers. The insistence on "successful and 'healed'" depictions of those who used to be represented exclusively as social victims is a reflex both of gains and changes in citizenship and respect, and of an adaptation to the spirit of the times and, in the case of academic criticism, professional prejudice and privilege. While earlier generations of critics sought to be ideologically correct by stressing exploitation, oppression and protest, our generation seeks ideological orthodoxy by stressing acceptance, reconciliation, salvation, transcendence, healing. In the age of superconductivity, the material world is totally transparent, so that these processes have the advantage of taking place in the mental and linguistic spheres which coincide with our professional domains, reinforcing our identity and role.

The insistence of contemporary Native American fiction on the spiritual healing power of religious and ritual traditions has generated readings which equate personal healing with social pacification, eventually belittling the stature and complexity of the characters themselves. In a chapter eloquently titled "Nobody's Protest Novel," Alan R. Velie combines the Baldwin-Ellison approach and the poetics of healing in a reading of N. Scott Momaday's *House Made of Dawn*.[8] Momaday has been described by anthropologist Michael E. Fisher as "the high priest of the healing power of the word."[9] His hero, Abel, rises from an "inarticulate" state[10] reminiscent of Bigger to regain his voice and "his emotional and spiritual health" (Velie, p. 62). Leslie Silko's *Ceremony* is an explicit story of healing; again, Velie points out that it is "not a protest novel" because in the end its protagonist, Tayo, "lives in triumph."[11] The ending of the novel, however, reiterates five times that the "witchery" which caused Tayo's suffering is "dead *for now*" (my italics): although Tayo is now in harmony with himself, the world around him is not forever pacified and justified (pp. 260–261). Abel also deals with the combined "witchery" of white encroachment and tribal rejection because of his half-blood status; his recovery of peace does not imply that these contradictions are also dissolved but only that he, like Tayo, is now ready to face them. Their "triumph" lies less in an ultimate cosmic pacification than in a regenerated power of resistance.[12]

In another context the Appalachian writer Gurney Norman uses the traditional form of the "Jack tale" to tell how imperialistic "witchery" has disrupted the lives of rural mountain people in "Ancient Creek." The story also culminates in a ceremony of magical healing; but Norman makes it clear that while the people are healed, the world is still sick. After they are cured of their physical and psychic wounds, the hero and his friends prepare to rise the next day to do what no ceremony can do: fight to wrest their land back from the invaders.[13]

The parallels between readings of Native American writers and of *Native Son* are reinforced by the striking parallels between Wright's novel and James Welch's *The Death of Tim Loney* (1979). Loney accidentally kills a hunting partner but assumes this act as his own: "That it was an accident did not occur" to him. He escapes into the reservation, where he is surrounded and sealed off by the police, like Bigger in the South Side, and is killed ("flushed off") as he stands on a high place, like Bigger captured by water on top of a building. In a phrase reminiscent of Wright, the place of Jim Loney's death is described as "looming walls."[14] The Native American critic Paula Gunn Allen insists that Loney achieves "personal integration through insight and action" by choosing, like a Sioux warrior (and unlike Bigger), the ritual time and circumstances of his own death.[15] This is, however, another way of defining suicide: the only "action" open to Loney, as to Bigger, is death. There is no way for the likes of them to be healed and live.

In fact, in a later novel, *Fools Crow* (1986), Welch openly rejects the metaphor of ceremonial healing: faced with smallpox epidemics and white invasion, "Fools Crow knew the ceremonies were futile—the healing and purifying were as meaningless as a raindrop in a spring water."[16] Fools Crow too changes, grows, and even survives; but he realizes that personal healing has limited power against social disease, and that self-knowledge and autonomy do not automatically bring freedom, because "any decisions [he could make] would be puny in the face of such powerful designs" (pp. 372–373).

If total victimization is a denial of the complex humanity of African Americans, Native Americans, Appalachians, women, so then is a pastoral and pacified version of their historical experience. One of the most articulate expressions of personal triumph that does not diminish the awareness of continuing "witchery" is the ending of Harriet Jacob's *Incidents in the Life of a Slave Girl;* as the protagonist rejoices in being free, she is also disturbed that her freedom was bought by a well-meaning friend. Slavery and paternalism do not end with her personal liberation, and the witchery of racism and sexism will not disappear even with the demise of slavery.

In fact, if it were only a matter of personal, spiritual, or mental healing, it would be only a matter of personal, spiritual or mental disease to begin with. The wounds are basically self-inflicted, and the world is ultimately innocent—or at least the world's disorder is a reflex of the characters.[17] Are we to assume that, if a last moment reprieve or pardon had come from the governor, the "articulate, pensive, tranquil Bigger that emerges from Book 3" could just go back to an edenic South Side and live happily ever after?

3. Whatever happened to Tea Cake?

The paradigm of healing and reconciliation became dominant especially after the re-discovery of Zora Neale Hurston's *Their Eyes Were Watching God* and its intertextual "signifying" with Alice Walker's *The Color Purple.* Hurston's novel has all but replaced Wright's in the African-American canon, and many recent re-readings of *Native Son* may be seen as attempts to legitimize it by remaking it according to the Hurston paradigm. Another look at *Their Eyes* becomes, therefore, necessary in order to balance our reading of *Native Son.*

Discussions of *Their Eyes Were Watching God* usually focus on the recovery of sexuality and nature in Janie's experience with Tea Cake and their life in the "muck." The experience, however, ends disastrously: when Tea Cake is bitten by a rabid dog, he attacks Janie, and she is forced to kill him in self-defense. This melodramatic plot-turn is bound to have some bearing on the meaning of the text as a whole, but it is hardly ever taken into consideration. Just as we need to remove Bigger's death in order to confer a positive ending to *Native Son,* so we also need to remove the wild violence of Tea Cake's aggression and his death at Janie's hands in order to find in her experience in the Everglades and in the metaphors of sexuality and nature it conveys nothing but reconciliation and peace of mind.

Henry Louis Gates, Jr., notes that while the image of the swamp in W. E. B. Du Bois's *The Quest of the Silver Fleece* "figures as uncontrolled chaos, for Hurston the swamp is the trope of the freedom of erotic love."[18] Hurston, however, may be "signifying" not only on a male writer of a generation before, but also on a woman's text of her own generation. Nella Larsen's *Quicksand* also uses the metaphor of the swamp to designate sexuality, as the heroine "returns" to a South identified with blackness and erotic love. Sexuality, however, appears to Larsen also in terms of disorder, chaos, loss of self, and as conducive to the "biological entrapment" of pregnancy.[19] Perhaps an undercurrent of chaos and loss of self also swells underneath Janie and Tea Cake's joyous sexuality and nature in the "muck," the flood, the hurricane.[20]

Tea Cake is bitten by a rabid dog in the flood's muddy waters, and in turn attempts to bite Janie—as if trying to penetrate her with his teeth. Biting as a figure of sexual aggression appears earlier, when Janie's grandmother sees a boy "*lacerating* her Janie with a kiss" (this is the grandmother's vision, but the wording belongs to Janie, who is supposed to be telling the story). A bite, then, is both Janie's first sexual experience, and her last. This is why Tea Cake could not die a natural death: Janie *had* to kill him, because by so doing she also kills the threat implicit in her own sexuality, and in the process destroys the joy which is extricably interwoven with the fear. At the end of the novel, Janie is preparing to live sexless for the rest of her life, "in a position of interiority so total it seems to represent another structure of isolation" (p. 248)[21]: deprivation is the price of reconciliation. Like Bigger's liberation, Janie's erotic life from now on takes place only in the mind, in the protected space of memory, away from the mud and teeth of the physical experience.

Their Eyes Were Watching God turns out, then, to be much more complex and problematic than a simplified pattern of liberation. Ironically, it shares with *Native Son* the liquid imagery of the region between love and death, sex and violence, orgasm and killing. Always read in opposition to each other, these two texts turn out to have more in common than we suspected. Maybe this is why they also share the critical removal by death of Bigger and of Tea Cake: in the first case, to remove Wright's view of social conflict; in the second, to obliterate Hurston's conflictual representation of sexuality; in both cases, to "transcend" their powerful materialistic implications.

4. I know how it sounds

I would like to conclude by returning to *Native Son* and the two scenes which are most frequently cited as evidence of Bigger's mastery of language, environment and fate: the writing of the ransom note and his final conversation with Max.

"As Bigger skillfully deceives the Daltons and evades detection by the police. . . . " Joyce A. Joyce writes, Wright "focuses on the change that begins to unfold in his psyche" (p. 44). After he has begun to recognize the meaning of his act, there is a new awareness in Bigger. He "begins to liberate himself from fear" (Smith, p. 108), and, instead of fleeing, he "defiantly remains among the Daltons, controlling and manipulating them through his awareness of the discrepancy between his reality and their illusions" (Joyce, p. 54). He thus begins "to articulate a story about himself that challenges the one that others impose on him" (Smith, p. 110).

This is all very well, except that Bigger's manipulation and defiance barely last the space of a morning. Although the whites are "trapped inside . . . stereotypical preconceptions" (Joyce, p. 44) that prevent them from imagining what has happened, they have no trouble adjusting to the news of his guilt: the stereotypes which power creates of the oppressed are always flexible and multiple enough to justify all forms of oppression, from paternalism to the electric chair. The white power structure is not trying to understand Bigger or to know him, but only to keep him in place, and is ultimately indifferent to which stereotype it uses, provided the chosen one works. On the other hand, if white people are trapped, Bigger is also trapped in their own stereotypes. The story he tries to create is not his own, but the repetition of white stories he has heard concerning Communists rather than blacks; it is, indeed, "based on poorly written models" and beset by "too many narrative inconsistencies." The only time Bigger surfaces is, as Barbara Johnson has shown,[22] not through controlled action but through a slip of control, his linguistic lapses in the writing of the ransom note ("do as this letter say") (Johnson, p. 119).

What Johnson fails to comment upon, however, is that none of the other characters seem to notice Bigger's deviation from standard into Black English because—I would submit—Bigger's language does not deviate from the white establishment's stereotype of how a Communist, stereotypically ignorant and foreign-born, would write. Both blacks and reds are beyond the pale of white American standard discourse: the former because they are nonwhite, the latter because they are un-American. The black remains invisible as long as society persists in seeing red.

Bigger eventually fails to control not only white stereotypes but his own actions: he betrays himself, forgets the money in Bessie's dress, kills her without being really aware of his reasons for doing so. No sooner has his growth begun than it is pushed back. *Native Son* shares with Douglass's *Narrative* the insight that the growth of consciousness is neither linear nor irreversible: just as Douglass finds "the pathway to freedom," loses it, and finds it again, whatever mastery Bigger has achieved is lost after his detection and capture, as he lapses back into silence and passivity and begins to recover only in his final confrontation with Max.

"Mr. Max, I *sort of saw* myself after that night," he begins; "And I *sort of saw* other people, too . . . Well, it's *sort of funny*, Mr. Max." The formulaic *sort of* indicates that Bigger's self-perception is still blurred, lacking definite shape and outline. Early in the novel he thought he knew what he wanted: he wanted to fly. Now he gropes: "It's sort of funny, Mr. Max . . . I always wanted *something*." After Max's socio-historical explanation, Bigger reiterates: "I always wanted to do *something*." And his final speech is still on the same blurred, unfinished note: "I *reckon* I believe in myself . . . I *kind of feel* what I wanted. It makes me feel I was *kind of right*. . . . *Maybe* it ain't fair to kill and I *reckon* I really didn't want to kill. But when I think of why all the killing was, I *begin to feel* what I wanted what I am!"[23]

There's a world of difference between "I begin to feel" and "I know"; and even Bigger's final shout of self-assertion is, at best, tentative: "But what I killed for I *am*! [Wright's italics] It must've been pretty deep . . . I must have felt it . . . What I killed for *must've been* good! It must've been good! When a man kills it's for *something*" (p. 849, my italics). But he yet does know not for what.

Bigger is groping for an understanding of himself, the self which he only dimly perceives, although he feels it with his whole being. "Seven times in the last page and a half of the novel," writes Paul N. Siegel, "Bigger cries out to Max, 'I'm all right.'"[24] While addressing Max, he is really talking to himself, reaching inside for understanding but also trying to persuade himself of what he is saying. "In him," the narrator says, "imperiously, was the desire to talk, to tell . . , and when he spoke, he tried to charge into the tone of his voice what he *himself* [Wright's italics] wanted to hear, what he needed."

"The tone of his voice" is not exactly "tranquil and pensive." His voice "boomed," "rushed on," "in a tone of hungry wonder," climbing to a climax "full of frenzied anguish." He is not exactly articulate either, but stammers and mumbles. "I know what I'm saying real good and I know how it sounds" (pp. 845–849): this immensely ironic passage dramatically contrasts the "what" and the "how," the words and the sound. "Sound" itself contains multiple, contrasting meanings and perspectives: metaphorically, it stands for the way Bigger's words are received by Max; literally, it describes the way the tone of his voice sounds to Bigger himself. This doubling of sound represents both the space between Max and Bigger as hearers of Bigger's speech, and the space between the outward sound and the "echoes" in Bigger's soul. Wright explores this gap to create a dramatic contrast between Bigger's assertion and Bigger's belief, between his effort to persuade (Max) and his failure to persuade (himself); between his urge to speak and the failure of language to do and say what he wants it to.

"I'm all right . . . Sounds funny": the space occupied by the ellipses in the text is the shadowy region Bigger has inhabited for so long. It is the psychic space within a divided self, the social space between the speaker and the hearer, the semantic space between the tranquilizing message and the "frenzy" in the sound, doubling the distance between incipient feeling and mastered knowledge in the distance between the discrete words of the language and the continuous sound of the human voice. Bigger is beginning to cross this space; but the violence of another sound—the clanging of steel against steel which, as Joyce Ann Joyce notes, "appropriately represents the power of the white world" (p. 50)—silences him forever before he makes it through.

Notes

1. James Baldwin, "Everybody's Protest Novel" and "Many Thousand Gone," in *Notes of a Native Son* (Boston: Beacon Press, 1955); "Alas, Poor Richard," *Nobody Knows My Name: More Notes of a Native Son* (New York: Dial Press, 1961); Ralph Ellison, 'The World and the Jug," in *Shadow and Act* (New York: Random House, 1964).

2. Donald B. Gibson, "Wright's Invisible *Native Son*," in *The Critical Response to Richard Wright,* ed. Robert J. Butler (Westport, Connecticut: Greenwood Press, 1905), p. 40 (my italics).

3. Katherine Fishburn, *Richard Wright's Hero: The Faces of a Rebel-Victim* (Methuen, New Jersey: Scarecrow Press, 1977), p. 71 (my italics).

4. Joyce Ann Joyce, *Richard Wright's Art of Tragedy* (Iowa City: University of Iowa Press, 1991), p. 69 (my italics).

5. Valerie Smith, *Self-Discovery and Authority in Afro-American Fiction* (Cambridge: Harvard University Press, 1987), quoted from *Richard Wright,* ed. Harold Bloom (New York: Chelsea House Publishers, 1988), p. 105 (my italics).

6. See Michel Fabre, *The Unfinished Quest of Richard Wright* (New York: Morrow, 1963); Addison Gayle, *The Ordeal of a Native Son* (Garden City, New Jersey: Doubleday/Anchor Press, 1980).

7. Interview with Laura Coltelli, in L. Coltelli, *Winged Words: American Indian Writers Speak* (Lincoln: Nebraska University Press, 1990), p. 166.

8. Alan R. Velie, *Four American Literary Masters* (Norman: University of Oklahoma Press, 1982), pp. 62, 11.

9. Michael E. Fisher, "Ethnicity and the Postmodern Art of Memory," in *Writing Culture: The Poetics and Politics of Ethnography*, ed. James Clifford and George E. Marcus (Berkeley: University of California Press, 1986), p. 225.

10. Mathias Schubnell, *N. Scott Momaday: The Cultural and Literary Background* (Norman: University of Oklahoma Press, 1985), p. 40 (in the context of a more articulate reading which also stresses healing).

11. *Ceremony* (New York: Viking Press, 1977), p. 11.

12. N. Scott Momaday, *House Made of Dawn* (New York: Harper, 1968).

13. Gurney Norman, "Ancient Creek," *Hemlock and Balsams* (Lexington, Kentucky: 1988).

14. James Welch, *The Death of Jim Loney* (New York: Penguin Books, 1987), pp. 129, 147, 170, 168.

15. Paula Gunn Allen, *The Sacred Hoop* (Boston: Beacon Press), p. 141.

16. James Welch, *Fools Crow* (New York: Penquin Books, 1987), p. 367.

17. Paula Gunn Allen writes that in Silko's *Ceremony* the ritual "can simultaneously heal a wounded man, a stricken landscape, and a disorganized, disappointed society" (p. 123). One fails to see, however, how the ceremony changes

the life of the people stranded under the bridges at Gallup, which Silko describes in an earlier chapter, or the attitude of the military-industrial machine that surrounds the reservation.

18. Henry L. Gates, Jr., *The Signifying Monkey* (New York: Oxford University Press, 1988), p. 193.

19. Mary Helen Washington, "Introduction," *Invented Lives: Narratives of Black Women 1860–1960* (Garden City, New York: Doubleday, 1987), p. xxiii.

20. Zora Neale Hurston, *Their Eyes Were Watching God* (New York: Harper and Row/Perennial Library, 1990).

21. M.H. Washington, *Invented Lives*. Washington notes that "even in this seemingly idyllic treatment of erotic love, female sexuality is always associated with violence" (p. xxiii). She, however, identifies this violence only with Tea Cake's slapping of Janie, not with his attempt to bite her and her self-defense homicide.

22. Barbara Johnson, "The Re(a)d and the Black," in *Modern Critical Interpretations of Richard Wright's "Native Son,"* ed. Harold Bloom (New York: Chelsea House, 1988), pp. 115–123; this essay is also included in *Reading Reading Feminist*, ed. Henry L. Gates, Jr. (New York: Penquin Books, 1990), pp. 145–154.

23. Richard Wright, *Native Son. Richard Wright, Early Works*, ed. Arnold Rampersad (New York: Library of America, 1991), pp. 845–849 (my italics throughout).

24. "The Conclusion of Richard Wright's *Native Son*," *PMLA*, 89 (May 1974), 521.

LALE DEMITURK

Mastering the Master's Tongue: Bigger as Oppressor in Richard Wright's Native Son

Racist ideology claims that individual "behavior is determined by stable inherited characters deriving from separate racial stocks and usually considered to stand to one another in relations of superiority and inferiority."[1] It is based on the racial precept referring to "an irrational group prejudice that assumes racial others to be inferior purely in terms of their racial membership biologically conceived."[2] Race stands out as the basic element of the discourse of difference that pervades interracial relations. The "images of 'others' depend not upon ethnic differences but upon particular types of hierarchical relationships."[3] Image-formation of the Other is determined by the power of the labelling group in relation to the labelled group. The labelling mentality defines the Other as the enemy, who is thus dehumanized by stereotyping. White stereotyping of blacks demonstrates the power of preconception over perception, leaving the white oppressor with no ability to "see," and the oppressed black with no chance to be "seen." Having limited power to control his/her own image, the black is turned into a victim of white stereotyping unless s/he controls his/her own image and defines a meaningful relationship to the white definitional framework.

In this context, Richard Wright's *Native Son* (1940) addresses the dire consequences of the whites' image-formation of blacks, as Wright analyzes the role of perception in interracial relations determined by the blinding

Mississippi Quarterly: The Journal of Southern Cultures, Volume 50, Number 2 (Spring 1997): pp. 267–276. Copyright © 1999 Mississippi Quarterly.

function of the prevalent image-domination. Stereotypical images of blacks as beast and savage, heathen, victim, devil, servant and entertainer, and the "merry nigger," which have all been part of colonialist discourse, also exist in the white stereotyping of Bigger Thomas. The opening scene, Bigger's violent act of killing the rat, juxtaposes Bigger's anger with the rat's fear. In the final scenes of the novel when he is trapped by the police—the legitimized release of white anger on him—Bigger will become the rat whose final cry of defiance is to no avail. But unlike the rat at the beginning, Bigger is able to attack both physically and mentally at the end.

Born in Mississippi, the twenty-year-old Bigger lives with his widowed mother, his sister Vera and his brother Buddy in one of the squalid apartments on Chicago's South Side. Bigger's violence directed to the rat is in fact the projection of his anger and hatred toward his own social role and family, for the rat, as Michel Fabre suggests, "symbolizes the family's poverty as well as Bigger's fierce hatred and the enormous forces that confront him. Eventually, too, Bigger himself will be caught like a rat."[4] Bigger hates his own family, not because he is inhuman but because "he was powerless to help them"[5] in the face of suffering. He feels that his mother's forcing him into taking on the responsibility of the family "had tricked him into a cheap surrender" (p. 15).Just like the rat he is cornered in a position where he does not have any freedom to go beyond the limited scope of action. His frustration in his "cornered" orbit of life prevents him from moving beyond the color-line, and knowing that he has to take the job with the Daltons fills him with despair: "It maddened him to think that he did not have a wider choice of action" (p. 16). His sense of powerlessness takes on a different form when he hangs around the gang, for he has absolutely no sense of direction. When Gus and Bigger watch the planes, they know that white boys "get a chance to do everything" (p. 19). Realizing that white skin and money are the two prerequisites for fulfilling of their dreams, Bigger and Gus "play white," recreating the roles of the white power structure "typical of the American capitalist system: warfare, high finance, and political racism."[6] The recreation of the white power structure reinforces for Bigger, rather than releases, the gap between dream and reality: "We live here and they live there. We black and they white. They got things and we ain't. They do things and we can't. It's just like living in jail" (p. 23). Being pinned down to a role in life with no outlets, Bigger finds in the movies those moments when "he could dream without effort" (p. 17).

Bigger is made to be highly conscious of his marginal social status, as he is pushed into the sign system of his peripheral position. The Black Code, which has already defined his social status, has also controlled his sexuality. When Mary gets drunk and Bigger has to carry her to her bed, he has the freedom to touch the body of a white woman. But he quickly remembers the myth of the black rapist of white women when Mrs. Dalton walks into

Mary's room. Her physical blindness does not reduce his hysterical fear: "A white blur was standing by the door, silent, ghostlike. It filled his eyes and gripped his body. It was Mrs. Dalton" (p. 84). He frantically presses the pillow to Mary's lips not to be caught, but after Mrs. Dalton walks out of the room, Bigger discovers that Mary is dead: "Her bosom, her bosom, her—her bosom was not moving!" (p. 86) Bigger becomes a murderer in order not to enact the white myth of the black rapist while he stands out as the very victim of the white myth itself, the myth that triumphs over black reality. He has been the victim of his own fear of the white world, as much as of his self-consciousness as a black which Mary and Jan have overly sensitized him to. The situation has worked against Bigger at the very moment when he tries to escape the stereotypical image of the black male as a sexual threat to white women.

Although it is an accident, Mary's murder has given Bigger a chance to reverse the power relationship between Mary and himself: for the first time he has been able to destroy the dominant image of the whites. No longer will Mary be able to manipulate his powerless image. By burning her corpse in the furnace to hide his crime, he can triumph over the white myth of black as totally powerless to act without white manipulation. Bigger finds power in white blindness to the individuality of a black person, in the whites' stereotypical images of blacks. That Bigger has done something that the whites do not know about provides him with a sense of superiority over them, regardless of the fact that the whites see him as inferior. He has now reversed the master-slave relationship between the Daltons and himself, for he has victimized the oppressor and has controlled the situation of which they are ignorant.

His counter-stereotyping of whites is his defiance of white power in image-formation. In his intentional counter-blindness to Mary through the process of stereotyping, he has made himself into an image-destroyer. He has long wanted to blot out all the images of whites as objects of fear in his life in order to erase fear from both his mind and life: "To Bigger and his kind white people were not really people; they were a sort of great natural force" (p. 109). He has found considerable freedom in attacking the very image that functions as the mere justification of his exclusion from the white definitional framework. He has turned the image of Mary into the image of a victim who has lost control of the situation and therefore he "felt that he had his destiny in his grasp" (p. 141). He has also killed the referential meanings of Mary, Jan, Mr. and Mrs. Dalton that create shame, fear and hate in him. His sense of powerlessness in the face of the taboos against his social conduct/status and sexuality that wipe the spirit of life out of his body is now replaced with the power he feels from violating those taboos, however covert the act of violation may be: "The knowledge that he had killed a white girl they loved and regarded as their symbol of beauty made him feel the equal of them, like a man who had been somehow cheated, but had now evened the score" (p. 155). He has been deprived of being any symbol of beauty, because his skin color has been the symbol of absence in the white society. He has now used his chance to kill the symbol that the white oppressor created in Mary: "Bigger Thomas," Houston A. Baker, Jr., points out, "struck America's most sensitive nerve; he attacked the white female, its 'symbol of beauty.'"[7] The white oppressor's image of beauty represents the very image of oppression for him. The whites' admiration for their object of purity and beauty has meant the rigid control of the black image of beauty and sexuality.

The private detective Britten's questions directed to Bigger about Mary and Jan reveal his stereotypical images of the blacks. Britten's remark "To me, a nigger's a nigger" (p. 154) reinforces Bigger's stereotyping of whites: "Britten was familiar to him; he had met a thousand Brittens in his life" (p. 154). His slander points to Jan as the potential murderer because he is a communist, and it reveals Bigger's ability to manipulate the stereotypical images of the white man. His wish to project his own fear of the white world onto whites like Jan and Britten reveals his repressed desire to shake the whites' image of him as submissive. He functions according to the white definitional framework as he writes the kidnap note. It is not only the murder or the kidnap note that "evens his score" with the whites, but also the clever manipulation—a white weapon long used against the blacks—through which he can match his wits with those of the whites. When the success of his manipulation of the stereotypical images of blacks is threatened by Bessie's fear, he has to kill her. Unlike Mary's accidental murder, Bessie's murder is an intentional one to prevent her telling on him. Since Bessie is in the same boat sharing the same lot with Bigger, he identifies himself with her, as opposed to Mary. He kills Bessie, for she represents his own self-image—his own blackness—to him. As Darwin T. Turner contends: "Bigger himself has escaped from the insecurities, the fears, the feelings of inferiority etched into the Negro psyche by centuries of repression in a white-dominated society. In Bessie, he sees a continuation of those mental chains. She is still lazily amoral, timid, compliant—in short, the Sambo personality which threatens the existence of the new Bigger. In order to live, Bigger must destroy her, the last link which reminds him of and binds him to his Negroness."[8]

On the one hand he lets the whites—the Daltons, Peggy, Britten, the Press—feel that they control him because they control his image, but on the other he controls his own life by controlling his own image outside of their frame of reference. In either case the whites and Bigger are not equals, for while he can violate the imagery of domination, by not fitting into it, he cannot change the mental set of white labelling that determines the social space he is confined to. Bigger is surrounded by the people whose stereotypical images work against his manipulation of these images: Bigger is "just like all the other colored boys" (p. 180) to Peggy; "just another black ignorant Negro" (p. 199) to the reporters; the "Negro rapist and murderer" (p. 230) to the police; "black ape" (p. 253) to the white people who yell at him. The newspapers set the rhetoric of their image-domination: "Police . . . feel that the plan of the murder and kidnapping was too elaborate to be the work of a Negro mind" (p. 229). Against these various forms of stereotyping we have Bigger's pride in achieving freedom of action and opening up a personal space for himself: the murder of Mary produces "a possible order and meaning in his relations" (p. 255) with the whites, but the relationship creates meaning only for him, not for the whites, because they still refuse to see Bigger as an individual. Once his crime is clear and he is arrested by the police, Bigger's image is controlled by the Press. The Tribunals images of Bigger—"like an ape"/"a jungle beast" (p. 260)—remind us of the actual imagery of the *Chicago Tribune* clips of Robert Nixon from which Wright borrowed. The stereotypical images of blacks—such as "just like an ape," "giant ape," "animal," "jungle Negro," connoting the racist perception of the black as "beast/savage"; "rapist," as the sexual threat to white women; "criminal," as the primitive outlaw; and "moron"[9] with no intellectual capacity— form a colonialist design for Bigger to fit into as the carbon-copy of all blacks.

The stereotypical image of Bigger as inhuman creature is shattered by Bigger's attitudes toward Jan and later toward Max. Bigger's stereotyping of Jan as a representative of all other whites disappears with Jan's understanding of his shame and guilt. His ability to go beyond his stereotypical image, when he is treated as being as human as any white, turns into a need for communicating to the white world that fails to see him as he is. He had "killed" any religious philosophy of life, for he knew he did not exist as part of the human universe in the eyes of the whites. He rejects whatever Reverend Hammond, the black preacher, tells him, not because he is incapable of faith in God but because he was pushed outside of the Christian scheme of the universe by the Christians themselves. He has always acted hard to his family, in order to protect himself from the sense of guilt they evoke in him by accepting the role of slaves of the Daltons. The sense of shame, hate and despair has been at the root of his anger that mounted to the violence toward Mary. And his despair now is the fact that "he could never make anybody know what had driven him to it" (p. 286). His violent attitude is his response to the white definitional framework that represses his individuality. The action is what the whites concentrate on and try to indict him for, but the narrator describes the thought-process behind his action that the white world motivated: "Bigger wanted to tell how he had felt when Jan had held his hand; how Mary had made him feel when she asked him about how Negroes lived; the tremendous excitement that had hold of him during the day and night he had been in the Dalton home—but there were no words for him" (p. 287).

Pride in committing an action that violates the white racist codes goes against the stereotypical image of the "merry nigger." Bigger has overturned the plantation myth that the blacks are happy with their lot because it is what they want. Mr. Dalton reenacts the plantation myth as he tries to keep the double-standard by hiring the Negro boys to make them the "merry niggers" in his house, a replica of the plantation mansion, while renting houses to the blacks only in the Black Belt, for he likes confining them to the "slave shacks" of his oppressive mind. It is a representative act of the whites who would like to keep the black plight out of sight and out of mind so that there will never be a reason for guilt and responsibility for their own crime. Dalton's evasion of any situation that would bring him into any confrontation of his own guilt is compensated for by Max who speaks in the name of all whites who have prescribed the conditions of black life in such a way that there is nothing else for the blacks to become other than criminals: "But to Mr. Dalton, who is a real estate operator, I say now: 'You rent houses to Negroes in the Black Belt and you refuse to rent to them elsewhere. You kept Bigger Thomas in that forest. You kept the man who murdered your daughter a stranger to her and you kept your daughter a stranger to him'" (p. 362). In this context, Max gets Mr. Dalton to verbalize the Daltons' blindness not only to the black plight but also to their own selves, in believing that they improve the blacks' living standards.

When Max says the whites hate the Reds as much as the blacks, he simply fails to see through Mary's condescending attitude to Bigger, and Bigger replies: "But they hate black folks more than they hate unions" (p. 322). Max is humane but is blind to the degree to which the white proscriptions of blacks' social conduct can push Bigger into such a frenzy. Max's interpretation of Mary's treatment of Bigger in the car as "being kind" is in full contrast to Bigger's reading that white sign system in Mary as condescension: "She acted and talked in a way that made me hate her. She made me feel like a dog" (p. 324). Max fails to read the unbearable pressure and the mental constructs of white myths, such as that of the black rapist, that can be imprinted on the black consciousness, and make the black unable to distinguish between what the white myth says about the black behavior and how the black "feels" about himself. Later, in the general explanation of the real motivation for his violent reaction to the white world, Bigger attempts to get Max to see the culturally prescribed role he has been put into by the whites: "Mr. Max, a guy gets tired of being told what he can do and can't do. You get a little job here and a little job there. . . . You don't know when you going to get fired, pretty soon you get so you can't hope for anything . . . . You ain't a man no more" (p. 326). Even if Max can't understand Bigger as an individual, he can at least explain to the white audience that white society's stereotyping of blacks is the real cause of the crime of such blacks as Bigger: "He was *living*, only as he knew how, and as we have forced him to live. The actions that resulted in the death of those two women were as instinctive and inevitable as breathing or blinking one's eyes. It was an act of *creation!*" (p. 366).

Max can give theoretical/impersonal explanations of Bigger's act of murder, but, much like Jan, he cannot move one step beyond seeing him as a type oppressed by the capitalistic system. Unlike Bigger, who searches for meaning, Max sees Bigger as "the Symbolic Oppressed Negro."[10] He sees the impact of the white power structure on the blacks' relationships with each other as the cause of Bigger's unhealthy relationship with the other blacks: "The attitude of America toward this boy regulated his most intimate dealings with his own kind" (p. 367). White supremacist ideology has been the main controlling force Bigger has known. He is unable to verbalize his gratitude to Max for at least having listened to and tried to defend his murder of Mary Dalton as a valid reaction to white supremacy, for Bigger "had lived outside of the lives of men. Their modes of communication, their symbols and images, had been denied him" (p. 386). But he is now able to articulate how he was made to feel by the whites who caused him to become a murderer: "But really I never wanted to hurt nobody . . . . They was crowding me too close; they wouldn't give me no room" (p. 388). The white American success myth, which necessitates a freedom of action and a sense of dignity in the white man is re-created by Bigger through a reversal process. Murder is the negative version of that success, but since it is an act of creation for him, it is the only success myth in the name of freedom that he can ever have: "But what I killed for, I am" (pp. 391–392).

Ironically enough Max fails to comprehend that white blindness to the black plight constitutes the problem of meaning in the sense that meaning refers "to the interpretation of messages."[11] Interpretation requires a mode of seeing, because it needs the definitional framework within which one looks at and understands the given situation in order to share the reality of experience. As Molefi Asante maintains: "Sharing of images is reasonable, valuable, and positive; image-domination, however, is the same as other colonial conquests, vile, repressive, and negative."[12] In this sense, Bigger's meaning is never shared by the whites to the extent needed to make any "communicative understanding" between them possible. Hence, stereotyping becomes for Bigger a way of "mastering the master's tongue [as] the sole path to civilization, intellectual freedom, and social equality."[13]

Bigger, who is forced to become the victim of stereotypical images at the beginning of the novel, now becomes a participant in the process of controlling images and meaning. He controls his own image and interprets the meaning of that image for his own self. He has succeeded in manipulating the whites' images of blacks and has turned to the stereotyping process as a weapon against the whites themselves. He has discovered that if he oppresses the oppressor with the same power of images, he will share the same power with the oppressor. Bigger, then, rebels against the blacks' lack of power to define themselves by operating within a white definitional framework. He exerts his power to destroy the whites by operating outside the white definitional framework. By acting out his role, defined by the white stereotypical image of a black man as a beast to be caged, yet by using his mind as untypical of the same image, he attacks the white definitional framework both physically and mentally, unlike the rat at the beginning of the novel. However, he ends up being trapped by the police for not operating within a white definitional framework. Since the white labelling group has already formed the image of the Other in him, as the member of the labelled group, he is punished according to the rules of the image-domination of the whites, because only the white oppressor has the right to act as the oppressor, as the master of the oppressive definitional framework, and not Bigger. He is punished with the death penalty, regardless of the fact that white stereotyping made him what he is—monster to the Press; victim to Jan and Max; heathen to the mother/minister; black worker to Mary, Peggy and the Daltons; "unhappy nigger," as opposed to the "merry nigger," to the white society, including the police and the press.

The image-domination pins him down to his prescribed role within the framework of these images. However, in the eyes of the reader, Bigger's acceptance of the individual responsibility for his own act of murder erases the image of Bigger as a type, as the novel itself shatters the white illusion that racist oppression produced minimal effects on the black mind. As James Baldwin remarks, if the black "breaks our sociological and sentimental image of him we are panic-stricken and we feel ourselves betrayed."[14] The sense of betrayal aroused in the white readers is carried further, for in the final scene Bigger is in full control of his image as an individual, and of the meaning that self-image holds for him. He has made a shift in his basic power relationship to the whites in murdering Mary and seeing her as a type. Unlike the stereotypical definition of the image, he has become a "merry nigger," not because he has enjoyed oppression but because he has managed to act as a "bad-nigger." Having victimized a white out of his free will, he has felt proud of it, for whites have been forced "to see the world through the eyes of a black man" who "reduce[s] the Whites to stereotypes, since Bigger always remains an outsider to their world" (Fabre, p. 185). Hence, he has challenged and threatened the whites' control of the black image in proving his intellectual capability by planning out and rationalizing the murder. He has taken on the role of the oppressor in determining and destroying the image-formation of the whites by the dynamics of his own blackness. He has treated the white image as the Other and in doing so he has redefined the logic of center and periphery in personal terms in an attempt to alleviate his marginal role in the oppressive definitional framework.

Notes

1. George M. Frederickson, "Toward a Social Interpretation of the Development of American Racism," in *Key Issues in the Afro-American Experience,* ed. Nathan L. Huggins, Martin Kilson, and Daniel M. Fox (New York: Harcourt Brace Jovanovich, Inc., 1971), p. 240.

2. David Theo Goldberg, "The Semantics of Race," *Ethnic and Racial Studies,* 15 (October 1992), p. 544.

3. Jan Nederveen Pieterse, *White on Black: Images of Africa and Blacks in Western Popular Culture,* trans. Jan N. Pieterse (New Haven: Yale University Press, 1992), p. 104.

4. Michel Fabre, *The Unfinished Quest of Richard Wright,* trans. Isabel Barzun, (1973; Chicago: University of Chicago Press, 1993), pp. 182–183.

5. Richard Wright, *Native Son* (1940; New York: Harper and Row, 1966), p. 13.

6. Keneth Kinnamon, "*Native Son:* The Personal, Social, and Political Background," in Yoshinobu Hakutani, ed. *Critical Essays on Richard Wright* (Boston, Massachusetts: G.K. Hall and Co., 1982), p. 125.

7. Houston A. Baker, Jr., "Racial Wisdom and Richard Wright's *Native Son,*" in Hakutani, p. 73.

8. Darwin T. Turner, "*The Outsider:* Revision of an Idea," *CLA Journal* 12 (June 1969), p. 313.

9. Charles Leavelle, "Brick Slayer is Likened to Jungle Beast: Ferocity is Reflected in Nixon's Features," *Chicago Sunday Tribune,* June 5, 1938, Sec. 1, p. 6.

10. Charles De Arman, "Bigger Thomas: The Symbolic Negro and the Discrete Human Entity," in *Bigger Thomas,* ed. Harold Bloom (New York: Chelsea House), p. 87.

11. Michael L. Hecht, Peter A. Anderson, and Sidney A. Ribeau, "The Cultural Dimensions of Nonverbal Communication," in *Handbook of International and Intercultural Communication,* ed. Molefi Kete Asante and William B. Gudykunst (with the assistance of Eileen Newmark), (1989; Newbury Park, California: Sage, 1990), p. 165.

12. Molefi Kete Asante, "The Ideological Significance of Afrocentricity in Intercultural Communication," in *Handbook,* pp. 5–6.

13. Henry Louis Gates, *Loose Canons: Notes on the Culture Wars* (1992; Oxford: Oxford University Press, 1993), p. 73.

14. James Baldwin, "Many Thousands Gone," *Notes of a Native Son* (1955; New York: Bantam Books, Inc., 1979), p. 19.

DESMOND HARDING

The Power of Place: Richard Wright's Native Son

The theory of architectural determinism, which has been linked to theories of environmental and physical determinism, is the assertion that the three-dimensional layout of the physical environment has a direct effect upon human behavior, that changes in "built form" can result in changes in human behavior.[1] The degree to which this deterministic theory has been held over from the nineteenth century by twentieth-century architects is clear from the design philosophies of individuals such as Le Corbusier and Frank Lloyd Wright. Contemporary studies supporting a theory of architectural determinism have, among other things, focused on the relationship between architectural environment(s) and human behavior. Architect Romaldo Guirgola, for example, writes: "The structure of the building articulates the interior spaces with a clear rhythm that reinforces rather than obscures the progress toward a coordination of a larger architectural environment,"[2] while the work of Charles Holahan and Susan Sagert concludes that where people have more clear-cut territories and opportunities to personalize them—"sociopetal" as opposed to "sociofugal" communal settings—more interaction occurs.[3] Further support for a determinative relationship between environment and human behavior can be found outside the design professions in the work of anthropologist Edward T. Hall, who has coined the term "proxemics" for the study of human behavior in space as

College Language Association Journal, Volume 40, Number 3 (March 1997): pp. 367–379.
Copyright © 1997 College Language Association.

part of a larger argument which points to culture and personal space as the behavioral bases of design.

Architectural determinism, however, also has its critics. Architect Brent Bolin writes: "[A]rchitectural determinism is a classic example of the simplistic cause and effect relationship between behavior and environment that still dominates planning and architecture, and that lulled modern architects into believing that they could change the way people live by modifying the physical surroundings."[4] Similarly, John Lang has argued that the theory delimits the agency of human behavior, both spatial and mental (a complex function of our intentions and habits), as well as the affordances of the physical and social environment.[5] In spite of the fact that the theory has been—indeed, continues to be—criticized as a simple behaviorist model, a conceptually clear statement of how the physical environment affects human behavior remains to be conceptualized. While many critics agree that the physical environment is *a* determining factor in the functioning of human behavior, commentators continue to maintain that it is not *the* determining factor: Social as well as spatial variables are just as important in determining patterns in human behavior.

In *Native Son* (1940) I would like to suggest, primarily, that Richard Wright confronts powerfully the theory of architectural determinism with regard to the ghettoized African-American community of Chicago's South Side. Indeed, for Wright the social and economic forces that inform the physical matrix of Chicago are inextricably linked to a Marxian correlation between material surroundings and human consciousness. Unlike the city's prosperous white eastern sector, the dilapidated, monolithic tenement buildings of the Black Belt—a cityscape composing "tall buildings holding black life"[6]—is an environment consisting of active and passive signifiers of flux and stasis. These structures embody historical layers of metropolitan life, palimpsests that have played host to the patterns of escape and assimilation within black and immigrant working-class experiences of the city. Furthermore, this is an environment controlled by a dominant white culture, and it is this social order that constricts and denies determinative control of the boundaries of both space and place, not only for Bigger Thomas but for the marginalized communities of the South Side.

While keeping this first proposition in mind, I would like to offer the following counter-argument: Though a powerful framework of reference is at work in the novel, Wright is careful not to foreground external environmental and social factors as sole causative agents of Bigger's tragic arc of development. Though certainly exacerbated by white social, cultural, economic, and political exploitation, Wright's Marxian formula cannot fully liberate Bigger from the complex articulation of an independent and destructive agency— what critic Houston J. Baker calls "conscious history,"[7] a menacing sense of self which Bigger possesses from the beginning of the novel. I would like to argue, ultimately, that it is precisely this sense of conscious history, with all its tragic repercussions, that is progressively and independently developed outside the template of Wright's seemingly determinative dialectic.

In his provocative essay "Richard Wright and the Dynamics of Place in Afro-American Literature," Houston Baker, Jr., focuses on the concept of "place" in a new historicist treatment of African-American male and female roles in *Native Son* against the background of Wright's own interpretation of Afro-American history in *12 Million Black Voices* (1941). In the course of the argument, Baker cites scholar Yi-Fu Tuan's own interpretation of the quality of "place" as a function of "space" and value thus:

> In experience the meaning of space often merges with that of place. "Space" is often more abstract than "place." What begins as undifferentiated space becomes place as we get to know it better and endow it with value. . . . The ideas "space" and "place" require each other for definition. From the security of and stability of place we are aware of the openness, freedom, and threat of space, and vice versa. (91)[8]

It is clear from Tuan's work—as well as Baker's interpretation of it—that the essential valuing of human agency within the construction of place as a valued locale demands the setting and maintenance of boundaries. For Tuan, the limitlessness of "space" represents possibility (we can also read this to also signify "desire"), while "place" (the achievement and/or frustration of that "desire" as signified), on the other hand, is a singular point invested by human agency with value. Developing the metaphor, Baker goes on to argue that in the context of the New World, "Afro-America was a PLACE assigned rather than discovered" (91). In the course of conscious [black] history, this "'second birth'" of experience was marked by "the closure of the whole experience, of the first floating instability and suffocation below deck at the hands of the European slave traders" (91). However, with regard to a theory of the semantics of place, this "'second birth'" was but another "deep hole of temporary placelessness" (91) within the system of American plantation agriculture. Extending the argument one step further, Baker, citing Charlotte Pierce-Baker's evocative image of the honeycombed tenements of Chicago's South Side as suggestive of "vertical slaveships," lays the foundation for the assertion that out of this hole a "'third birth'—a new Afro-American" was born, a generation that, like Wright's protagonist Bigger Thomas, rejects the "brittle tenuous folk family of black America" (97) as represented by his mother, Vera, and the pastor, in an attempt to ally itself with the forces of Western technological power and modes of social activism.

In *Native Son* African-American experience, as such, is denied determinative control of the boundaries of space and place across the urban aggregate. Bigger, like his family and the black community at large, is confined, ghettoized in a prescribed corner of the city, an area "tumbling down from rot" (*NS* 164). In this part of the city the urbanization of capital dictates that the vector's desires are controlled, consequently, by the "interlocking institutional arrangements" (Baker 87) of corporations such as Mr. Dalton's "SOUTH SIDE REAL ESTATE COMPANY" (*NS* 164), which owns the Thomases' rat-infested tenement.

In the opening chapter, entitled "Fear," Wright immediately establishes the boundary between these discrete units of mutually exclusive space/place—that of the South Side (African American/poor) and the eastern sector (white/affluent)—with Bigger's odyssey "across the line" (*NS* 164) to the Dalton home on Drexel Boulevard. Bigger quickly realizes that this privileged bastion is radically different from the intoxicating images of white America mythologized by cinema and the media (pop-culture fodder that he and his gang, Gus, Jack, and G.H. have consistently dieted upon). Far from being glamorous and alluring, Wright tells us that this eastern sector was a "cold and distant world; a world of white secrets carefully guarded. He [Bigger] could feel a pride, a certainty, and a confidence in these streets and houses" (45).

Bigger's tension and frustrations mount further as he enters the Dalton home: In the sumptuous surroundings of a domain geometrically constructed around principles of space and light, Wright tells us, "He [Bigger] had not expected anything like this; he had not thought that this world would be so utterly different from his own that it would intimidate him" (*NS* 47). Given all that Wright unveils thus far, it comes as no surprise that this epiphanic experience evokes in Bigger a concrete realization of the absence of any notion of benign space or light in his own family's squalid tenement. Returning home,

> He [Bigger] looked round the room, seeing it for the first time. There was no rug on the floor and the plastering on the walls and ceiling hung loose in many places. There were two worn iron beds, four chairs, an old dresser, and a drop-leaf table on which they ate. This was much different from the Dalton's home. . . . He hated this room and all the people in it, including himself. (*NS* 100)

Bigger's developing sense of "conscious history"—an awareness of the fractured nature of his existence which dictates that he forever be aware of "that black skin" (*NS* 67) trapped in the "strange labyrinth" and "chaos" (225) that is Chicago—is further elaborated upon later in the novel during the climactic chase sequence over the South Side rooftops. Following the discovery of Mary Dalton's incinerated remains, and with the fury of the white mob closing around the derelict tenement in which Bigger is hiding, Wright explicitly enunciates a sense of the deterministic forces that have allegedly contributed to Bigger's tragic condition. In a world of fear, hate, and brutality, it was

> only under the stress of hate that the conflict was resolved. He had been so conditioned in a cramped environment that hard words or kicks alone knocked him upright and made him capable of action—action that was futile because the world was too much for him. It was then that he closed his eyes and struck out blindly, hitting what or whom he could, not looking or caring what or who hit back. (*NS* 225)

In the frenzy of Bigger's futile effort to escape the hate of this white world, it is inevitable that the attempt to establish a contained and stable space is denied by the steady and methodical uncovering of the unstable, marginalized ghetto—one of the two major principles around which the text has been constructed. In time, Bigger is caught, tried, and executed.

In the space of one day, the Dalton killing paradoxically catapults Bigger into "another life" (*NS* 100) of "terrifying pride," one with a "hidden meaning" (101) beyond the fear of myths constructed and supported by a dominant white culture, the gang, and his own family: "They might think he would steal a dime, rape a woman, get drunk, or cut somebody; but to kill a millionaire's daughter and burn her body?" (108). Released from blindness into insight, Bigger believes that, along with his family, "Jan was blind. Mary had been blind. Mr. Dalton was blind. And Mrs. Dalton; yes, blind in more ways than one" (102)—blind to the fact that it was now possible to "act like other people thought you ought to act, yet do what you wanted" (108).

At this point, I would like to pick up an earlier argumentative thread with the suggestion that our awareness of a concept of agency with regard to Bigger's psychological character, independent of a theory of architectural determinism, can tell us much about Wright's protagonist and, indeed, the work as a whole. Such an understanding can do much to isolate Bigger's actions from a behaviorist model in that his increasing sense of self-empowerment—Baker's "conscious history"—is evident from the very beginning of the novel.

In the role of omniscient narrator, Wright informs us of Bigger's psychological character thus: "These were the rhythms of his life: indifference and violence; periods of abstract brooding and periods of intense desire; moments of silence and moments of anger" (*NS* 31). In the course of the novel these twisted forces of Eros and Thanatos are energizing principles; they comprise the "invisible force" of Bigger's sense of Self and, consequently, manifest themselves as agents in the construction of a particular brand of "conscious history." Wright's point-of-view narration justifies this violent strain of soul-destroying schizophrenia:

> He was bitterly proud of his swiftly changing moods and boasted when he had to suffer the results of them. It was the way he was, he would say; he could not help it, he would say, and his head would wag. And it was his sullen stare and the violent action that followed that made Gus and Jack and G. H. hate and fear him as much as he hated and feared himself. (*NS* 31)

As the novel progresses, this nascent sense of black Self reveals itself in two very different ways: First, in pathological acts of violence and sadism; and secondly, performatively, with Bigger's keen sense of masquerade. With reference to the latter, as the Daltons attempt to provide a new environment for Bigger as part of his "fresh start," Bigger responds by projecting the image of a docile Negro. The subtext of this masquerade, however, is quite different: In proffering a stereotypical facade, Bigger, in fact, successfully structures a diametrically opposed and aggressive self-awareness which runs counter to the "identity" perceived proposed by the Daltons:

> He [Bigger] stood with his knees slightly bent, his lips partly open, his shoulders stooped; and his eyes held a look that only went to the surface of things. There was an organic conviction in him that this was the way white folks wanted him to be when in their presence; none had ever told him that in so many words, but their manner had made him feel that they did. (*NS* 50)

Indeed, the connection between Bigger's developing dramatic sense and his repeated use of the word "idea" at points in the text where that agency manifests most clearly as a terrifying logic of progression, is of paramount importance as the novel progresses. For example, on the night of Mary Dalton's murder, Bigger is faced with two problems: The disposal of the corpse and—in spite of the fact that he is ignorant of Jan's personal brand of Communist ideology—successfully implicating Jan in Mary's murder. In the case of the first problem, the knowledge that Mary was expected to leave for Detroit early the following morning initially fills Bigger with "another idea" (*NS* 87), that of hiding Mary's corpse in her own trunk.

However, seeing the basement furnace ablaze, Bigger decides to follow the logic of a more expedient and horrifying alternative: "He stared at the furnace. He trembled with another idea. He—he could, he—he could put her, he could put her in the furnace. He would burn her!" (*NS* 89). Furthermore, as the plan to incriminate Jan unfolds, the Communist pamphlets given to Bigger by Jan the same night of the murder take on a dramatic importance. Wright tells us that, once more, Bigger was "filled with a cunning idea" to "show them to the police if ever he were questioned" (94), for he "knew the things that white folks hated to hear Negroes ask for. . . . And he knew that white folks did not like to hear these things asked for even by whites who fought for Negroes" (184). It is with the ransom attempt, finally, that Bigger's developing sense of Self reaches apocalyptic fruition in the desire to "be an idea in their minds; that his black face and the image of his smothering Mary and cutting off her head and burning her could hover before their eyes as a terrible picture of reality which they could see and feel and yet not destroy" (123).

In *Native Son* I would like to suggest further that, with obvious exception taken to the sensationalistic "hack" rhetoric of the Chicago newspapers regarding Mary Dalton, Bigger Thomas commits two acts of brutal, premeditated rape in the space of the novel, the first homosexual, the second heterosexual. In the case of the former, as the gang looks on in the fight scene in Doc's poolroom, it is Gus, Bigger's alleged friend and fellow gang member, who first succumbs to Bigger's frenzied psychosexual violence. Standing triumphantly erect over the defeated figure of Gus and holding a knife to Gus's open lips, Bigger forces him to symbolically perform fellatio on his blade-as-phallus:

> "You want me to slice you?"
> He [Bigger] stooped again and placed the knife at Gus's throat. Gus did not move and his large black eyes looked pleadingly. Bigger was not satisfied; *he felt his muscles tightening* again.
> "Get up! I ain't going to ask you no more!"
> Slowly, Gus stood. Bigger held the open blade an inch from Gus's lips.
> "*Lick it,*" Bigger said, his body *tingling with elation.*
> Gus's eyes filled with tears.
> "*Lick it,* I said! You think I'm playing?"
> Gus looked round the room without moving his head, just rolling his eyes in a mute appeal for help. But no one moved. Bigger's left fist was slowly moving to strike. Gus's lips moved toward the knife; he stuck out his tongue and touched the blade. Gus's lips quivered and tears streamed down his cheeks. . . .
> Bigger watched Gus with lips twisted in a crooked smile. . . .
> His *eyes gleamed hard again, pregnant with another idea.* (*NS* 40–41; my italics)

In this particular instance, Wright frames Bigger's sadistic agency within the signifying framework of a rape scenario, with the knife-as-phallus representing the dominant power position in the act of Gus's psycho-sexual humiliation. Wright, however, gives the scene an interesting "twist" in that as Bigger's desire to further humiliate Gus gathers momentum toward "climax," Wright "inverts" the structure of the brutal scenario—and it is at this point in particular that the phenomenon of Bigger's conscious agency manifests itself most clearly. In short, after forcing Gus to symbolically perform fellatio on the blade, there is a sudden slippage in Bigger-as-signifier: The position of Bigger-as-male-violator is transplanted or attributed metaphorical connotations of female gendering (*"eyes gleamed hard again, pregnant . . ."*). In the act of sadistic psycho-sexual *plaisir,* Gus's reactions—his fear—symbolically "inseminates" Bigger's violent agency further, rendering it symbolically androgynous, thus producing *"another idea."* But with Gus's escape, Bigger fails to consummate (and/or conceive of) his desire—the *idea*—to "slice" his victim. This frustration of desire, I would like to add, can be seen again metaphorically, as a case of "coitus interruptus": Sexual failure, coupled with the fear of both the gang and of breaking taboo by robbing the white man Blum, induces, therefore, a characteristic act of violence in the damage that Bigger does to the pool table with the knife. It is this strain of pathological behavior—which finds its root in sadistic pleasure—that, ultimately, hallmarks Bigger's distorted sense of "conscious history" from very early on in the novel.

In marked contrast to the castrating figure of the "valued" white Mary Dalton—the apex of inaccessibility to potential black experience—Bessie, the black domestic, Houston Baker, Jr., argues, is the "unprotected," the "accessible woman who institutes folk history as opposed to conscious modernism" (Baker 111). Bessie, like Gus, is a victim of rape, only in her case, the act is followed by murder. Throughout the novel she has come to symbolize a naturalistic force that is incongruent with both Wright's and Bigger's conception of black urban modernism. As Bigger makes love to Bessie, Wright variously describes her as a "fallow field," "cloudy sky," "rain," "warm night sea," and a "fountain" (*NS* 128). Bigger uses Bessie as a repository for sexual appetite, and there is a menacing self-satisfaction with regard to this economy of desire in that as far as Bigger is concerned, the relationship is one based on commercial relations: "Most nights she was too tired to go out; she only wanted to get drunk. . . . So he would give her the liquor and she would give him herself" (132). Scaling his operations one step higher, Bigger brutally implicates Bessie in the megalomaniac plan to ransom the missing body of Mary Dalton. However, dissatisfied with merely mutilating and burning Mary's corpse, Bessie is used by Bigger as part of the ransom attempt in order to further "deny" the Daltons a "security he [Bigger] had never known"—to "even the score" (155).

Bigger's "terrible picture of reality" is such that he rapes and murders Bessie Mears in a delapidated South Side tenement which is much like the home that his family rents from Mr. Dalton. What contributes to the totality of Bigger's brutal action is that Bessie's forced compliance in the act of distortion is repaid by Bigger's premeditated decision to dispose of her presence *before* Mary's body is discovered. Wright informs us: "He [Bigger] was afraid that he would have to kill her before it was all over. She would not do to take along, and he could not leave her behind" (*NS* 170). Bessie's murder marks the death of the folk trace in the novel and Bigger's complete and tragic embracing of his own tragically constructed fate in the chains of Western urban culture. Richard Wright's *Native Son* is an act of ideological defiance that articulates a profound sense of fear, deprivation, and hatred toward white America. However, as Wright points out in the preface "How 'Bigger' was Born," his protagonist could just as easily have been white as opposed to black. For Wright, the dimension of class added to that of caste through contact with Marxist thought was of profound importance: "The extension of my sense of the personality of Bigger was the pivot of my life; it altered the complexion of my existence. . . . It was as though I had put on a pair of spectacles whose power was that of an x-ray enabling me to see deeper into the lives of men."[9] It would seem, therefore, that Wright's position as laid out in the "Bigger" article denies, to a certain extent, a reading of the novel as a black nationalist repudiation of Marxism. As Keneth Kinnamon states: "Wright's effort in the novel is to reconcile his sense of black life with the intellectual clarity and the possibility of social action provided by Communism, to interpret each group to the other."[10]

However, in privileging my remarks in this paper that Bigger Thomas possesses an individual consciousness in all its subjectivity independent of existential qualities of "primal fear and dread"[11] as well as the theory of architectural determinism, the final section of the novel plays a significant part. For Bigger, attorney Boris Max's arid theorizing in the courtroom scenes and beyond is redundant. Not only does Bigger consciously and consistently reject all notions of African-American "communitas"; he also denies the potential of social activism as evinced by Communist ideology. Bigger's final and irrevocable statement is a plain: "What I killed for must've been good! I feel all right when I look at it that way" (*NS* 358).

Wright is surely correct when he states that Bigger's destructive desire is not necessarily a "white" one, nor, indeed, even a "black" appropriation of white desire. Bigger's agency is unique in its own fearful autonomy, its anger, and its blindness. As such, his attempt to separate the Self from the community in order to come into a new sense of conscious history is nothing more than a tragic fallacy.

Notes

1. John Lang. "The Built Environment and Social Behavior: Architectural Determinism Reexamined," *Via: Culture and the Social Vision,* vol. 6, ed. Russell Versaci (Philadelphia: University of Pennsylvania Press, 1980): 147.

2. Romaldo Guirgola, "Reflections on Buildings and the City: The Realism of the Partial Vision," *Perspecta: The Yale Architectural Journal* 9.10 (1965): 110.

3. See Charles J. Holahan and Susan Sagert, "Behavioral and Attitudinal Effects of Large Scale Variations in the Physical Environment of Psychiatric Wards," *Journal of Abnormal Psychology* 82 (1968): 454–462.

4. Brent Bolin, *The Failure of Modern Architecture* (Princeton, N.J.: D. Van Nostrand, 1976): 162.

5. Lang, 149.

6. Richard Wright, *Native Son* (New York: Harper, 1966): 70. Hereafter cited as *NS* in the text.

7. Houston Baker, Jr., "Richard Wright and the Dynamics of Place in Afro-American Literature," *New Essays on Native Son,* ed. Keneth Kinnamon (Cambridge: Cambridge University Press, 1990): 98. Hereafter cited parenthetically in the text.

8. See Yi-Fu Tuan, *Space and Place* (Minneapolis: University of Minnesota Press, 1974).

9. Richard Wright, "How Bigger Was Born," *Native Son* (Harper, 1966): xi.

10. Keneth Kinnamon, ed., *New Essays on* Native Son (Cambridge: Cambridge University Press, 1990): 3.

11. Wright, "How Bigger Was Born" xviii.

DAMON MARCEL DECOSTE

To Blot It All Out:
The Politics of Realism in Richard Wright's
Native Son

The strategies of the classic realist text divert the reader from what is contradictory within it to the renewed recognition (misrecognition) of what he or she already "knows," knows because the myths and signifying systems of the classic realist text re-present experience in the ways in which it is conventionally articulated in our society.

Catherine Belsey, Critical Practice

But what enabled me to overcome my chronic distrust was that these books—written by men like Dreiser, Masters, Mencken, Anderson, and Lewis—seemed defensively critical of the straitened American environment. These writers seemed to feel that America could be shaped nearer to the hearts of those who lived in it. And it was out of these novels and stories and articles . . . that I felt touching my face a tinge of warmth from an unseen light.

Richard Wright, Black Boy

I

Although now almost twenty years old, Belsey's forceful dismissal of a realism that, to her mind, "performs . . . the work of ideology" (67) remains,

Style, Volume 32, Number 1 (Spring 1998): pp. 127–147. © 1998 *Style Journal*, Northern Illinois University.

to this day, a virtual axiom of Anglo-American literary criticism. Despite Rita Felski's more recent claim that "the 'conservative' status of realism as a closed form which reflects ruling ideologies has been challenged by its reappropriation by . . . oppositional movements such as feminism" (161), recent scholarship, implicitly or explicitly deploying what Belsey dubs "[p]ost-Saussurean work on language" (3),[1] has tended to take the diagnosis of realism as reactionary as its starting point in discussions of the realist novel. Indeed, even such a recent reclamation of American realism as William Solomon's 1996 essay, "Politics and Rhetoric in the Novel in the 1930s," begins by conceding realism's effectively conservative character as a mode of ideological "closure" (799). If the ostensibly realist fiction of the 1930s is to be rescued from critical scorn here, this is to be done by demonstrating that it is not in fact realist at all, but rather an attempt to go "beyond" realism and toward a rhetorical form exhibiting a healthy and "at times extreme skepticism towards the referential reliability of realist modes of narration" (800). Nor has the Wright who, in our second epigraph, praises realism as a kind of personal and political epiphany escaped scholarly censure for just this allegiance. To be sure, Wright's work, and *Native Son* in particular, was initially praised by reviewers for nothing other than the power of its realism. Thus critics who praised *Uncle Tom's Children* for its "brutal reality" and "authenticity" would likewise applaud in Wright's first novel an "authentic, powerful writing" and a "factual quality as hard and real as a paving stone" (Reilly, *Critical Reception* 2, 28, 50, 61). More importantly, as regards recent formulations of the politics of literary realism, these first critics and reviewers would see this realism itself as at the very heart of a potent and oppositional political act, as "a considerable factor in awakening a social sense and conscience willing at last, after much evasion and self-deception, to face the basic issues realistically and constructively" (Locke 20).

By 1963, such readings of Wright's achievement in *Native Son* were so current that Irving Howe could claim of the novel that it was not only a disclosure of the facts of racist oppression, but further, a form of literary liberation from the "protest" novel for those black American writers who came after it ("Black Boys" 137). Yet it is instructive that such an argument should come some two years after Howe's own fearful eulogy for Wright, which lamented that his works were now largely unread, his name unknown (Reilly, *Critical Reception* 350). For indeed, by the 1960s, Wright's literary fortunes had waned—so much so, in fact, that his 1954 novel, *Savage Holiday*, would receive not a single American review (Reilly, *Critical Reception* 239)—and had done so in step with the declining esteem in which the realist novel was held in American literary circles. In fact, as early as 1949, the acuity and oppositional character of Wright's brand of realism would come under fire from his own one-time protegé, James Baldwin. Seeing in the realist novel only "an accepted and comforting aspect of the American scene" (19), Baldwin would further charge *Native Son* with being no more than "a continuation, a complement of that monstrous legend it was written to destroy" (22). Such arguments would be echoed some fifteen years later by Ralph Ellison, who, in response to Howe's 1963 attempt to redeem Wright from relative obscurity, would accuse Wright's realism of a politically suspect falsehood, of endorsing "the ideological proposition that what whites think of Negro reality is more important than what Negroes themselves know it to be" (114). If Wright's realism had, at least by the time of *Native Son*'s publication, been seen by reviewers as the weapon with which his fiction assailed American racism, by the early 1960s it had, in Belsey-like terms, become a weapon directed against Wright's own politics.

The late 1960s, however, witnessed a further reversal in Wright's canonical fortunes—witnessed, indeed, his "emergence" as a respectable subject for scholarly research and comment[2]—and one once again tied to new responses to the question of the politics of realism. For as the Civil Rights movement of the 1950s and early '60s gave ground slowly to the more militant discourse of Black Power, Wright himself—the originator, as Robert Buffer notes, of the very term (Introduction xxxiii)—experienced a literary resurrection and a new political cachet. As Michel Fabre observes, "racial events, totally independent of literary fashion, began to bring Wright's work back into the limelight. As the civil rights movement tended more and more toward Black Power, its leaders became increasingly aware of the relevance of Wright's message" (vii). And, again, this new literary stature and political relevance were seen as stemming from Wright's critical insight as a writer in the realist mode. Thus for so outspoken a proponent of "Black Power" as Eldridge Cleaver, Wright becomes the chosen literary father figure, precisely because, in his fiction, we find a *true* picture of an oppressive America that must be changed. For Cleaver, Wright "reigns supreme for his profound political, economic, and social reference" (105), and represents *therefore* both a useful tool for an oppositional politics and a valuable literary model. But this age of renewed respect for Wright as realist and, as a consequence, political critic, would itself soon give way to a new era in the academy that had so recently accredited him, namely that exemplified by Belsey's "post-Saussurean work on language" and its profound suspicion of the politics of referentiality and, thus, of realism itself.

What have become common, then, are analyses of Wright and, especially, of his most famous work of fiction, which undertake, *à la* Belsey and Baldwin, to reveal the political conservatism Wright's commitments to realism inevitably entail, or, in ways paralleling Solomon's recent argument, to show how oppositional politics survive in this fiction precisely because it in fact eschews realism. Graham Clarke, praising a later African-American

fiction that jettisons referentiality in favour of letting "language and style become the dominant forces of the novel's impetus" (48), sees Wright's *Native
Son* as still mired in a realism "constrained by the limits of social determinism" (43). Indeed, even Laura Tanner, who, in the face of Clarke's charges
"of narrative conservatism," comes to the defense of Wright's novel, does so
by first granting that realism is both reaction and "distortion" (132, 134). If
Native Son is worth defending, it is because, for Tanner, it effectively deconstructs the realism of its own narrative presence; says Tanner of her "alternative reading," the novel offers a "surprisingly radical critique of the type of
narrative conservatism attributed to it" (132). A similar argument may be
traced in John M. Reilly's recent essay, "Giving Bigger a Voice: The Politics
of Narrative in *Native Son*." Here, Reilly sees Wright's novel as subverting
the discursive monopoly of the ruling class "by use of a narrative point of
view that draws readers beneath the externals of surface realism, so that as
they are led into empathy with Bigger, they will be denied the conventional
attitudes of American racial discourse" (46).

Yet such "exculpatory" readings fundamentally misconstrue Wright's
realist and political commitments. If realism is worthy of that admiration he
lavishes on it in our second epigraph, this is so, in part at least, because realism is for Wright a mode not of narrative conservatism, but of oppositional
potential and force; it is, in his view, the primary way in which "words [can]
be weapons" (*Black Boy* 272). Indeed, *Native Son* is a realist text that does effectively critique American class and race relations, in ways that would seem
to baffle the charges of reaction and conservatism Belsey and more contemporary critics would level at the realist mode. Moreover, in ways largely overlooked by champions of the novel *as* both realist and oppositional, *Native
Son* is a novel *about* realism, an argument that proffers realism as precisely
that mode of discourse which can, *contra* Belsey, highlight political contradictions and shatter those conventional and shared political "truths," Belsey's
"myths," it reveals to be mere illusion and elision. In Wright, realism becomes
self-consciously politicized as an analysis of the ways misrepresentation and
fantasy foster both oppression on the basis of class and race, and a murderous alienation in the oppressed themselves. More, Wright's realism is here
the proposed medium in which such oppression and alienation may be overcome. In *Native Son,* realism itself, as discursive mode, is cast as a struggle
against not only poverty and racism, but the popular American myths and
values that perpetuate this poverty and racism. If, as Dorothy Redden has
argued, Bigger becomes "almost a stereotype of the skulking black brute who
violates and kills pale virgins in their beds" (74), the black rapist of lynch
mob rationalizations, he does so not only because of the power of this myth
to write his story for him, but also because his own renunciation of a realist
discourse precludes, in Wright's eyes, the possibility of struggle against this

power. Himself committed to the erasure, the blotting out, of both his own reality and its potentially unifying role as a common ground between himself and others, Bigger ends up abetting his *own* erasure, and effecting the murderous blotting out of other African Americans.

II

Wright's Bigger Thomas is, as we first meet him, an unemployed black man of twenty, living in a one-room, rat-infested kitchenette with his mother, brother, and sister, and rankling at the restrictions placed upon his life by the tenets and practices of American racism. Indeed, at the outset of the novel, Bigger is presented as a very acute observer of the realities of American racism. As Bigger complains to Gus, his partner in petty crime, "They don't let us *do nothing*" (20), but, apparently, make whites money. For as Bigger knows, the lines of race that cordon off the squalid South Side are ones that turn a profit for those white landlords and shopkeepers who live elsewhere. Bigger *knows* "that black people could not go outside of the Black Belt to rent a flat," and knows moreover that, so caged, they pay twice the rent whites do for their slum dwellings (288). Indeed, as he muses sardonically to himself, even bread is one cent more expensive in South Side grocery stores (289). Everywhere Bigger's aspirations turn, these same lines loom, keeping him, in every sense, in his place, and he knows only too well the risks attendant upon straying from this place. As he walks through a wealthy white neighbourhood, Bigger understands fully that he is a target here, a figure perceived as a threat, a criminal, the dread black rapist of Southern lynch-mob rhetoric: "Suppose a police saw him wandering in a white neighborhood like this? It would be thought he was trying to rob or rape somebody" (49). His boyhood dreams of being a pilot or a soldier have run into this same barrier, the school of aviation barring black students as the army of Uncle Sam admits them only "to dig ditches" and "scrub floors" (409). Thus the lessons young Bigger has learned well are ones of his own imprisonment, of American blacks being yoked to the service of the white world. As he himself articulates his experience of African-American reality, white Americans "own the earth [and] say black folks are dogs. They don't let you do nothing but what they want" (406).

Yet if Bigger *knows* these facts of his own oppression, his response is an attempt to erase this reality, to deny its status as fact and to retreat to a position where its factuality cannot reach him. Rankling at his own circumscribed existence, Bigger withdraws from it, from the world that rebukes him, from those other blacks as sorry and powerless as he, finally from his own consciousness of the real itself. Indeed, *because of* what he knows of this reality, Bigger pursues a studied rejection of it:

> He shut [his family's] voices out of his mind. He hated his
> family because he knew that they were suffering and that he was
> powerless to help them. He knew that the moment he allowed
> himself to feel to its fulness how they lived, he would be swept
> outside of himself with fear and despair. So he held toward them
> an attitude of iron reserve; he lived with them, but behind a wall, a
> curtain. And toward himself he was even more exacting. He knew
> that the moment he allowed what his life meant to enter fully into
> his consciousness, he would either kill himself or someone else. So
> he denied himself and acted tough. (9)

What is most remarkable in this passage is the portrait of an existence that
is its own self-conscious negation. Bigger, who knows only too well the
limits placed on his existence, assiduously obliterates such knowledge from
his mind, denying both the suffering of those closest to him and his own
frustration. Thus if Bigger is proffered as a character of acute insight into
the realities of American racism, he is one also in deliberate flight from
these realities.

Indeed, Bigger only lives by a process of erasing his own life. Anxious
always "to do something to evade looking so squarely at this problem" (18), he
strives towards a denial of it that is its ostensible eradication. Thus the desire,
indeed the phrase, predominant in Bigger's tale is that of "blotting it out."
Squirming awkwardly in the face of Mr. Dalton's questioning, Bigger aches
"to wave his hand and blot out the white man who was making him feel this"
(53). Caught in the Daltons' car by the friendly overtures of Mary Dalton and
her Communist boyfriend, Jan Erlone, he yearns "to seize some heavy object
and grip it with all the strength of his body and in some strange way rise up
and stand in naked space above the speeding car and with one final blow blot
it out—with himself and them in it" (80). Faced with the claustrophobic existence of his family, he longs not only for a curtain behind which to hide, but
also "to wave his hand and blot them out", erasing them as he would those
whites who befuddle and terrify him (112). Bigger's persistent desire is for the
wholesale erasure of a reality he cannot bear to acknowledge, for the oblitera-
tion not only of the whites who oppress, but of those blacks with whom he
suffers, of, indeed, his own existence itself.

And this desire has, in Wright's novel, its readily available outlet. If Bigger yearns for something that will enable him to forget his own circumstances,
this longing is met in *Native Son* by popular media catering precisely to the
wish for fantasy rather than realism. As Ross Pudaloff notes, Bigger's world
is one "dominated by movies, magazines, newspapers and detective stories"
(90), and it is indeed toward these media that Bigger hungrily turns. What
they offer him is precisely that for which he longs, an erasure of world that

is also an erasure of self. Thus leaving his family's flat, restless and dissatisfied even with his imminent job interview at the Dalton home, Bigger aches "to see a movie; his senses hungered for it. In a movie he could dream without effort; all he had to do was lean back in a seat and keep his eyes open" (13). The appeal here is twofold: movies are desired both because they offer dreams rather than that knowledge of reality which only torments him and because they are the kind of dreams requiring no dreamer, because they permit that erasure of *self* Bigger so desires. Such movies, and with them the pulp fiction of detective magazines, the sensational headlines of the Chicago dailies, and the lyrics of the latest dance tune, provide Bigger with a dream, a diversion, itself powerful enough to suppress the facts of his life. This indeed, as Bigger himself articulates it, is the very heart of their desirability: "He longed for a stimulus powerful enough to focus his attention and drain off his energies. He wanted to run. Or listen to some swing music. Or laugh or joke. Or read a *Real Detective Story Magazine.* Or go to a movie" (31).

But if Bigger longs for such stimuli as an erasure of self and world, what these media in fact present him with is an alternative world, a vision of an existence beyond his experience but not, thanks to these conventional sources, his ken. What Bigger finds, and indeed loves, in the movie-house and pulp magazine is a portrait of life defined not, as is his own, by limitations, poverty, and impotence, but rather by possibility, wealth, and power. Bigger's immersion in popular culture thus emerges here not only as a denial of the realities of his own oppression, his own experience, but also as an identification with and endorsement of the wealth and power of those who oppress him. Happily watching the matinee newsreels, Bigger sees a world of white American luxury, a world of "*the daughters of the rich taking sun baths in the sands of Florida,*" a sight that, the commentator informs him, "*represents over four billion dollars of America's wealth*" (34). Next to this vision, both his own experience and the feature film's portrait of "naked black men and women whirling in wild dances" (36) recede into insignificance. Bigger's mind is instead occupied with an awe-filled longing for that other world, that "real" world of Hollywood fantasies. Consciousness of self and world, as indeed of the black "savages" of B-movies, is here "replaced by images in his own mind of white men and women dressed in black and white clothes, laughing, talking, drinking and dancing" (36). Not only *Trader Horn's* African scene, but his own experience as a black American are effectively occluded by media-fostered dreams of a white world, a "realer" because desired reality of opulence and power.

But for Wright as realist, this erasure of self and world represents only Bigger's schooling in submission, an endorsement of the power others hold over him. In *Native Son* to accept the dream, to eschew realism, is only to perpetuate the realities of oppression. In Bigger's eyes, then, those well-dressed whites of his movie-house fantasies are "smart people; they knew how to get hold of money, millions of it" (36–37). The wealth and power of white America become here, in Bigger's attempts to blot out his reality, his own standards of value. In his mass media evasion, Bigger ends up not only retreating from his world, his people, indeed himself, but identifying himself with those powerful whites who, as he *knows*, will not let him do anything. Scorning poor whites as "stupid" for their inability to get hold of millions (37), Bigger spends his free time "playing white," assuming the roles of J. P. Morgan, the President, and white generals, speaking lines "heard . . . in the movies" (19). Having found his proper objects of respect and value in the wealthy whites he himself knows to own the earth, Bigger seeks a final erasure of himself in the dream of *being* these whites, of dispensing with their wealth, of making their decisions, of, indeed, dealing in their fashion with "the niggers . . . raising sand all over the country" (20). Thus if, as Wright himself describes him, Bigger is a man "trying to react to and answer the call of the dominant civilization whose glitter [comes] to him through newspapers, magazines, radios, movies" ("How Bigger" 513), he is one also who makes his answer by assenting to the values of those who oppress him, by, indeed, contradicting and denying the reality he suffers.

For the Marxist Wright of 1940, this assent, of course, is no strange phenomenon. As he himself, paraphrasing Lenin, wrote in 1938, "oppressed minorities often reflect the techniques of the bourgeoisie more brilliantly than some sections of the bourgeoisie themselves. The psychological importance of this becomes meaningful when it is recalled that oppressed minorities . . . strive to assimilate the virtues of the bourgeoisie in the assumption that by doing so they can lift themselves into a higher social sphere" (*Richard Wright Reader* 38). While we shall soon see how Bigger himself, after his accidental killing of Mary Dalton, makes this assumption, what is most important in this identification is how it feeds both Bigger's own sense of terror and powerlessness in the face of white America and his alienation from all those—his fellow blacks, the poor whites, "Reds" like Jan and Boris Max—with whom he might struggle not to evade but to change the world. Certainly Bigger's identification with the wealth and power of the oppressor leads to a contempt for those whites who will not play this role. Of the Communists who will become first his scapegoats and then his defenders, Bigger has only the vaguest, most caricatured of notions, one gleaned from that mass media dream-world with which he blots out his experience: "He remembered seeing many cartoons of Communists in newspapers and always they had flaming torches in their hands and wore beards and were trying to commit murder or set things on fire. People who acted that way were crazy" (*Native Son* 74). Yet if Bigger has learned through newspaper stereotypes that the "Reds" are crazy, what most repels him is their manifest lack of identification with that world he himself holds dear. As Bigger sees it, the problem with the "Reds," as with the stupid poor whites, is precisely their exclusion from the world of wealth and power: "He didn't want to meet any Communists. They didn't have any money" (73).

If Bigger's scorn thus reveals a contempt for the common, for those who share in some sense that world of dispossession and disempowerment which is his own, this contempt is all the more acute and alienating in Bigger's relations with other African Americans. For at the heart of Bigger's admiration for the white world captured in matinee newsreels is, as we have seen, a hatred for, the desire to erase, his own poverty and powerlessness. Bigger retreats behind a curtain in his dealings with other blacks because, identifying with wealth and power, he can see in others like himself only contemptible weakness, indeed only a reflection of that position he occupies and loathes. Bigger's dealings with his family, "friends," and lover, then, are all governed by feelings of shame and self-hatred, feelings bound up in his education in, and identification with, the values of wealth and power learned in newspapers and movie houses. Toward the family for whom he announces his contempt at the very opening of the novel Bigger can feel only a scornful pity and shame. Even as they weep and plead for him as he awaits trial, Bigger can only recoil in disgust at what he sees as the revelation of that weakness he wants to erase. They are for him no solace, but rather only the badge of his shameful impotence, something therefore to be obliterated, denied: "Bigger wanted to whirl and blot them from sight . . . . He felt that all of the white people in the room were measuring every inch of his weakness. He identified himself with his family and felt their naked shame" (341).

If Bigger here "identifies" with his family, it is only in terms of ascribing to them that shame and loathing he feels, a shame and a loathing that stem rather from his identification with the scorn he sees in the eyes of white onlookers. This dynamic of loathing and withdrawing from those who suffer as he does governs all of Bigger's relations with other African Americans, such that his dealings with them become rehearsals of rejection. Bigger does not "think enough of" the gang with whom he pulls his petty heists to care what they think of him, or ever to attempt to explain himself to them (47). Likewise, toward his "girl," Bessie, he feels, as he admits to Communist lawyer Boris Max, neither love nor hate; she is, in his own words, "just my girl. I don't reckon I was ever in love with nobody . . . . You have to have a girl, so I had Bessie" (408). And, indeed, precisely insofar as this compulsory "girl" assumes a human significance, a black face and a black life like his own, she is to be denied: "he felt that there were two Bessies: one a body that he had just had and wanted badly again, the other was in Bessie's face; it asked questions . . . He wished he could clench his fist and swing his arm and blot out, kill, sweep away the Bessie on Bessie's face and leave the other helpless and yielding before him" (159).[3] With family, friends and lover, Bigger can only re-enact that erasure of self he

pursues throughout the novel, an eradication of a reality that is for him, looking on it through an admiration for and identification with a white American
dream, not only unbearable but contemptible. What is to be sought instead is
an identification with the oppressor in such dreams, an identification that may
permit Bigger's assertion of difference from the weak and indeed from himself,
but that marks the death of the very possibility of solidarity with the oppressed:
"There were rare moments when a feeling and longing for solidarity with other
black people would take hold of him . . . . [B]ut that dream would fade when he
looked at the other black people near him. Even though black like him, he felt
there was too much difference between him and them to allow for a common
binding and a common life" (129).

Yet if Bigger's rejection of the reality he knows thus significantly sounds
the death knell for any possibility of unity with those like himself, his admiration for the affluent whites of Hollywood film leads him to actual assaults on
other blacks and, indeed, to that barely conscious act, the killing of Mary Dalton, which is his own undoing. For if Bigger is awe-struck in the face of those
wealthy white figures in his movie-house dreams, it is awe holding terror as
well as admiration, a terror which leads him to an actual and violent blotting
out of black victims—and ultimately of himself. The white world with which
he seeks to erase his own experience figures in Bigger's imagination no longer
as a social system or an aggregate of individuals, but as a powerful, indeed
fearsome, natural force; it is for him both the paradise of power and wealth
and "that looming mountain of white hate," something both inhuman and
terrifying in that very power he covets in it (333). Moreover, although Bigger
himself sees this fearsomeness as somehow different from his imagining of
this world in the pre-fabricated dreams of American cinema, his schooling
there in an identification with the powerful white force that hates is itself also
an education in terror before this force. While Bigger, when confronted with
Mary Dalton in the flesh rather than in her celluloid projections, muses "in
amazement how different the girl had seemed in the movie. On the screen
she was not dangerous and his mind could do with her as it pleased" (62),
the lesson he leaves the theatre having learned is one of fear rather than of
empowerment. Identifying with the white power and affluence on the screen,
Bigger becomes increasingly anxious about his gang's imminent robbery of a
white man and leaves the theatre "with a mounting feeling of fear" (38). The
mythical world with which he attempts to blot out himself and those like him
becomes, in this very attempt, "a sort of great natural force, like a stormy sky
looming overhead, or like a deep swirling river stretching suddenly at one's
feet" (129). It is as such a mythic force that this world becomes the motive
behind the violence Bigger enacts on those closest to himself.

For having learned the lesson not only of an admirable and validated
white pre-eminence, but also of the fearsome character of this pre-eminence,

Bigger's first concern is to derail that "violation of ultimate taboo"—his gang's plan to rob Blum's Deli (14). What this derailment significantly involves is violence against other blacks, those "friends" with whom he commits his petty crimes. As cohort Gus appears at the appointed time, making the robbery an imminent reality, Bigger, gripped by terror, not only assaults him, but pulls a knife on him and makes him, on his knees and helpless, lick it (41-44). This whole performance, the beating and humiliation of another African American, is both the result of Bigger's own helpless fear before the endorsed white power of his dreams and itself a blotting out or coveting up of this fear, both for their and his own benefit: "His confused emotions made him feel instinctively that it would be better to fight Gus and spoil the plan of the robbery than to confront a white man with a gun. But he kept this knowledge of his fear thrust firmly down in him; his courage to live depended on how successfully his fear was hidden from his consciousness" (47). Bigger's violence issues not only from his own persistent need to erase what he *knows* to be the case, but also from that denied fear which is itself the product of this attempt. Moreover, as with his early drawing of that curtain which separates him from his family, the result here is not only a bleeding and humbled Gus, but a Bigger Thomas once more cut off from those closest to, and most like, himself: "he knew that what had happened today put an end to his being with them in any more jobs" (47).

III

If Bigger's negation of self and world, tangled as it is with a love for and fear of the white world of fantasy, only alienates him from those who share his reality, this separation, figured as violence, is most extreme in the case of his girlfriend, Bessie. Bigger, as noted, is already effectively alienated from Bessie, viewing her not as person, but only as a potential source of oblivion and gratification. Insofar as she might be anything more, insofar as she might take on any human reality or substance, she is herself to be denied in the most violent of fantasies. Indeed if, as I am arguing here, Wright's *Native Son* presents an argument as to the murderous and oppressive consequences of living the ethics of blotting out, it is in the case of Bessie, who is in fact blotted out by Bigger, that this argument is most forcefully made. Yet in order to understand this fulfilment of Bigger's desire to sweep away the Bessie on Bessie's face, we must turn first to that earlier blotting out, the death of Mary Dalton. What is central in this fateful "murder," and indeed that cold-blooded killing of Bessie which follows, is again a fear and a violence born of the lie.

The Bigger who loves the Hollywood idiom of white power knows only too well the myths by which such figures enact their *real* power over him and his fellow black Americans. As revealed in that reflection on his own vulnerability to the charge of rape noted above, Bigger knows both the myths white America maintains about itself and those by which it defines his reality. The logic of the lynch mob, the white stereotype of the black rapist, are hardly foreign to his consciousness. As he tells Max, all he knows of Mary Dalton is that "they kill us for women like her" (405), and do so with a rhetoric of the rape and the black rapist: "They say black men do that. So it don't matter if I did or if I didn't" (404). Here racist myth, with good reason, figures both as a determinant of his reality and as part of his own dreaming identification with the white world that produces this oppressive reality. Earlier, admiring and affirming that white power and luxury captured in newsreel images of lounging, billion-dollar debutantes, Bigger in this very endorsement jokes that if friend Jack were indeed part of this fantasy world, "[he]'d be hanging from a tree like a bunch of bananas" (34).

Yet if this myth of the black rapist, a myth that bears strange if real and bloody fruit, is thus part of the fantasy Bigger himself pursues as the erasure of self and experience, its issue once more is a deadly terror. For if Mary Dalton dies unviolated, she dies because of the myth of the black violator and the fear it inspires in Wright's desperate dreamer. Indeed, the scene of Mary's death is scripted by this myth, which, for Bigger, as much as for the whites with whom he identifies, is accepted as truth. Having carried the drunk Mary to her room, Bigger is caught in her bedroom as the blind Mrs. Dalton enters. Knowing all too well the lethal power of a fantasy that would label him criminal and rapist here, Bigger is seized by "a hysterical terror" (97), a terror itself part of his immersion in a fiction whose true effects he knows by heart: "He felt strange, possessed, or as if he were acting upon a stage" (95). Gripped by the fear this fantasy produces, seemingly bound by the role it would assign him, Bigger, in a desperate attempt not to be discovered, silences Mary with her pillow, inadvertently smothering her (100). Here the very terror produced by his understanding of the racist myths of his coveted white world pushes Bigger toward a final blotting out, and towards his assumption of that very role, that of the black criminal, such myths would assign him. And, significantly, Bigger himself assents to the logic of these myths, assumes that identity they insist upon: "He was black and he had been in a room where a white girl had been killed; therefore he had killed her. That was what everybody would say anyhow" (119).

If this killing reveals the murderous aspect of Bigger's programme of denial, it also marks the fulfilment of his greatest wish, his immersion in that world of white American fantasy he has always admired and feared. Indeed, Bigger himself, in assuming that identity of murderer and rapist which is his in this world, revels in this immersion. It is, for him, the beginning of a new life, the erasure of the old. Now he is, in his own eyes, the self-made and powerful man of Hollywood's American story, and one moreover on the make and on the rise. With this act, he feels, he has made "a new life for himself. It was something that was all his own" (119).[4] By this act, he sees himself as having become that man of action and power he has never been but has dreamed of being, the hero of that American movie narrative of wealth, power, and success with which he has identified in the past. Now in possession of the money roll from Mary's purse, he flatters himself as the man of wealth and power looking forward to his next enterprise: "he was a man who had come in sight of a goal, then had won it, and in winning it had seen just within grasp another goal, higher, greater" (148). That this higher, greater goal is his plan to extort more money from the Daltons, by leading them to believe Mary kidnapped by the Communists, is itself significant. For in having arrived, by way of dreams and the fear they foster, as the man of power and decision, Bigger himself conceives and enacts this new identity as a living of the lie. The great insight won over Mary's body is one of universal delusion, a blindness from which he alone, he feels, is exempt. People, he now "sees," are "blind to what did not fit. They did not want to see what others were doing if that doing did not feed their own desires" (120). The lesson here, for Bigger, is to use this blindness to one's own advantage, to perform the quotidian, all the while pursuing that higher goal of personal satisfaction; the new self-made man of his own Hollywood drama, his task is "to act just like others acted, live like they lived, and while they were not looking, do what you wanted" (120).

Thus made "murderer" by that tangle of fear and fantasy outlined above, Bigger insists that by this act he has transcended fear and understood the reality of American society. If he feels he may assume the identity of that white American hero with whom he has so long identified, this identification is for him not the acceptance of the lie, but the canny use of it. Yet the results of this manipulation are eerily familiar. For through the lie of his ransom note, and indeed the new ethos of the lie just articulated, Bigger brings about only his further alienation from all around him and finally his own destruction by the lies of white racism. The new and improved Bigger, bankroll in hand and new plans on the go, feels now "cut off from [the old gang] forever" and doles out packs of cigarettes to them as a sign of his new power and distinction (125). His family, too, recede from him to join the malleable ranks of the benighted, the secret of his "murder" itself becoming another "natural wall from behind which he could look at them" (119). Finally, Bessie, who will soon suffer the true violence of the lie, also fades further into the distance. If she remains important to him as a sexual diversion, as a way indeed to keep from seeing the truth of his crime, "that terrible image of Mary's head" (150), her voice and very presence are themselves blotted out by Bigger's new, big-money dreams: "Bigger was not listening. The world of sound fell abruptly away from him and a vast picture appeared before his eyes . . . . why could he not, not send a letter to the Daltons, asking for money?" (155).

If Bigger's living of the dream he has so long cherished represents only a further retreat into isolation, his writing of this letter, his new *creation* of the lie, becomes the tool by which he can target for violence all those who would seek strength in speaking truly and overcoming such isolation. Having learned from his own media-fed dreaming that the "Reds," like Chicago blacks, are hated and vulnerable, Bigger resolves to make the note appear to be the work of the Communist Party: "Bigger knew the things that white folks hated to hear Negroes ask for; and he knew that these were the things the Reds were always asking for" (225). What here might be the identification of purpose and struggle becomes, rather, for the Bigger who seeks the world offered in media dreams, a tool for profiting by the blood of others who might be allies. Indeed, Bigger's primary target in the construction of his "story" for the Daltons is Mary's boyfriend Jan, the very "Red" who has argued for such an alliance: "Don't you think if we got together we could stop things like that [the murder of Bigger's father]?" (85). Rather than responding to such appeals, Bigger begins instead composing lies that will be headlines out of headlines he himself has read and taken to heart. Thus he is cast here by Wright as parrot rather than creator, the idiom of his ransom note, as of his earlier playing white, borrowed from the mass media with which he has sought to blot out the real: "*Get ten thousand in 5 and 10 bills and put it in a shoe box* . . . . That's good. He had read that somewhere" (203). With this letter, itself designed by the news of the dailies, Bigger starts making this news, making, as the reporters at the Dalton home note, great copy. But what this copy means is not only the reiteration of lies about, and persecution of, a political organization whose demands are his own, but the promulgation of those lies and myths by which his people are oppressed. As one of the reporters exclaims, "What a story! Don't you see it? These Negroes want to be left alone and these Reds are forcing 'em to live with 'em, see? Every wire in the country'll carry it!" (246). If, then, Bigger has become the powerful man admired on the movie screen, he has done so not only by a further retreat from those who would fight against oppression, but also by himself becoming the reproduction of the lies that serve oppression.

Bigger's insistent rehearsal of mass media ideals, as one achieved only by the maintenance of lies that oppress, becomes all the more lethal when his own lie is dashed. When Mary's remains are found, Bigger becomes even greater copy, and *a* copy, now not of the caricatured "Reds" of Sunday-paper cartoons, but of that myth of the black criminal and rapist that was indeed the source of his "self-creation." While scarcely free of the fear that made this crime when he dreamed of himself as the hero of newspaper copy (see, e.g., 176; 207), Bigger, discovered, is now wholly returned to that terror and to the myths inspiring it. Watching the discovery of Mary's remains, Bigger feels the fantasy of the self-made man quickly dissolve: "There was just the old feeling, the feeling he had had all his life: he was black and had done wrong; white men were looking at something with which they would accuse him. It was the old feeling, hard and constant again now" (253). Bigger's living of the lie has thus only surrendered him all the more forcefully to its identification of him as the accused, and has further made of him the stuff of racist myth and headlines, myth and headlines that drive him to terrified flight and target both Chicago blacks and "Reds" for violence and persecution. If he is now, as "AUTHORITIES HINT SEX CRIME" (281), the stuff of headlines as the black rapist of racist myth, he is also the occasion, as such copy, for massive assaults on the black community he has scorned and on the Communists whose appeals for solidarity he himself has targetted. These headlines have themselves effected other news, as blacks throughout the South Side are terrorized by police and vigilantes: "Police reported that many windows in the Negro sections were smashed . . . . Reports were current that several Negro men were beaten in various North and West Side neighborhoods" (282). If blacks are beaten and harassed, so too are Bigger's cartoon "Reds," as the Communist headquarters are raided and hundreds of members arrested (297).

Thus Bigger's own programme of blotting it all out ends in the violent triumph of the lies of those rich whites he sought to become. It ends indeed not only in violence against those whom he has scorned but also in the erasure, the mortal blotting out, of himself and others. For Bigger himself is, before his final erasure, already erased by the racist stereotype of his own newspaper copy. No longer the terrified man who killed in fear of this stereotype and its consequences, he is now, for the media he has cherished, "a beast untouched by the softening influences of modern civilization" whose "central crime . . . is *rape!*" (323; 481). Yet if Bigger is thus blotted out by the myth of the black rapist, this is an erasure Bigger himself helps to effect, and not only by that nurtured fear which led to Mary's death. For while, as Bigger knows, "when they killed him it would be for Mary's death" (351), the unraped and accidental victim of his own terror, Bigger, in living out his newspaper dreams of success, has made himself *in fact* the murderer and rapist this myth holds him to be, a murderer and rapist who, like this myth itself, victimizes African Americans. While Bigger dreams his headline dreams of extortion and personal advancement, he is already plotting to make his desired erasure of Bessie complete. For the Bigger who fancies himself a man on the rise, Bessie is a useful, but disposable tool, one to be rubbed out when she becomes a liability. And here, too, her lethal liability is figured in terms of fear, Bigger's own fear of discovery: "He was afraid that he would have to kill her before it was all over. She would not go with him and he could not leave her behind" (207). Once this discovery is made, once Bigger has become the rapist of myth, Bessie's fate is sealed. No longer a stepping stone for his advancement but an object for his fear, she is now to be used one last time and irrevocably blotted out. Thus Bigger, seizing here that sexual diversion she has always represented to him, rapes her in an act that fulfills his desire for her erasure. While she protests and resists, her voice comes to a Bigger still living only the fantasy "from out of a deep, far-away silence and he paid her no heed" (270). This violent silencing, however, is for him insufficient; her irritating intrusions on his fantasy, her very human reality, must be obliterated finally in murder (274).

If, then, the Bigger who lives only by eliding his own reality and living the dreams generated by those who oppress him becomes himself the violent oppressor, he does so by his transformation into the very figure these whites hold him to be. And this transformation is fatal not only for Bessie, but, ultimately, for Bigger himself. For if by this brutal act he becomes the rapist and murderer as whom he has always dreaded being accused, he also thereby provides the myths that will kill him with the proof of their validity and justice. At the coroner's hearing, which will produce the charges of rape and murder for which he will be condemned to death, Bessie figures not as victim, but as damning testimony, proof that he is, now in reality and not just in racist myths, the black rapist everyone expects him to be. Here Bessie's raped and mutilated body is actually presented as *evidence* against him, evidence of his being, as indeed he has become, the stereotype of white fantasies. What's more, as Bigger knows, this evidence, his own violent transformation into myth by his own urge to deny the real, is already his death sentence: "They were bringing Bessie's body in now to make white men and women feel that nothing short of a quick blotting out of his life would make the city safe again. They were using his having killed Bessie to kill him for his having killed Mary, to cast him in a light that would sanction any action taken to destroy him" (383). Thus Bigger's own desire for the dream leads, by way of his transformation into myth, to his own final erasure, his own fatal blotting out. And as Bigger himself understands, this final erasure and alienation are things he himself has helped to bring about: "There was no one to whom he had anything to say, for he had never given himself whole-heartedly to anyone or anything, except murder . . . . Of the old gang, only Jack had been his friend, and he had never been so close to Jack as he would have liked. And Bessie was dead; he had killed her" (489).

IV

If Wright thus demonstrates the denial of the real to entail the oppression of the group denied, his novel also posits as the empowering and indeed life-saving alternative to this cycle of killing a solidarity and struggle born not of denial, but of a discourse of disclosure, of indeed a realism attuned to the contradictions of conventional myth. Central here are Bigger's encounters with those very Communists he himself has set up for persecution. While the arguments of Jan Erlone and lawyer Boris Max are dismissed by such critics as Dan McCall as "the forensic slag, the endless clichés, and awkward set of speeches" (367)[5], they figure in the text itself as Bigger's only experience of communication with, rather than erasure of, the other. Jan and Max are virtually the only characters in the novel ever to question Bigger about anything other than his crimes, and to do so as a means not of accusation but of understanding and common struggle. If Jan argues, as we have seen, for a common fight against oppression, he does this by way of a desire to discover, understand, and communicate the real. Like Mary, he wants "to see . . . . to *know* these people" (79), and to do so through a language at odds with Bigger's own silencing fantasies. Yet perhaps most important here is Bigger's extended, pre-trial interview with Boris Max. Max, who holds that disclosure is itself the medium of struggle—"Not if we fight. Not if I tell them how you've had to live" (427)—uses the fact, the real, as his weapon both in court and in his assaults on Bigger's own cocoon of withdrawal. His language, one that draws forth Bigger's thoughts and experiences, also ties these to a larger world of persecution and resistance, disclosing a world of common interest at odds with Bigger's own contempt for that which is like his own suffering: "They [the powerful whites] hate trade unions. They hate folks who try to organize. They hate Jan" (402). Although such potential for identification with those like himself, an identification and a struggle to be born out of a discourse rather than a denial of the real, comes too late to change Bigger's fate, the recognition of such potential serves for Bigger himself as an epiphany resonant of Wright's own in *Black Boy*. It is Bigger himself who insists upon the significance of this interview, of the brand of communication it represents, and he does so by seeing it as a form of empowerment, an empowerment that stems from acknowledging and working with, rather than mentally and physically blotting out, others like himself: "Mr. Max, I sort of saw myself after that night. And I sort of saw other people, too" (496). Bigger has "spoken to Max as he had never spoken to anyone in his life, not even to himself" (417), and what this very act has revealed to him is the appeal and power of communication with the reality of other human beings; he sees now that "in [this] touch, response of recognition, there would be union, identity; there would be a supporting oneness, a wholeness which had been denied him" (420). If Bigger's own case is hopeless, he nonetheless dies a rather different figure, one now filled with the hope such recognition inspires. Thus his last words are an uncharacteristic appeal to an other he has once scorned and scapegoated: "Tell . . . . Tell Mister . . . . Tell Jan hello" (502; ellipses in text).

In all of this, I would argue, we see Wright executing through his realism a subtle and detailed dissection of the costs of racism in both physical and psychic terms, one that mobilizes realist narrative as a means to critique both the violence of racist oppression and the disabling power of racist discourse. The realist mode in *Native Son* enables an oppositional political analysis that flies in the face of recent theses, in Wright criticism and elsewhere, as to the inherent conservatism of realist conventions. Indeed, the text itself highlights the importance of the realist mode to its own emancipatory concerns by arguing, via the tale of Bigger Thomas, *for* realism, for referential and documentary language, as the prime weapon against an oppression that is seen to thrive on elision and misrepresentation. Despite Tanner's assertion that *Native Son* assumes its radical stature by its undermining the "conservatism" of its own apparent realism (132), it is a language of realism the novel itself champions as the means by which we may fight both conservatism and oppression. Words that attend to and express the facts of lived experience are here not only Wright's medium for his own analysis of racial and class oppression in America, but the message of this medium itself, and the strategies of the classic realist text are here deployed not, as Belsey would have it, to do, but to expose and undermine the work of ideology. Wright's work thus points to the descriptive poverty of such recent formulations of the politics of realism, not only as regards his own corpus, but potentially a whole tradition of realist political fiction, as well. Perhaps now, in the age "post" Belsey's post-Saussurean thought[6], it is time to begin reassessing not only Wright's political concerns and achievements as realist, but the oppositional as well as reactionary potential of literary realism more generally.

Notes

1. Indeed, the durability of this critical truism attests, I would argue, to the on-going importance of post-structuralist premises to the critical practice of the academy of the 1990s. While Belsey herself derives her critique from the works of such French thinkers as Barthes and Althusser (see, especially chapters 2 and 3 of *Critical Practice*), this assault on the drive to representation that is realism is common to most contemporary French thought. If Barthes, in "The Reality Effect," attacks the ideological force of "the *referential illusion*" (148), more recent work by such thinkers as Jean-François Lyotard would seem merely to extend such an assessment. For Lyotard, literary realists must always be "apologists for what exists" (6), and he discerns in the desire for realism a palpable political evil: "we hear [in calls for realist work] murmurings of the desire to reinstitute terror and fulfill the phantasm of taking possession of reality" (16). Though less explicitly concerned with realism as a literary mode, Jacques Derrida, in his own attacks on a logocentric desire for the referent that is "nothing but the most original and powerful ethnocentrism" (3), would seem implicitly to concur with such dismissals, and indeed himself charges literature *tout court* with having "almost always and almost everywhere, according to some fashions and across very diverse ages, lent itself to this *transcendent* reading, in that search for the signified" (160). If such anti-realist, poststructuralist premises no longer require Belsey's brand of polemical introduction, they are nonetheless still

assumed and operative in much contemporary scholarship, and stand, as I hope the present work will demonstrate, in need of their own critical re-assessment.

2. Examples of the mini-explosion in Wright studies in the late 1960s and early 1970s include not only such biographical works as Constance Webb's *Richard Wright: A Biography* and Michel Fabre's more comprehensive *The Unifinished Quest of Richard Wright*, but also a wide array of works of criticism and introduction, treating, often in eponymous fashion, the re-emergence of Wright as a writer of critical, as well as political, interest. Of these latter, see, for example, Robert Bone's *Richard Wright*, Dan McCall's *The Example of Richard Wright*, Milton and Patricia Rickels's *Richard Wright*, Keneth Kinnamon's impressive study, *The Emergence of Richard Wright*, and collections of criticism edited by Richard Abcairn and (collaboratively) David Ray and Robert M. Farnsworth under the respective titles of *Richard Wright's Native Son: A Critical Handbook* and *Richard Wright: Impressions and Perspectives*.

3. Indeed it is such passages as these, with their violent expression of Bigger's desire to erase his world and the other blacks who populate it, that have led many critics to attack Wright's fiction for its apparent misogyny. Since, at least, Michele Wallace's 1978 identification of Wright as the founding father of the cult of "Black Macho," Wright scholars have targetted what they see as his fiction's attempt "to appropriate (and thus dehumanize) women by reducing them to objects of male status conflict" (France 414). Such criticisms are echoed by Caesar Blake, who sees the women of *Native Son* as functioning only as targets of male violence (195), Nagueyatti Warren, who argues Wright labels all his women either "bitches" or "whores" (60), and Houston Baker, who reads Wright as the champion of an ascendant and essentially misogynist modernity (222). Indeed one-time friend and biographer Margaret Walker even makes the claim that in Wright's "subconscious mind all black women were whores, bitches or cunts and deserved to be treated as such" (163). Such critics, however, would seem to equate Wright with his protagonist, and fail to note how Wright casts Bigger's violence against women as both the product of that studied anti-realism Wright is attacking and indeed as the very source of Bigger's own ultimate destruction.

4. Critics of the novel have been quick to agree with Bigger's own assessment on this score, and have thus missed a central component of Wright's argument for the oppositional politics of realism. Robert Bone, Milton and Patricia Rickels, Charles De Arman, Robert Butler, and Valerie Smith all agree with Bigger in viewing Mary's slaying as a liberating act, one by which Bigger frees himself from his fear and takes on, for the first time, the task of defining himself. Such readings, which I would argue have helped foster those of Wright as misogynist, ignore the ways in which the novel reveals Bigger's crimes to be the result of a fear itself the product of his acting out others' definitions of himself and the world. While Bigger, living a fantasy of new-found power, claims this "murder" as a liberating act, such claims are undercut by the novel. In this very passage, in which Bigger first exults in his crime, the text itself questions the extent to which this act is Bigger's at all: "Though he had killed by accident, not once did he feel the need to tell himself it had been an accident" (*Native Son* 119). Once his crime is discovered, moreover, even Bigger's own belief as to his transcendence of fear and powerlessness are dashed: "his whole body was wrapped in a sheet of fear . . . . It was the old feeling, hard and constant again now" (253).

5. Houston A. Baker also bemoans what he sees as Wright's lamentable "lack of immunity to the lure of a peculiarly materialist historiography" (222), yet I agree

rather with Barbara Foley in her assertion that even Max's lengthy speeches serve, in a novel that deals with the deadly consequences of the denial of experience by popular myth, to "question the very self-evidence of 'experience'" (198) and to force the reader to confront actual social conditions rather than the easy stereotype (191).

6. While the persistence of the caricature of literary realism I am contesting here reveals the extent to which poststructuralist thinking and assumptions remain very much operative in literary criticism of the 1990s, recent work has been arguing for myriad alternative theoretical paths to bring literary study "beyond" poststructuralism. See in particular collections edited by Nancy Easterlin and Barbara Riebling—*After Poststructuralism: Interdisciplinarity and Literary Theory*—and Wendell V. Harris—*Beyond Poststructuralism: The Speculations of Theory and the Experience of Reading*. Although these volumes devote relatively little space to the ways in which poststructuralist readings often entail a blindness to the oppositional politics of literary texts, Riebling's own essay, "Remodeling Truth, Power and Society" (Easterlin and Riebling 177–201), provides a cogent critique of the ways in which the subversion-containment model adopted by New Historicist Renaissance scholars from Foucault involves a view of political history as effectively static and immune to meaningful critique or transformation. As I hope the present essay demonstrates, however, there remains much work to be done in this "post" age on how literary texts themselves, as well as literary theories, can enact an oppositional politics.

Works Cited

Abcaim, Richard, ed. *Richard Wright's* Native Son: *A Critical Handbook*. Belmont, CA: Wadsworth, 1970.

Baker, Houston A., Jr. "On Knowing Our Place." Gates and Appiah 200–225.

Baldwin, James. *Notes of a Native Son*. Boston: Beacon, 1955.

Barthes, Roland. "The Reality Effect." *The Rustle of Language*. Trans. Richard Howard. New York: Hill and Wang, 1986. 141–148.

Belsey, Catherine. *Critical Practice*. London: Methuen, 1980.

Blake, Caesar. "On Richard Wright's *Native Son*." *Rough Justice: Essays on Crime and Literature*. Ed. M. Friedland. Toronto: University of Toronto Press, 1991. 187–199.

Bloom, Harold, ed. *Bigger Thomas*. New York: Chelsea, 1990.

Bone, Robert. *Richard Wright*. Minneapolis: University of Minnesota Press, 1969.

Butler, Robert J. Introduction. *The Critical Response to Richard Wright*. Ed. Robert J. Butler. Westport, CT: Greenwood, 1995. xxv–xxxix.

———. Native Son: *The Emergence of a New Black Hero*. Boston: Twayne, 1991.

Clarke, Graham. "Beyond Realism: Recent Black Fiction and the Language of 'The Real Thing'." *Black American Literature Forum* 16.1 (1982): 43–48.

Cleaver, Eldridge. *Soul on Ice*. New York: Dell, 1970.

de Arman, Charles. "Bigger Thomas: The Symbolic Negro and the Discrete Human Entity." Bloom 83–89.

Derrida, Jacques. *Of Grammatology*. Trans. And Intro. Gayatri Chakravorty Spivak. Baltimore: Johns Hopkins University Press, 1976.

Easterlin, Nancy, and Barbara Riebling, eds. *After Poststructuralism: Interdisciplinarity and Literary Theory*. Foreword Frederick Crews. Evanston, IL: Northwestern University Press, 1993.

Ellison, Ralph. *Shadow and Act*. New York: Vintage, 1972.

Fabre, Michel. *The Unifinished Quest of Richard Wright*. Trans. Isabel Barzun. New York: William Morrow, 1973.

Felski, Rita. *Beyond Feminist Aesthetics: Feminist Literature and Social Change*. Cambridge: Harvard University Press, 1989.

Foley, Barbara. "The Politics of Peotics: Ideology and Narrative Form in *An American Tragedy* and *Native Son*." Gates and Appiah 188–199.

France, Alan. "Misogyny and Appropriation in Wright's *Native Son*." *Modem Fiction Studies* 34.3 (1988): 413–423.

Gates, Henry Louis, Jr., and K. A. Appiah, eds. *Richard Wright: Critical Perspectives, Past and Present*. New York: Amistad, 1993.

Harris, Wendell V., ed. *Beyond Poststructuralism: The Speculations of Theory and the Experience of Reading*. University Park: Pennsylvania State University Press, 1996.

Howe, Irving. "Black Boys and Native Sons." Abcairn 135–143.

Kinnamon, Keneth. *The Emergence of Richard Wright*. Urbana: University of Illinois Press, 1972.

Locke, Alain. n. t. Gates and Appiah 19–25.

Lyotard, Jean-François. *The Postmodern Explained: Correspondence, 1982–1985*. Trans. Don Barry, et al. Afterword Wlad Godzich. Minneapolis: University of Minnesota Press, 1992.

McCall, Dan. *The Example of Richard Wright*. New York: Harcourt, Brace and World, 1969.

———. "Wright's American Hunger." Gates and Appiah 359–368.

Pudaloff, Russ. "*Native Son* and Mass Culture." Bloom 90–102.

Ray, David, and Robert M. Famsworth, eds. *Richard Wright: Impressions and Perspectives*. Ann Arbor: University of Michigan Press, 1973.

Redden, Dorothy S. "Richard Wright and *Native Son:* Not Guilty." Bloom 73–82.

Reilly, John M. "Giving Bigger a Voice: The Politics of Narrative in *Native Son*." *New Essays on* Native Son. Ed. Keneth Kinnamon. Cambridge: Cambridge University Press, 1990. 35–62.

———, ed. and intro. *Richard Wright: The Critical Reception*. n. p. Burt Franklin, 1978.

Rickels, Milton, and Patricia Rickels. *Richard Wright*. Austin: Steck Vaughn, 1970.

Smith, Valerie. "Alienation and Creativity in the Fiction of Richard Wright." Gates and Appiah 433–447.

Solomon, William. "Politics and Rhetoric in the Novel in the 1930s." *American Literature* 68.4 (1996): 799–818.

Tanner, Laura. "Uncovering the Magical Disguise of Language in Richard Wright's *Native Son*." Gates and Appiah 132–148.

Walker, Margaret. *Richard Wright: Daemonic Genius*. New York: Warner, 1988.

Wallace, Michele. *Black Macho and the Myth of the Superwoman*. New York: Dial, 1979.

Warren, Nagueyatti. "Black Girls and Native Sons: Female Images in Selected Works by Richard Wright." *Richard Wright: Myths and Realities*. Ed. C. James Trotman. New York: Garland, 1988. 59–77.

Webb, Constance. *Richard Wright: A Biography*. New York: Putnam, 1968.

Wright, Richard. *Black Boy: A Record of Childhood and Youth*. New York: Harper & Row, 1966.

———. "How 'Bigger' Was Born." *Native Son*. Intro. Arnold Rampersad. New York: HarperCollins, 1993. 503–540.

———. *Native Son*. Intro. Arnold Rampersad. New York: HarperCollins, 1993.

———. *Richard Wright Reader.* Ed. Ellen Wright and Michel Fabre. New York: Harper & Row, 1978.

JONATHAN ELMER

Spectacle and Event in Native Son

So prevalent is the vocabulary of trauma in contemporary criticism that one is drawn to inquire into the nature of its appeal and ask what cultural work it is performing. From one point of view, the focus on trauma might seem an expression of humility, of a desire to forestall overzealous lesson-drawing from history, or worse, "comparative victimology."[1] So unimaginable and so unremitting are the horrors we have perpetrated on one another, according to this view, that we must assume that we suffer from radical disorientation. We do not know what we have done, and we do not know what has been done to us, which must be why we keep committing such horrors, compulsively. This humility can produce a querulous uncertainty about our own historical agency that for some feeds impotent liberal guilt while offering others a ready explanation of continued victimization. There is a less sentimental version of this humility, however, aptly summarized in Claude Lanzmann's influential phrase, "the obscenity of understanding."[2] Lanzmann's exacting aesthetic demands a continual presentation of the fact of the Holocaust, but in such a way that it never takes the shape of an event that might be apprehended by the objectivist epistemology of history. To make the Nazi destruction of European Jewry understandable, Lanzmann argues, is to categorize it, which is perforce to relativize it—which is "obscene." Jean-Francois Lyotard's philosophy of the

American Literature, Volume 70, Number 4 (December 1998): pp. 767–798. Copyright ©1998 Duke University Press.

"different" exemplifies a related humility before the depredations committed in the name of Western cognitive regimes. Over and against the "rules
for linking" put in place by the law, historiography, or science, Lyotard
attempts a recuperation of an ethics of obligation and witnessing, one that
aligns an oppositional politics with the aesthetic and the affective.[3]

In the American context, it is the history of slavery and the African
diaspora that most often induces meditations about trauma. Indeed, it is difficult to offer any general interpretation of the shared history of Africans
and Europeans in the Americas without invoking the idea of a catastrophe
that still grips us and that seems at times to determine all the repetitions
and impasses that characterize the dismal state of race relations today. Toni
Morrison's great meditation on trauma and survival, *Beloved* (1987), is only
the most searching work in a long tradition of African American creativity
and criticism that confronts its history as both a destructive and necessary site
of witnessing and testimony. "This is not a story to pass on," writes Morrison
at the close of *Beloved,*[4] and one can extract from this sibylline phrase a warning similar to Lanzmann's or Lyotard's: be wary, the phrase seems to say, of
communicating this; its effects may be more wounding than healing, or (what
may be worse) its effects might not wound or heal enough. But if this is not a
story to pass down, neither is it a story to be passed up. Morrison implies that
there are certain stories—the story of Margaret Garner, perhaps, on which
she based *Beloved*—that simply cannot be laid aside, refused, as one might
"pass on," give a miss to, something being offered.[5] The compulsive return
to traumatic encounters is both the subject and the mode of this novel, and
its most powerful lesson is the difficulty and the possibility of surviving this
confusion of the traumatic event and its narrative recapitulation.

In psychoanalytic theory, trauma names the problematic relation between experience and affect. Psychoanalysis attempts to understand how a
single event can be simultaneously experienced and not experienced, and how,
consequently, the psychic life of the traumatized individual is infected by belatedness: "hysterics suffer primarily from reminiscences," to recall Freud and
Breuer's early formulation of the problem. In responding to an event after the
fact, and then only through some resonating trigger or reminiscence, the traumatized person exhibits the radically ambiguous temporality that has come
to seem emblematic of a wide range of historical conditions. What trauma
theory attests to, one might say, is an uncertainty about the relation between
event and condition. Indeed, trauma theory offers a way to fudge the distinction between them, since the phenomenon of trauma extends from the originally inapprehensible event to the condition of having to compulsively revisit
this event. Looked at epistemologically, trauma theory is a way of having our
cake and eating it too, for it insists on narratives of origin—the primal scene,
the historical catastrophe—that it also insists are never available as such.

Rather than accuse psychoanalysis of a lack of rigor, however, we might observe that it is here extending previous developments, earlier alignments of the discourses of affect and event. Frances Ferguson has recently argued that the parallel developments of the beginning of modern historiography and the rise of the novel in the eighteenth century (let's call them the cognitive and the aesthetic discourses, to recall the antagonists in Lyotard or Lanzmann) can both be seen as having been prepared for by Locke's inquiries into the relation between memory and personal identity, a relation that disturbs in a productive way what Ferguson calls the "theater of immediate experience." I want to draw attention to a kind of perturbation in the notion of observation within both psychological and historiographical discourses, as described by Ferguson, both because it brings to mind the language of witness so common in trauma theory and because the figure of the witness plays a large role in what I have to say about Richard Wright and racial trauma. On the one hand, Locke ratifies what Ferguson calls a "remarkable feature of everyday life—that we don't imagine that the continuity of an individual's identity rests on a series of ocular proofs." We might say that individual identity is verified by recourse to a historical archive removed from the spectacular visibility of the theater of everyday life. On the other hand, writes Ferguson, the historiographical impulse of the eighteenth century was to install an "archaic" notion of history as its regulative ideal, one that considers history to be that which would "record actual events that are confirmable by more than one witness."[6] Even as the personal experience of identity takes us away from the certainties promised by the language of observation, the ideal of occular confirmation asserts itself as normative elsewhere. Already, Ferguson's remarks suggest, the eye begins to unhinge itself from concepts of self, to begin its career as the apparatus and ideal so definitive of our televisual world.

I invoke Ferguson's commentary here to suggest that both contemporary critical and earlier psychoanalytic vocabularies of trauma revisit epistemological terrain that has been much crisscrossed in the modern period. "Everything that was directly lived has moved away into a representation," lamented Guy Debord three decades ago,[7] but Locke worried the same problem three centuries ago. The antinomy between experience and representation only seems to gain urgency as it becomes more and more precarious. Indeed, one might surmise that trauma theory's emphasis on experiences of sublime, incommunicable affect are actually the leading edge of an ongoing attempt to save experience by redirecting attention to its radical ambiguities.[8] But if affective experience undergoes this strange volatilization in discourse, so too does the event. For modernity at once exorbitantly aggrandizes and radically attenuates the event. The more we problematize the discourses of affect and event, the more crucial they become. The less certain we are about what we feel or about what has happened, the more we talk about both.

The symbiotic antagonism between discourse and experience reaches its apogee in the assaultive iterations of television because the televisual world amplifies existing problematics. Television itself has been analyzed as traumatized, driven by a repetition compulsion beyond the pleasure principle. It is, for instance, notoriously hard to distinguish between television's vicarious extension of its viewers' affects and its tendency to narcotize their receptivity. And this undecidable oscillation is accompanied by the vexed problematics of the visible, of witness, and of the fixing of the event that I have begun to tease out. Samuel Weber points out that we think we are looking at something when we watch television, but we are really looking at a way of looking; in this way our naive expectation of conjoining event and witness is both indulged and undermined by the apparatus of its delivery. It is in this sense that Weber remarks that the "technological novelty of television must be understood both as the consummation of a very old tradition and at the same time as a heightening of its internal ambivalences."[9] Mary Ann Doane suggested some time ago that the ambivalences of witnessing are more than matched by television's contradictory relation to the problem of the event and its temporal containment:

> [C]atastrophe's discontinuity is embraced as the mirror of television's own functioning, and that discontinuity and indeterminacy ensure the activation of the lure of referentiality. In this sense, television is a kind of catastrophe machine, continually corroborating its own signifying problematic—a problematic of discontinuity and indeterminacy which strives to mimic the experience of the real, a real which in its turn is guaranteed by the contact with death.[10]

As we all know, television comes into its own during catastrophes, which allow it to "corroborate" most compulsively its own "signifying problematic," namely, its ever-renewed, because always baffled, promise to align witness and event, to "put us there."

But put us where? With these various threads in hand, I want to focus on contemporary race relations in the United States. If we ask, with respect to some of the more notorious televisual race spectacles of the last ten years, where television promises and fails to "put us," we might answer, "at the scene of the crime." Let us recall the Hill-Thomas Hearings—that "high-tech lynching," in Thomas's words— or the visage of Willie Horton in the 1988 presidential campaign, or Rodney King, or O. J. Simpson. In each instance what ostensibly brought the individuals involved before the televisual eye was that a crime had been committed or alleged. But in each case, the transformation of the case into spectacle caused it to break away from the events of history, created a field of implication or resonance that took on a life of its own.

In the case of the Willie Horton ad, his having committed another crime after his release on Governor Dukakis's furlough program was, we might reasonably argue, a mere pretext for the Bush campaign's cynical manipulation of race fear; one had the feeling that the mug shot alone (which might as well have been labeled "dangerously violent black man") would have triggered the required narrative if the Bush campaign had not had one to hand. The excruciating spectacle of the Hill-Thomas hearings only began to reach closure when Thomas brazenly substituted "lynching" for "sexual harassment" as the crime under discussion. Thomas thus managed to exploit the uneasy recognition that his exposure before a panel of white men as an embodied black man with a taste for pornographic videos resonated so powerfully with earlier scripts of violent "judiciary" disciplining of black men that he could usurp Hill's position as victim.

In the case of the Rodney King and O. J. Simpson verdicts, the sense that spectacle and event are in an antagonistic symbiosis is even more powerful. The Simi Valley jury that could look at the videotape of King's beating and decide that it was not what it looked like could do so, it would seem, only through reference to a script different from the actual performance. The power of spectacle, ostensibly supported by the prestige long accorded to ocular proof, took, we might say, a notorious beating there. In the case of O. J. Simpson, the hyperbolic spectacularization of the "story" substituted, in many eyes, for an event that was not seen and recorded, the double homicide. Hence the starkly divided response to the verdict: those who were dismayed by the finding of innocent did not understand that an event different from the murder—the merciless spotlighting of the administration of "justice" to a black man—was being watched by others. Indeed, one could say that both crime and punishment were entirely idealized, even fantasized, events in these cases. What is traumatic about them is that they demonstrate, in fruitlessly compulsive detail, that justice in America is catastrophically damaged, deeply fissured by the chasms that separate black from white and that also separate the history of justice from its concept. This catastrophe, at once formal and historical, means that in contemporary America the hope of locating and defining the events called crime and punishment is forever infected by the ambiguities of "gaze, script, and spectacle."[11]

• • •

I have been probing some of the problematics of the contemporary language of trauma, particularly as they pertain to race in America, because I wish, in good literary-critical fashion, to so overdetermine the field of implication that the scene I will analyze from Richard Wright's *Native Son* (1940) will achieve maximum traumatic toxicity. Wright's novel can certainly be inserted into the series listed above.[12] Here again we are invited several times to the "scene of the crime," only to find the same uncertainties and disruptions present in even more unbearably protracted and pronounced form. And like those recent televisual spectacles, Wright's text can never be entirely free of the suspicion that its representations are repetitions rather than revisions, contributions to racial impasse and the violence of stereotype rather than exposés of them. Of course, Wright's novel does not need my efforts to make it shocking; Wright himself saw to that. In his essay on the writing of *Native Son,* "How 'Bigger' Was Born," Wright describes his creation as at least in part an overt act of aggression against his white audience:

> I had written a book of short stories under the title of *Uncle Tom's Children.* When the reviews began to appear, I realized that I had made an awfully naïve mistake. I found that I had written a book which even bankers' daughters could read and weep over and feel good about. I swore to myself that if I ever wrote another book, no one would weep over it; that it would be so hard and deep that they would have to face it without the consolation of tears.[13]

Although Wright professes to worry that he might be playing into the hands of the racists by depicting their worst nightmare, it seems clear that Bigger is meant to evoke that same nightmare: "I knew that I could not write of Bigger convincingly if I did not depict him as he was: that is, resentful toward whites, sullen, angry, ignorant, emotionally unstable, [and] depressed, [though] unaccountably elated at times" (523). How better to prevent the bankers' daughters from weeping over poor Bigger's unkind fate than to have him suffocate, decapitate, and incinerate Mary Dalton, a sympathizing white girl—not the daughter of a banker, true, but of a real estate magnate, which is close enough—an action that leaves Bigger "unaccountably elated" for some time afterward.

My focus here is the scene in which Bigger suffocates Mary Dalton by holding a pillow over her head as her blind mother stands in the doorway. Any interpretation of the novel must consider it central, if only because the murder is the crime that inaugurates Bigger's excruciating descent to the electric chair. But even as we remark the scene's centrality, we must take note of an ambiguity. Bigger murders accidentally, as it were. He does not intend to suffocate Mary Dalton, merely to keep her quiet so that he will not be discovered in her room, where he has carried her inebriated body after having chaperoned her through the South Side on the first night of his employment as the Daltons' chauffeur. At the heart of the novel, then, is an act that seems at once a logical—perhaps we should say, ideological—inevitability, and a terrible, irreducibly ambiguous accident.[14] It is not that Bigger is incapable of such an act. Indeed, the novel goes out of its way to suggest that were it a matter of mere intention Bigger would be a daily felon; and he proves later how capable he is of premeditated murder in the bludgeoning death of his girlfriend Bessie. But in the Dalton murder, homicidal intent and the act itself—while both real—are somehow out of phase, nonsynchronous. The immediate cause of this temporal and logical anomaly is the arrival of Mrs. Dalton. Bigger must escape detection, and it is, as it were, to prevent anything from happening that he unwittingly commits his crime. The scene at the heart of novel, at the navel of the nightmare, is both overwhelmingly vivid and irreducibly ambiguous: a murder that is and is not witnessed, that is and is not intended.

It is not merely the horror of this scene that renders it traumatic. For sheer nauseating power, Bessie's death is arguably more overwhelming. What makes this scene particularly interesting for an analysis of trauma, however, is the essential, structuring role played by the crisscrossing axes of visibility and temporality traced in my introductory comments. In traumatic reminiscence the subject's psyche is invaded by intrusive memories, scenes remarkable for their vividness. But even as such scenes rise up in all the "intensification of their colours," these memories do not feel like normal seeing, in which we might be able to locate ourselves at some point external to the representation. As Lacan writes about vision in dreams in *The Four Fundamental Concepts of Psycho-Analysis,* "in the final resort, our position . . . is . . . that of someone who does not see." The temporal axis in trauma is similarly fissured by paradox, for though the trauma is irrefutably from the past, it remains strangely suspended, out of time, unassimilated. I want to suggest that the scene of Mary's murder constitutes what Lacan calls in discussing trauma "the encounter with the real"—"an appointment to which we are always called with a real that eludes us," the "real . . . as essentially the missed encounter."[15] This encounter is missed both in the field of visibility, where an apparent face-to-face meeting between Bigger and Mrs. Dalton does not quite come off, and along the axis of temporality, where the event takes place in a kind of temporal suspension. To discuss the resonances of this scene in terms of trauma, however, requires a double strategy, for trauma is at once historical and formal. If trauma is a paradoxically historical disruption of historical time, then its status is perforce formal; for what measure internal to historicity can define that which is incommensurable with it? On the other side of this disjunction, we could say that from within those structures that operate according to a formalist paradigm—here we might implicate legal procedures—trauma signals the eruption of a certain historicity that exposes the contingency of form. It is in recognition of this division reflected in the language and experience of trauma that I have arranged this essay as a weaving back and forth between historical and formal observations.

To begin, then, where Wright begins and ends: Is the power of the stereotype a historical or formal phenomenon? One could argue that the stereotype is more than a mere representation. To invoke it is to repeat it, perhaps even in the strong sense of repetition compulsion, which Lacan characterizes as the subject's dragging his "thing" into a "path that he cannot get out of," after which it is the subject who ends up being hauled, as if along a "towpath."[16] The double power of the stereotype to function as both cause and result of the subject's repetitions is the very subject of Wright's novel and the reason for his vexed place in literary history. In Bigger Thomas, Wright self-consciously creates a limited creature, apparently mercilessly determined by his environment. Bigger's limitations have come in for a good deal of criticism, and I see no possibility of this criticism being convincingly answered. We are dealing not with a fully realized, complex character, this criticism runs, but with a cartoon, a stereotype. Ralph Ellison, in "The World and the Jug," characterizes such a creation as nearly an example of bad faith on Wright's part: "Wright could imagine Bigger, but Bigger could not possibly imagine Richard Wright. Wright saw to that."[17] Ellison's comment is made in the context of an argument with Irving Howe over the value of authenticity as an aesthetic or political ideal for African American Literature, and Wright's work has often been caught up in such debates.[18] One effect of this debate is the way Wright's commitment to a naturalist aesthetic, his presentation of the violence and horror of black life in the United States, and his desire to make his fiction part of a political struggle have caused him to be viewed as a version of Bigger himself. Wright contributed to this impression in various ways. In "How 'Bigger' Was Born," for example, he figures his anxieties about white reaction as the intrusion of a monitoring figure explicitly parallel to the "white blur" created in Bigger's eyes by Mrs. Dalton: "Like Bigger himself," he writes, "I felt a mental censor—product of the fears which a Negro feels from living in America— standing over me, draped in white, warning me not to write" (523). Bigger's and Wright's acts, this comparison implies, are equally caught up in an agon between white and black; both men are forced into a symbolic encounter marked by compulsion and reaction.[19]

But how satisfactory is it merely to point out the factitious quality of such encounters, their stereotypical character? It was, and is, perfectly clear that Wright knew Bigger was an incompletely realized character, as much a product of cultural fantasy as anything else. Wright's point would seem to be that such incompletely realized characters are everywhere walking the streets. He writes that he needed to "make [Bigger] a living personality and at the same time a symbol of all the larger things I felt and saw in him" (524). While many will say Bigger never is realized as a "living personality," perhaps this is because the aim of the novel is to present him as never having been one, but instead an individual perennially mortifying himself, or being mortified, into the crudest of symbols. The agonizing drama of the book would then be the protracted tempo of this transformation, amounting to a sense of impasse or suspension between fantasy and reality, individual and symbol.

Something like this analysis of stereotype seems to be on James Baldwin's mind in his great essay on Wright, "Many Thousands Gone":

> In our image of the Negro [throughout the essay Baldwin uses "our" to indicate that he is looking at the Negro with "us"] breathes the past we deny, not dead but living yet and powerful, the beast in our jungle of statistics. It is this which defeats us, which continues to defeat us. . . . Wherever the Negro face appears, a tension is created, the tension of a silence filled with things unutterable. It is a sentimental error, therefore, to believe that the past is dead; it means nothing to say that it is all forgotten, that the Negro himself has forgotten it. It is not a question of memory.

It is not a question of memory because the past has been recorded, archived, somewhere *beyond* conscious memory. Indeed, Baldwin explicitly invokes instances of trauma:

> The man does not remember the hand that struck him, the darkness that frightened him, as a child; nevertheless, the hand and the darkness remain with him, indivisible from himself forever, part of the passion that drives him wherever he thinks to take flight.[20]

In this final image of an agonizing "passion"—a compulsive flight "driven" by an unmasterable and self-mutilating violence—I believe Baldwin means us to encounter the terrifying visage of Wright's most powerful creation, Bigger Thomas.

But if the traumatized Negro cannot escape himself, no more can the white imagination escape the Negro face rising up before it as a traumatic "intrusive memory": "it is we who, . . . every hour that we live, reinvest the black face with our guilt; and we do this—by a further paradox, no less ferocious—helplessly, passionately out of an unrealized need to suffer absolution." What keeps coming back is the "fantasy Americans hold in their minds when they speak of the Negro: that fantastic and fearful image which we have lived with since the first slave fell beneath the lash."[21] Baldwin faults Wright for his participation in the dynamics of the stereotypical face-to-face encounter between black and white, a constellation of imagistic and narrative fragments that fail to cohere but, like fantasy or dream, have no less power for that. His eloquent dissection of this fantasmatic encounter can be usefully linked to Kimberly Benston's analysis of the pervasive topos of the face-to-face in the

African American literary tradition. Benston examines a series of scenes of heightened drama, perhaps the most influential of which is the young Frederick Douglass negotiating the terrifying change in his mistress Sophia Auld's countenance as she moves from angelic to demonic in a few short paragraphs. Benston concludes his essay by suggesting that

> the end of the tradition imagined in the topos of facing would be the effacement of an encounter face-to-face, the scene beyond the vertiginous exchanges of master-slave and oedipal positions, where the spatial and temporal predicaments of tradition are suspended, where immediacy is no longer an illusion of scopic power but the dissolution of specular relations altogether.[22]

Whether or not Benston is justified in locating such a utopian moment behind the insistent scenes of encounter, his argument does serve to historicize what can seem a rigidly formalistic topos, whether it is the face-to-face of fantasy—oedipal or otherwise—or the ideologeme of the specular encounter.

Such a historicization goes some way toward supporting Paul Gilroy's contention in *The Black Atlantic* that Wright's meditation on, and manipulation of, the symbolizing power of the stereotype, far from signaling his entrapment in a limiting concept of authenticity, is what makes him a profoundly modernist writer. For Gilroy, it is less the specificity of black experience that is Wright's ultimate subject than the way that experience epitomizes in a peculiarly intense way various social and psychological patterns of modernity *tout court:* "In Wright's mature position, the Negro is no longer just America's metaphor but rather a central symbol in the psychological, cultural, and political systems of the West as a whole." Wright's work "situates the philosophical and political problems of black America in the provocative progression from a mode of literary realism defined by race to a metaphysics of modernity in which notions of racial particularity appear trivial and inconsequential." Because Wright's "distinctive visions of modernity . . . are mediated by the historical memory of slavery"—he speaks elsewhere, in a brush with the problematics of trauma, of "the impossible memory of slavery," —"the tension between the claims of racial particularity on one side and the appeal of those modern universals that appear to transcend race on the other arises in the sharpest possible form."[23] This tension, visible in the shape of Wright's career, is also present in Mary Dalton's bedroom.

• • •

With these observations about spectacle, event, and stereotype in mind, let me now turn in earnest to the scene of Mary Dalton's murder. The "fantastic and fearful image" Wright both conjures up and negates in Bigger is that staple of white supremacist fantasy, the black man as rapist of white women.[24] In the scene of Mary's murder, Bigger goes some distance towards enacting this fantasy: "He eased his hand, the fingers spread wide, up the center of her back and her face came toward him and her lips touched his, like something he had imagined" (96). Bigger's progressive absorption into this script is painfully clear:

> He lifted her and laid her on the bed. Something urged him to leave at once, but he leaned over her, excited, looking at her face in the dim light, not wanting to take his hands from her breasts. She tossed and mumbled sleepily. He tightened his fingers on her breasts, kissing her again, feeling her move toward him. He was aware only of her body now; his lips trembled. Then he stiffened. The door behind him had creaked. (96–97)

Both the compulsive quality of his actions and his sense of having left his body—"he was aware only of her body now"—are signs that Bigger is caught up in a dynamic of fantasy. If Bigger knows this script, if in all his dealings with the drunken Mary he feels "strange, possessed, or as if he were acting upon a stage in front of a crowd full of people" (95), it is because this scene has been well-rehearsed. Just hours earlier Bigger had encountered Mary, had consumed her desirability. In a scene that Wright subsequently modified, Bigger and his pal Jack go to the movies, where they see a newsreel about debutantes in Florida, one of whom is the naughty Mary Dalton, filmed cavorting with her communist boyfriend Jan Erlone: "The close-up faded and the next scene showed only the girl's legs running over the sparkling sands; they were followed by the legs of the man running in pursuit. The words droned on: 'Ha! He's after her! There! He's got her! Oh, boy, don't you wish you were down here in Florida?'" (35). This invitation, the two boys know, both is and is not extended to them. "'Some babies,' Jack said. . . . 'I'd like to be there.' 'You can,' Bigger said. 'But you'd be hanging from a tree like a bunch of bananas'" (34). The boys can, indeed must, consume this scene, but they can do so only from a position structurally excluded from it. The only way they could ever be in the scene is as a stain on the picture, as lynched and mutilated bodies, strange fruit.

Wright underscores the contradictory position of the two boys vis-à-vis the image through an odd plot device. When Wright changed his text at the request of the Book-of-the-Month Club, he took out the scene I've just described as well as this more shocking one, which immediately precedes it:

> The picture had not yet started and they sat listening to the pipe organ playing low and soft. Bigger moved restlessly and his

breathing quickened; he looked round in the shadows to see if any attendant was near, then slouched down in his seat. He glanced at Jack and saw that Jack was watching him out of the corners of his eyes. They both laughed.

"You at it again?" Jack asked.

"I'm polishing my nightstick," Bigger said. They giggled.

"I'll beat you," Jack said. (32).

It is hardly surprising that this scene of competitive masturbation was cut before publication. Wright evidently wishes us to follow the lateral associations and overdeterminations of the terms "nightstick" and "beating" until we recognize that the need for stimulation to which Bigger has just attested is here enacted as a kind of self-flagellation. This is a self-administered beating with a nightstick; the two black boys beat each other, in a metaphoric condensation of a central motif in the novel—namely, the rebounding of black violence and rage onto other blacks, a motif culminating in the murder of Bessie.

But what is most bleak and bizarre about the scene is its apparent lack of direct incitement, for there is nothing on the screen; the curtain has not even gone up. In other words, if there is a link between the masturbation and the subsequent newsreel, it is only Wright and the reader who see it. A logic might appear to link them, but that logic is not present as motivation for Bigger and Jack. The elements of an enduring and toxic cultural fantasy are all here—the rich white girl, at once pure and naughty, the desiring and violent black man, even the punishment of lynching (in Bigger's disquieting joke about the bananas)—but the fantasy is not realized in any plausible way. Rather, the elements function like the discrete images one often finds in dreams, images that do not organize themselves according to the norms of naturalistic narrative. Wright makes obvious here what is often misunderstood, namely that certain fantasies exist apart from their vehicles, that fantasy's order of significance is transpersonal.

This would also seem to be the case in the more catastrophic repetition of the rape fantasy in Mary Dalton's bedroom. For there, too, a temporal disjunction is paired with a scene of spectacle. The arrival of Mrs. Dalton interrupts Bigger's descent into the fantasy, but the fantasy does not cease to be enacted just because Bigger is trying to do nothing. The strange suspension brought on by Mrs. Dalton's arrival instead exacerbates the unfolding of the drama, which is now in a terrible, insupportable way both personal and transpersonal. For both Mary and Bigger are victimized symbolically and as individuals. Bigger's decision to incinerate Mary's corpse amounts to a gruesome realization of the ideal of disembodiment subtending the fantasy of Southern white womanhood.[25] And Bigger himself is catapulted from the disembodiment attending his immersion in fantasy to a "stiffened" synecdoche of the phallic role he plays in the drama: "Mrs. Dalton was moving slowly toward him and he grew tight and full, as though about to explode" (97). This scene is, if anything, even more scandalous than the one Wright excised, for what Wright ruthlessly delivers here is the image of Bigger becoming the fantasmatic phallus of the white supremacist fantasy. The various associations clustering in Bigger's name now come into full force. Bigger becomes bigger than himself at this moment, an aggrandizement that is also, excruciatingly, the definitive reduction to stereotype. To be Bigger is to be a "big, bad nigger," certainly, but it is also to be frozen into a relation of comparison that can always only be registered as threat and affront. Perhaps this is the crucial subtext for Boris Max's histrionic announcement during the trial that "his very existence is a crime against the state!" (466). In becoming fused with his name, Bigger is literally stiffened into the symbolic register of the signifier; he both becomes the signifier of pure physicality and is removed altogether from any proprietary relation to his own body, which has now become the contentless aggravation of his mere existence as "bigger" than he ought to be, than I am, than can be adequately policed.

Wright follows through with merciless consistency on this simultaneous presentation and negation of the primal white-supremacist fantasy by describing Bigger's suffocation of Mary as though it were an actual rape:

> [H]e grew tight and full, as though about to explode. Mary's fingernails tore at his hands and he caught the pillow and covered her entire face with it, firmly. Mary's body surged upward and he pushed downward upon the pillow with all of his weight, determined that she must not move or make any sound that would betray him. His eyes were filled with the white blur moving toward him in the shadows of the room. Again Mary's body heaved. (97–98)

We have here an articulation of racial and sexual antagonism. Abdul Jan-Mohamed has recently used the example of Wright's work to explore the intrication of racial and sexual economies. Jan Mohamed argues that "racialized sexuality" operates within a set of relations and media different from those Foucault analyzes in *The History of Sexuality* as bourgeois sexuality. While bourgeois sexuality is marked by an analytic will to knowledge and a vast net of discursive practices—a "dense discursivity," as JanMohamed calls it—"racialized sexuality" is under the sign of prohibition, more tightly linked to the institutional juridical networks associated by Foucault with the structures of "alliance." But at the same time that it seems to escape the analytically exfoliating discursivity of bourgeois sexuality, racialized sexuality exerts a continuous pressure as something that cannot be adequately integrated into the social order, cannot be adequately understood or discursively placed. This constitutes it as pathological in the same way that desires that have been repressed emerge as pathological variants: "In this dynamic structure, where silence and repression play a strategic rather than a tactical or local role, sexuality becomes an even more dense transfer point for relations of power."

As a result, "racialized sexuality is structured by a set of *allegorical* discourses: silence and repression weave a limited configuration of symbols and desires that are deeply resonant but never available to pseudo-scientific methods." We might say that what Wright gives us in the scene of Mary's murder is the emergence of racialized sexuality. The very nearly baroque allegorizing at work in the stiffening of Bigger and the surging of Mary is a terrifying reminder of just how "limited" the "configuration of symbols and desires" that exerts power in this domain is, a limitation narrowing finally to the "hystericized, oversexualized body of the black male."[26] JanMohamed rather boldly goes on to assert that in this pathologized, allegorical discourse of racialized sexuality, rape itself—both trope and reality—constitutes what Foucault called a "positivity," "an historical a priori that defines a field in which formal identities, thematic continuities, translations of concepts, and polemical interchange may be deployed."[27]

The status of "rape" as at once a magnet and transfer point for various lines of force leads Bigger, JanMohamed suggests, to accept his inadvertent suffocation of Mary as in fact the rape Wright makes visible in the text:

> Had he raped her? Yes, he had raped her. Every time he felt as he had felt that night, he raped. But rape was not what one did to women. Rape was what one felt when one's back was against a wall and one had to strike out, whether one wanted to or not, to keep the pack from killing one. He committed rape every time he looked into a white face. (262–263)

JanMohamed glosses this passage as an expression of Wright's view that "regardless of gender, the racialized subject is always already constructed as a 'raped' subject. . . . Rape thus subsumes the totality of force relations on the racial border, which is in fact always a sexual border."[28] Rape here becomes a pathological discursive event, one that attracts or allows for unconscionable substitutions and metaphorizations, scrambles agents and victims, and generally destroys the most basic ethical landmarks. This scrambling cannot avoid wounding and affronting those exposed to it. Is rape an event ("he had raped her") or a condition ("rape was what one felt")? There is no way out of this interpretive ethical impasse except via the violence of metaphorization that lies at the heart of the crisis. Wright's brilliant stroke is to make Bigger his own first defender and first condemner, so that we who come after must make Bigger meaningful in the shadow of his own disturbing efforts to do so.[29] And it is precisely the fixing of meaning that is at stake in this self-interpretation: "the hidden meaning of his life—a meaning which others did not see and which he had always tried to hide—had spilled out" (119). If the revelation of his meaning was initially a seepage, an uncontrolled overflow, with the hindsight of the day after, the "spill" can be defined, not so much placed in time as made to establish an altogether new temporal series: "His crime was an anchor weighing him safely in time" (119). But if Bigger's acceptance of the idea that he had raped Mary makes him complete, his "act of creation" (466) comes with unimaginable costs and cannot be understood outside his absolute victimization by the gaze, script, and spectacle of the white world in which he lives.

In both the scene of Mary's murder and the one in the theater, then, Wright presents us with the elements of fantasy narratives, but he scrambles or displaces the links between agents, problems, and events. In this ostensibly naturalist novel, an irreducibly allegorical level of reality is insistently brought out. Things are happening: they are happening to people, and though they could be happening because of people—that is, the requisite subjective intentions are certainly possible—they are not. Rather, things are happening to some people through other people. The passive construction is appropriate here; events are being precipitated. What Wright delivers here is a vision of our concept of event being split apart by what I've called the naturalist and the allegorical levels of reality.

Some thirty years ago, in *The Logic of Sense*, Gilles Deleuze offered some remarkable reconsiderations of the notions of sense and event that might help us here. Deleuze's book is organized around two series defined variously in terms of heights and depths, the order of propositions and the mixtures of bodies, speaking and eating, and so on. Riding along a ridge articulating these series, "sense" and "event" are at once enabling and excessive — enabling because they constitute transfer points between bodies and propositions, excessive because sense and event are never reducible to their "meanings" or their corporeal "states of affairs." Events are "singularities"—"turning points and points of inflection; bottlenecks, knots, foyers, and centers; points of fusion, condensation, and boiling." Mary's murder answers just this description; we have there a blockage and bottleneck building up pressure, which results in the change of state figured in Deleuze's metaphors of fusion, condensation, boiling—or Wright's of "spilling." The event here is thus not the murder itself but the change of state, the relation between the accumulation of meaning and the precipitation of the act. Deleuze insists on the ideal dimension; the event can never be fully reduced to its "spatio-temporal realization in a state of affairs." "Events are the only idealities," he writes; they are phenomena of meaning, of sense, beyond the dimensions of "denotation, manifestation, or signification." They are, importantly, phenomena of the "surface": "to the extent that the incorporeal event is constituted and constitutes the surface, it raises to this surface the terms of its double reference: the bodies to which it refers as a noematic attribute, and the propositions to which it refers as an expressible entity."[30]

The Deleuzian "line-frontier between things and propositions" is the line on which Bigger rides throughout the opening of the novel and across which his meaning "spills" in Mary's bedroom.[31] Bigger experiences this strange surface—which both allows communication across and disarticulates the series of bodies and propositions—in his own skin. This is why the horripilation and anxiety he experiences as he stands by Mary's bed trying not to be there are at once catastrophically embodying and radically disembodying, why his "stiffening" before the blind gaze of Mrs. Dalton can be at once the experience of anxious self-absenting and a violent "mixture of bodies" surging on the bed. Phenomenality and metaphysics, things and propositions, communicate in this strangely distorted world of racial impasse. Such is the force of the stereotyping gaze Bigger has felt the entire evening leading up to the murder:

> His entire mind and body were painfully concentrated into a single sharp point of attention. He was trying desperately to understand. . . . He was very conscious of his black skin. . . . [T]hey made him feel his black skin by just standing there looking at him, one holding his hand and the other smiling. He felt he had no physical existence at all right then; he was something he hated, the badge of shame which he knew was attached to a black skin. (76)

To concentrate one's mind and body into a "point of attention," as he also does beside Mary's bed later on, is to be simultaneously radically embodied and allegorically mortified; it is to feel "no physical existence" but to feel that negation in one's skin; it is to become merely a propositional entity attached to the pathological surface of a "badge of shame." The trauma presented by the scene in Mary's bedroom, then, can be ascribed neither to the event as "state of affairs" nor to its discursive meaning; it resides on neither the empirical/naturalist nor the ideal/allegorical side of this divide but rather in the pathological convergence of the two, a convergence that exceeds the orders of experience and of meaning. Trauma would be the impossible experience of the self-dividing of the event, the change of state. It is not the fantasy of rape that traumatizes; and it is not the accidental murder of Mary that traumatizes. It is in the "in-between" that the traumatic event resides.

•••

The passage about rape contains a disquieting slippage from the word "pack," behind which we are meant to see the lynch mob, to a single and not obviously threatening "face": "Rape was what one felt when one's back was against a wall and one had to strike out, whether one wanted to or not, to keep the pack from killing one. He committed rape every time he looked into a white face" (262–263). This terrible slide brings us back to Mrs. Dalton, for it is the sudden appearance of her face, with its sightless eyes, that precipitates the event in question. We must now look more closely into her role. If we can characterize the scene of Mary's murder as being suffused with a sense of suspension, it is not because things don't keep happening. Rather, it is the provenance of these happenings that seems in suspense. The feeling for both Bigger and the reader is of being caught and held somewhere between dream and reality. Bigger's dreamlike absorption in the proximity of Mary's taboo body gives way, with the arrival of her mother, to a sense of "falling from a great height in a dream" (97). He doesn't land until after he realizes he has killed Mary: "The reality of the room fell from him; the vast city of white people that sprawled outside took its place" (100). Between the dream and the awakening everything happens, despite Bigger's efforts to ensure that nothing happens, and despite Mrs. Dalton's blindness to what is happening. It is to just this in-between state that Lacan directs our attention in his discussion of trauma in *The Four Fundamental Concepts of Psycho-Analysis*. I have already invoked his troping of trauma as a kind of missed encounter to which we are compulsively called. Lacan considers trauma to involve a strange relation between two levels of reality. His famous example, drawn from Freud, concerns the relation between the overturned candle in the next room, even then burning the son's corpse, and the father's dream in which he is reproached with the words, "Father, can't you see I'm burning?" It is neither the corpse burning nor the son's question in the dream that is the real in Lacan's account, but rather the relation between the two: "the encounter, forever missed, has occurred between dream and awakening." Such encounters, "radical points in the real," alert us to the imbrication of reality and desire even as they manifest the nonsynchronous relation between the two; what we attain here is an experience of the suspension of a reality "en souffrance . . . in abeyance, awaiting attention."[32]

What governs all such encounters, in Lacan's view, is what he calls the tuché, the chance event, the "accident, the noise, the small element of reality which is evidence that we are not dreaming."[33] What might it mean that the tuché in this scene, Bigger's evidence that he is not dreaming, which nevertheless does not deliver him to awakening, is an actual missed encounter? For it is Mrs. Dalton's sightless eyes that govern this traumatic suspension. What, then, does she represent?

Most obviously, Mrs. Dalton represents for Bigger the white world in its threatening totality, at once real and indeterminate. This is what is implied in her "flowing" presence as a "white blur." When this white blur blocks his exit, we have a fictional realization of the phenomenological impasse that lies at the heart of Bigger's deformed experience: we have racial aporia, huis clos.[34] This moment of blockage is an example of what Toni Morrison sees as a recurrent topos in an American literature traumatized by racism. Again and again, in texts from Poe to Hemingway, a blinding, obstructing whiteness rises up as at once symbol and wishful erasure of racial antagonism.[35] Morrison's central example is the huge shrouded figure "of the perfect whiteness of the snow" that emerges at the close of Poe's racialist fantasy, *The Narrative of Arthur Gordon Pym*. Wright has Poe much in mind in his creation of Mrs. Dalton, since he also equips her with a white cat that compensates for her blindness in witnessing Bigger's gruesome exploits. When a picture is taken later of Bigger with the white cat on his shoulder, we are meant to remember the betrayal by the black cat in Poe's tale of the same name. Wright thus repeats Poe with racial inversion, an inversion that is hinted at in a different register when he concludes "How 'Bigger' Was Born" with the statement, "If Poe were alive, he would not have to invent horror; horror would invent him" (540).[36] Mrs. Dalton's flowing presence thus extends to her cat and, in an echo of Poe's *Pym*, to the snow that begins to blanket Chicago at this moment. At the end of Book Two, when Bigger has been cornered by the mob, he throws himself suicidally, Pym-like, at a snow-covered watertower, "something huge and round and white looming up out of the dark: a bulk rising up sheer from the snow of the roof and swelling in the night" (307).

It is this white world flowing around him, blocking his exit, covering him up, that Bigger confronts in Mrs. Dalton. But why must she be blind? Here we might recall the fact that Lacan's influential discussion of the "eye and the gaze" in the *Four Fundamental Concepts* follows immediately his discussion of trauma and repetition. Indeed, Lacan claims in the seminar that he was "diverted" into "developing the concept of the gaze to such an extent" "by the way in which [he] presented the concept of repetition." The articulating question is, How is "tuché represented in visual apprehension?"[37] As gaze, comes the answer.

Recall that for Lacan, the field of the visible is split between what he calls the eye and the gaze. Correlative to what Lacan calls the "geometral point" from which the eye as consciousness essays the field of its own representation is a point that emits light:

> This is the function that is found at the heart of the institution of the subject in the visible. What determines me, at the most profound level, in the visible, is the gaze that is outside. It is through the gaze

that I enter light and it is from the gaze that I receive its effects. Hence it comes about that the gaze is the instrument through which light is embodied and through which . . . I am photo-graphed.[38]

In a scenario reminiscent of the scene in Mary's bedroom, Lacan borrows from Sartre the example of a fellow peeping through a keyhole: "A gaze surprises him in the function of voyeur, disturbs him, overwhelms him and reduces him to a feeling of shame."[39] Bigger's reaction to the arrival of Mrs. Dalton is more momentous and catastrophic than mere "shame," but it is clear that her role in disrupting his fantasy is to make him visible, to project him onto a screen. Both Sartre and Lacan insist that what distinguishes the shaming gaze from the voyeur's "eye" is that the gaze creates the field of visibility while remaining external to it. Mrs. Dalton's blindness, then, is an example of the kind of witnessing beyond sight characteristic of the gaze.

But Mrs. Dalton's status as bearer of the gaze is more complex still. Bigger's first vision of her is as a revenant:

> [H]e saw coming slowly toward him a tall, thin, white woman, walking silently, her hands lifted delicately in the air and touching the walls to either side of her. . . . Her face and hair were completely white; she seemed to him like a ghost. . . .
> "That was Mrs. Dalton," her husband said. "She's blind."
> "Yessuh."
> "She has a very deep interest in colored people." (52–53)

Wright's dialogue indulges in ironic juxtaposition here. While Mrs. Dalton's well-meaning liberalism might seem appropriately figured as "colorblindness," Wright makes clear that her "deep interest in colored people" is fed by springs more subterranean than regimes of surface visibility. Her liberalism and her blindness, in fact, go hand in hand. Even as she exempts herself from the coercive visual economy regimenting race relations, she supports and makes possible that system, just as the gaze is both external to and productive of the field of visibility.

Mrs. Dalton's implication in a system of racial exploitation she personally opposes is clarified by another feature of her status as representative of the gaze. Kaja Silverman has recently argued that Lacan may have been more historically precise than he intended when he likened the gaze to the camera. Invoking Jonathan Crary's *Techniques of the Observer*, Silverman notes what we had occasion to remark early in this essay—namely, that the trope of vision (or of observation or witnessing) is quite fundamentally riven in modernity between a humanist appropriation of vision as the property of the self and the ever-accelerating development of vision as a technology independent of embodiment or identity. Silverman sees the camera and related media as instantiations or historical crystallizations of the atemporal structure of the gaze.[40] With this argument in mind, we can note the striking fact, one consonant with the novel's depiction of Bigger as a victim of a media blitz, that the blinding whiteness of Mrs. Dalton (Bigger says that the blur "filled his eyes," and earlier that "[h]e had the feeling that talking to a blind person was like talking to someone whom he himself could scarcely see" [69]) is forcefully linked by Wright to the blinding flashes of the cameras and thus to the mass-mediated world that so irrevocably fashions Bigger's desire and demise: "Then suddenly, so suddenly that the men gasped, the door behind Mr. Dalton filled with a flowing white presence. It was Mrs. Dalton, her white eyes held wide and stony, her hands lifted sensitively upward toward her lips, the fingers long and white and wide apart. The basement was lit up with the white flash of a dozen silver bulbs" (232).

Her logical priority with respect to the field of visibility is matched— and this should no longer seem coincidental—by a kind of temporal priority as well. We have seen how Bigger sees her as a kind of "ghost." She embodies a function of time profoundly alienating to Bigger, who seems anxiously sensitive to the passing of time throughout his first few hours in the Dalton's employ: "Mr. Dalton said nothing. Bigger heard a clock ticking somewhere behind him and he had a foolish impulse to look at it" (56). Later, in his second unnerving encounter with Mrs. Dalton, the association is repeated:

> Mrs. Dalton in flowing white clothes was standing stone-still in the middle of the kitchen floor. There was silence, save for the slow ticking of a large clock on a white wall. . . . He went to the sink, watching her as he walked, feeling that she could see him even though he knew that she was blind. . . . Her face was still, tilted, waiting. It reminded him of a dead man's he had once seen. (68)

As far as Bigger is concerned, Mrs. Dalton is simply the function of waiting, a role that reaches crisis intensity as she stands in the doorway of her daughter's room. Because she is not exactly alive, it seems to Bigger that she has all the time in the world. Logically, temporally, structurally, Mrs. Dalton represents for Bigger a threat he cannot counteract: the anteriority of privilege. Wright does not neglect to dot his *i*'s here. Although her husband makes the executive decisions, it is Mrs. Dalton's capital, we are told, over which he presides.

Her status as a blinding "photographic" gaze, her mortified and mortifying presence, her embodiment of anteriority—all these features suggest that Mrs. Dalton functions as the apparition of what Lacan called the symbolic. What we see in the murder scene is the traumatic incursion into the visual field of the gaze as tuché. It may seem that what Wright gives us in the scene is precisely the dream of perfect witnessing—the "you are there" of the gaze as apparatus, the televisual ideal. But his racializing of the encounter shows us that not only can this scene not be adequately witnessed (the gaze is blind) but that its very arrival induces the resurgence of an unmasterable anteriority that precipitates the traumatic rupture between imaginary and symbolic, experience and representation, around which all the actors thenceforth merely orbit according to their places in the racialized symbolic structure. Mrs. Dalton both anticipates and recapitulates historical constructions of the white gaze. If she can be understood as an avatar of CNN, the force of Wright's presentation also requires us to see her as simply a naive but well-intentioned woman and mother, a version of Douglass's initially kindly Mrs. Auld or some eighteenth-century humanitarian. Julie Ellison has written provocatively about the "preoccupation with the gaze" so central to various liberal-humanitarian and sentimental discourses over the past two hundred and fifty years: "Liberal guilt, which from the very beginning is bound up with self-conscious racial difference, is repeatedly staged through stories of cross-racial spectatorship. It relies on visual practices of seeing pain and being seen to be afflicted by it." In a rhetorical flourish that parallels the sweeping historical linkages I traced in the opening pages of this essay, Ellison asks, "Are the Age of Sensibility and the Age of Mechanical Reproduction the same thing?"[41] Mrs. Dalton's overdetermined symbolic and narrative presence, her status as sightless witness of the catastrophe she also induces, suggests that Ellison's question is on the mark. For Wright, such ideally reciprocal exchanges across the divide of race, such "face-to-face" personal encounters, are themselves sites of trauma, not because of the liberal "preoccupation with the gaze" but because of a prior and less human "preoccupation of the gaze." The excruciating scene in which Mary and Jan try to bond with Bigger as equals makes it perfectly clear that attempts to communicate are powerfully distorted by the precedence of the symbolic asymmetry governing any exchange. The intractable quality of race relations in this country may have much to do with the sense that we are forever called to a face-to-face meeting of equals—"Can't we all just get along?"—that we nevertheless forever miss. Confronted with the asymmetry between imaginary and symbolic as that takes shape racially, confronted with the realization that our vision is supported by stony blind eyes, that our history and our experience are linked in the precipitation of acts at which we were neither present nor absent, and that, consequently, we will never have subjectively available as experience the way in which we have been mortified into meaning, we all follow our own itineraries in the return to the missed encounter.

Those itineraries may share a similar traumatic structure but are nevertheless finally determined by where one is in that structure. Most of Wright's
book—far more than this essay has suggested—is taken up with following out
Bigger's compulsive repetitions, which include most cruelly the murder of Bessie, during which the intrusive memory of the white blur recurs, and most profoundly his attempt to claim as subjectively meaningful ("he had murdered and
created a new life for himself" [119]) what is in fact his utter sacrifice to, and
destruction by, a meaning far beyond his control. The white world's compulsions run to the details of the fantasized crime, a compulsion most grotesquely
manifested in the scene in which the press tries to force Bigger, unsuccessfully,
to pose for pictures looming over the bed in which he killed Mary Dalton.
Once again the media's determination to conjoin spectacle and event is foiled.
But what about Wright's and his readers' compulsions? Wright situates the
reader's consciousness beyond both Bigger and the white world that destroys
him. If there is a repetition compulsion specific to our traumatic engagement
with *Native Son*, perhaps it is figured in the trial itself, and most specifically in
the speech of the communist lawyer Boris Max. Critics have long objected to
Wright's habit of recapitulating his action through explicit commentary; the
trial scene in *Native Son* has been particularly criticized in this regard. And
indeed, in the trial's compulsively detailed retelling of the first half of the book,
Bigger is made once again to undergo his mortification by meaning.[42] Just as
Wright himself intends to do, Max must make Bigger at once an individual—he argues to spare Bigger's life—and a representative creature deformed by
the world he was born into, "a test symbol," as Max says, like a "germ stained
for examination under a microscope" (444). Such is Bigger's send-off into his
posthumous life as a problem for interpretation. Max's arguments seem at once
powerfully cogent and entirely futile. He repudiates a liberal-humanitarian approach based on sympathy, as well as all arguments based upon a notion of
justice, since the notion of justice here, with its "premise of equal claims," simply
institutionalizes an illusion of reciprocity. Max seems to insist that the court
spare the life of an individual whose very individuality is, as he says, "a crime
against the state" (466). There is no position, Max demonstrates, from which we
might be able to assess the relation between Bigger's acts and his meaning. We
cannot find the original crime, cannot represent it; that is the primal trauma
that Max does not so much represent as repeat, his speech itself an expression
of the racial impasse it denounces.

But such repetition by recapitulation should be seen as extending the
presentation of the mortifying consequences of meaning-making in this racially "nonsynchronous" world from the action to the institutions and discourses that try unsuccessfully to comprehend it. That is, Wright's presentation of racial trauma implies, as its most comprehensive lesson, the failure
of explanation, a failure at once legal (Bigger's execution is neither just nor

unjust), ethical (there is no comfortable position from which one might observe the failures of the legal system), and artistic (the novel's attempts to "understand" itself command no more conviction that Bigger's attempts at understanding himself). Much recent trauma theory, implicitly or explicitly, makes claims for aesthetic understanding as a prerequisite for ethical action, a claim based on the belief that aesthetic experience attests to, brings back into visibility, that which has been excluded or repressed by cognitive discourses. But there is no communication of any sort without the pressure to select among meanings, no meaning without decision; the aesthetic and the cognitive are not opposed, and the way in which we hurtle from a state of delay and suspension to implication in catastrophe can no more be adequately explained or resisted by aesthetic discourse than by legal, psychological, or historiographical discourses. After nearly sixty years, *Native Son* continues to be a problem, continues to pressure us toward conflicting conclusions that share only their unacceptability.

NOTES

1. William Egginton, "On Relativism, Rights, and Differends, Or, Ethics and the American Holocaust," *qui parle* 9 (Fall/Winter 1995): 68.

2. Claude Lanzmann, "The Obscenity of Understanding: An Evening with Claude Lanzmann," *American Imago* 48 (Winter 1991): 473–495.

3. See Jean-François Lyotard, *The Differend: Phrases in Dispute* (Minneapolis: University of Minnesota Press, 1988), and *Heidegger and "The Jews"* (Minneapolis: University of Minnesota Press, 1990). Of particular interest also is "Logos and Techne, or Telegraphy," in *The Inhuman* (Stanford, Calif.: Stanford University Press, 1991), pp. 47–57.

4. Toni Morrison, *Beloved* (New York: Penguin, 1987), p. 275.

5. The criticism on *Beloved* is extensive. Of particular relevance here, because it explicitly places the novel in the context of current trauma theory, is Naomi Morgenstern, "Mother's Milk and Sister's Blood: Trauma and the Neoslave Narrative," *differences* 8 (summer 1996): 101–126.

6. Frances Ferguson, "Romantic Memory," *Studies in Romanticism* 35 (Winter 1996): 509, 511.

7. Guy Debord, *Society of the Spectacle* (Detroit: Black and Red, 1983), par. 1; translation of *La Société du Spectacle* (Paris: Editions Buchet Chastel, 1967).

8. Some recent expressions of skepticism about the language of trauma seem animated by a concern similar to the one I express above. See Walter Benn Michaels, "'You Who Never Was There': Slavery and the New Historicism, Deconstruction and the Holocaust," *Narrative* 4 (January 1996): 1–16; and Dominick La Capra, "Lanzmann's Shoah: 'Here There Is No Why,'" *Critical Inquiry* 23 (winter 1997): 231–269.

9. Samuel Weber, "Television: Set and Screen," in *Mass Mediaurus: Form, Technics, Media,* ed. Alan Cholodenko (Stanford, Calif.: Stanford University Press, 1996), p. 123.

10. Mary Ann Doane, "Information, Crisis, and Catastrophe," in *Logics of Television*, ed. Patricia Mellencamp (Bloomington: Indiana University Press, 1990): p. 234.

11. This is the subtitle of the powerful collection of essays edited by Toni Morrison and Claudia Brodsky Lacour on the O. J. Simpson trial, *Birth of a Nation'hood: Gaze, Script, and Spectacle in the O. J. Simpson Case* (New York: Pantheon Books, 1997). For a powerful reminder of why the legal order remains the site of trauma in American race relations, as well as an honorable attempt not to succumb to its pervasive effects, see Randall Kennedy, *Race, Crime, and the Law* (New York: Pantheon Books, 1997).

12. Introducing his collection of essays on Bigger Thomas, Harold Bloom draws attention to the parallels between Bigger Thomas and Willie Horton; see *Bigger Thomas*, ed. Harold Bloom (New York: Chelsea House, 1990), p. 1. Ishmael Reed has published a characteristically witty, ferocious, and tendentious essay titled "Bigger and O. J." in Morrison and Lacour, *Birth of a Nation'hood*, pp. 169–195. Let me note here as well Shoshana Felman's recent essay discussing the O. J. trial in terms of trauma theory and the relations between aesthetic and legal modes of understanding, "Forms of Judicial Blindness, or the Evidence of What Cannot be Seen: Traumatic Narratives and Legal Repetitions in the O. J. Simpson Case and in Tolstoy's 'Kreuzer Sonata,'" *Critical Inquiry* 23 (summer 1997): 738–788. Felman's analysis shares many terms with mine, most obviously the conjunction of narrative trauma and the thematics of witnessing and blindness. I hope it will be clear, however, that I do not share her faith in the ethical efficacy of aesthetic procedures as contrasted with legal ones. Wright's novel, it seems to me, indicates the mutual infection of aesthetic and cognitive representational operations.

13. Richard Wright, "How 'Bigger' Was Born," in *Native Son* (New York: Harper Perennial, 1993), p. 531. This is the restored text as established by the Library of America; all subsequent quotation from *Native Son* and Wright's essay are from this edition and are cited parenthetically in the text.

14. In this regard, *Native Son* is quite like many other twentieth-century American novels in focusing intently on a central traumatic murder that it then renders ambiguous in some essential way. Think of Clyde Griffith's bungled drowning of his girlfriend in Dreiser's *American Tragedy*, or Truman Capote's leisurely elaboration of doubts as to who killed whom in *In Cold Blood*, or DeLillo's artfully confused reconstruction of the Kennedy assassination in *Libra*.

15. Jacques Lacan, *The Four Fundamental Concepts of Psycho-Analysis*, ed. Jacques-Álain Miller, trans. Alan Sheridan (New York: W. W. Norton, 1977), pp. 53, 55, 75.

16. Ibid., p. 51.

17. Ralph Ellison, "The World and the Jug" (1953), in *Shadow and Act* (New York: Vintage, 1972), p. 114.

18. Paul Gilroy's recent reassessment of Wright has much to say about this topic; see *The Black Atlantic: Modernity and Double Consciousness* (Cambridge: Harvard University Press, 1993), chap. 5.

19. The relation between Wright and his creation has been of vital concern for analyses of the book that focus on the crucial role played by violence against women. Here the antagonism in which Wright and Bigger are equally ensnared is not so much between white and black as between men and women. As I will suggest in looking at the scene in Mary's bedroom, it is indeed the case that the novel articulates

racial and gender antagonism in ways that lead to equally appalling mortifications in both registers. On Wright's readiness to depict violence against women, see Mariah K. Mootry, "Bitches, Whores, and Woman Haters," in *Richard Wright: A Collection of Critical Essays*, ed. Richard Macksey and Frank Moorer (Englewood Cliffs, N.J.: Prentice-Hall, 1984), pp. 117–127; Alan W. France, "Misogyny and Appropriation in *Native Son*," in Bloom, *Bigger Thomas*, pp. 151–160; Farah Jasmine Griffin, "On Women, Teaching, and *Native Son*," in *Approaches to Teaching Wright's "Native Son*," ed. James A. Miller (New York: MLA, 1997), pp. 75–80. For an article focusing on Bigger's contempt for the women in his world, see Trudier Harris, "Native Sons and Foreign Daughters," in *New Essays on "Native Son*," ed. Kenneth Kinnamon (Cambridge: Cambridge University Press, 1990).

20. James Baldwin, "Many Thousands Gone" (1951), in *Notes of a Native Son* (1955; reprint, Boston: Beacon Press, 1985), p. 29.

21. Ibid., pp. 25–26, 34.

22. Kimberly W. Benston, "Facing Tradition: Revisionary Scenes in African American Literature," *PMLA* 105 (January 1990): 106. Let me call attention here to another powerful essay concerned with themes and theoretical problems similar to those in my essay but that, like Benston's, works toward a passage beyond the ruptures and impasses generated by the face-to-face and its theoretical inscription as the faulty relation between imaginary and symbolic registers: Lee Edelman, "The Part for the (W)hole: Baldwin, Homophobia, and the Fantasmatics of 'Race,'" in *Homographesis: Essays in Gay Literary and Cultural Theory* (New York: Routledge, 1993), pp. 42–75.

23. Gilroy, *The Black Atlantic*, 159, 164, 179, and 147.

24. An authoritative historical account of certain so-called theories of "regression" underlying the crystallization of the narrative of the black beast can be found in George M. Fredrickson, *The Black Image in the White Mind: The Debate on Afro-American Character and Destiny, 1817–1914* (New York: Harper & Row, 1971; reprint, Middletown, Conn.: Wesleyan University Press, 1987), especially chaps. 8 and 9. Over the last fifteen years or so, a remarkable body of work has been produced on the intrications of race and gender, both in white supremacist imaginations and within various traditions of African American thought. Some of the debates and lines of contention and solidarity threading through this body of work are surveyed and interestingly analyzed by Robyn Wiegman in *American Anatomies: Theorizing Race and Gender* (Durham, N.C.: Duke University Press, 1995). For a window on the debates among historians, with special reference to the historiography of lynching, see the fascinating "Round Table" in *The Journal of American History* 83 (March 1997): 1221–1272. The Round Table consists of a self-reflective essay by Joel Williamson and replies—many of them the original readers' reports—by other historians in the field.

25. The contrast here between white and black women could not be more stark; it is posed as a difference of "evidence." After having seen but not registered the significance of the small chips of bone recovered from the furnace, Bigger reflects: "Never did he think he could stand and look at the evidence and not know it" (271). The near-total lack of forensic evidence from Mary's body allows the false charge of rape to go uncontradicted in the trial (though one could also chalk this up to lousy lawyering; see Michael Bérubé, "Max, Media, and Mimesis: Bigger's Representation in *Native Son*," in Miller, *Approaches to Teaching Wright's "Native Son*," pp. 112–119). Mary's symbolic status beyond evidence is secured, both

ideologically and within the narrative itself, by Bessie's complementary reduction to pure evidence. District Attorney Buckley actually wheels Bessie's battered corpse into the courtroom to secure the tendentious charge about Mary. Bessie could hardly signify better what Hortense J. Spillers has analyzed as a baseline tendency in white uses of black bodies to reduce them to a state of ungendered corporeality; see Spillers, "Mama's Baby, Papa's Maybe: An American Grammar Book," *Diacritics* 17 (Summer 1987): 65–81.

26 Abdul R. JanMohamed, "Sexuality on/of the Racial Border: Foucault, Wright, and the Articulation of 'Racialized Sexuality,'" in *Discourses of Sexuality: From Aristotle to AIDS,* ed. Domna C. Stanton (Ann Arbor: University of Michigan Press, 1992), pp. 99, 105, 105, 105.

27. Michel Foucault, *The Archaeology of Knowledge,* trans. A. M. Sheridan Smith (New York: Pantheon, 1972), p. 127. The passage is cited by JanMohamed on p. 108.

28. JanMohamed, "Sexuality on/of the Racial Border," p. 109.

29. Here I am implicitly arguing against the interpretation of the novel as representing Bigger's tragic assumption of his own meaning, his achievement of articulate self-understanding; the paralysis of language and meaning in the novel seems to me too intractable a phenomenon to sustain this view. But see Valerie Smith, "Alienation and Creativity in *Native Son,*" and Joyce Anne Joyce, "The Tragic Hero," in *Richard Wright's Native Son,* ed. Harold Bloom (New York: Chelsea House, 1988), on pages 105–114, and 67–87, respectively.

30. Gilles Deleuze, *The Logic of Sense,* ed. Constantin Boundas, trans. Mark Lester with Charles Stivale (New York: Columbia University Press, 1990), pp. 52, 53, 53, and 182; translation of *Logique du sens* (Paris: Editions de Minuit, 1969).

31. Ibid., p. 182.

32. Lacan, *The Four Fundamental Concepts of Psycho-Analysis,* pp. 59, 56.

33. Ibid., p. 60.

34. The problems of event and expression that I have been insisting are both linguistic and experiential in this scene might be considered in relation to some of Jacques Derrida's recent questions about the very possibility of experiencing aporia: "We are dealing here with names (event, decision, responsibility, ethics, politics—Europe) of 'things' that can only exceed (and must exceed) the order of theoretical determination, of knowledge, certainty, judgment, and of statements in the form of 'this is that,' in other words, more generally and essentially, the order of the present or of presentation" *(Aporias* [Stanford, Calif.: Stanford University Press, 1993], p. 20). In aporia, we can have it "right before our eyes" and still not see the "present." It is implicitly argued throughout this essay that race is traumatic very generally in modernity because it so insistently re-presents this impossible presentation. Philosophical and historical problematics join hands here. Paul Gilroy's words resonate with Derrida's when he discusses violence as that which "mediates racial differences and maintains the boundary between racially segregated, non-synchronous communities" *(The Black Atlantic,* 174). The nonsynchronicity, the temporal hitch in racialized violence is both historical and formal.

35. Toni Morrison, *Playing in the Dark: Whiteness and the Literary Imagination* (Cambridge: Harvard University Press, 1992).

36. The porousness of the boundaries between literary and social histories implied in Wright's epigram is no mere offhand observation. One could argue that the relation between Bigger and Robert Nixon—the Chicago youth whose

sensationalized crimes and punishment Wright used for some details in *Native Son*—is an example of this porousness, inasmuch as Nixon was in no direct way a "real-life" source for Bigger, merely a convenient parallel instance.

37. Lacan, *The Four Fundamental Concepts*, pp. 79, 77. This drift from temporal problems to scenarios of vision and blindness is central to much of Lacan's thinking. Both in his 1945 essay on "logical time" and in his early seminars, Lacan had joined visual and temporal problematics in his attempt to understand the relation between the Imaginary and the Symbolic. Whether it is the prisoners with white and black disks on their backs or his description of the dance of vision and blindness in Poe's "Purloined Letter," the presence of the symbolic as logically and structurally prior to the intersubjective realm of the imaginary is consistently expressed in Lacan via metaphors of blindness and temporal paradox. The symbolic is, Lacan writes in his second seminar, "like an image in the mirror, but of a different order." "It isn't for nothing that Odysseus pierces the eye of the Cyclop," he writes, suggesting that the symbolic is experienced as a mutation process within the imaginary, in which vision and reflection are first inflated to the monstrous proportions of the singular Cyclopean eye, and then blinded, passed beyond. Correlative to this blindness is what Lacan characterizes as a temporal lurch between imaginary and symbolic registers, a kind of transpersonal "precipitation in the act." Here Mrs. Dalton's function as pure waiting would be powerfully set off against Bigger's anxious haste. Lacan speaks of a "relation to time peculiar to the human being. . . which is neither belatedness nor being in advance, but haste"; see Jacques Lacan, *The Seminar of Jacques Lacan, Book II: The Ego in Freud's Theory and in the Technique of Psychoanalysis, 1954–1955* (New York: W. W. Norton, 1988), pp. 185, 289, 291.

38. Lacan, *Four Fundamental Concepts*, p. 106.

39. Ibid., p. 84.

40. See Kaja Silverman, *The Threshold of the Visible World* (New York: Routledge, 1996), especially chaps. 4 through 6.

41. Julie Ellison, "A Short History of Liberal Guilt," *Critical Inquiry* 22 (winter 1996): 352, 361. It is tempting to see Wright's presentation of Mary's murder as a kind of revision of the following scene, which combines in nearly pornographic luridiness a promiscuous visibility transcending individual blindness, the fact of confinement and enclosure, and racialized violence:

> [H]orrid to think and painful to repeat, I perceived a Negro, suspended in the cage and left there to expire! I shudder when I recollect that the birds had already pecked out his eyes. . . . I found myself suddenly arrested by the power of affright and terror; my nerves were convulsed; I trembled; I stood motionless, involuntarily contemplating the fate of the Negro in all its dismal latitude. The living spectre, though deprived of his eyes, could still distinctly hear, and in his uncouth dialect begged me to give him some water to allay his thirst. . . . I guided it to the quivering lips of the wretched sufferer. . . . Tanky you white man, tanky you." (J. Hector St. John de Crèvecoeur, *Letters From an American Farmer* [1782], ed. Albert E. Stone [Harmondsworth: Penguin, 1986], p. 178).

42. Bérubé details this in "Max, Media, and Mimesis."

HAZEL ROWLEY

Backstage and Onstage:
The Drama of Native Son

In the spring of 1940, on his farm outside Chapel Hill, North Carolina, the dramatist Paul Green walked through the woods, musing about *Native Son*, Richard Wright's best-selling novel published on March 1 as a Book-of-the-Month Club choice. "Found it horrifying, brutal, and extraordinarily vivid," Green noted in his journal. "Reminiscent a bit of 'Crime and Punishment.' Doubt I could do anything with it. However, I feel it's the most vivid writing I've seen by any Negro author in America."[1]

Cheryl Crawford, director of the communist Group Theater in New York, had asked Green whether he might be interested in dramatizing Wright's novel. Green was not tempted until he heard that Orson Welles and John Houseman were likely to get the stage rights. Welles, currently working on his movie *Citizen Kane*, was the buzz of Hollywood.

Wright was in Mexico that spring, reeling from the backlash against *Native Son* that had quickly followed the praise. He was both flattered by and anxious about the frenzied interest in the stage rights. "I realize the limitations of the screen and stage in America," he wrote to Houseman and Welles. "Can such a book be done in a light that presents Bigger Thomas as a *human being*? . . . To be honest, I'm more interested in that than I am in seeing the book on the stage or screen."[2]

Mississippi Quarterly: The Journal of Southern Cultures, Volume 52, Number 2 (Spring 1999): pp. 215–237. Copyright © 1999 Mississippi Quarterly.

Houseman wrote back at length, reassuring Wright. "The more of your help we can have, the more you can transmit to us of the intention and the spirit of your book, the better pleased we shall be."[3]

Wright told Green that his offer to write the script interested him more than any other. "But I would very much like to know (if it is not asking too much!) just what you think you can do with the book."[4] He added that·he would like to have the right to go through the script; would that be acceptable to Green? Green wrote back suggesting that they formally collaborate. That way, said Green, "all matters could be discussed as we went along."[5]

Wright was enthusiastic. Paul Green, a well-known Southern liberal, was the only white playwright to produce serious drama about the Negro experience. His play *In Abraham's Bosom* had won the Pulitzer Prize in 1927. He knew his craft, and he could be hardhitting when he wanted to be. It appeared that he was not afraid of controversy: his plays had been attacked as much as praised. Wright believed he could "handle a boy like Bigger" (May 22, 1940). He and Green had very different perspectives, but if they worked on the play together, Wright was sure he could impart his own vision, showing the social forces that create a Bigger Thomas.

John Houseman was not at all keen on working with Paul Green. He did not see how Green's moralist religious perspective could possibly be compatible with Wright's radical vision or with his realism. Houseman could foresee Paul Green turning a forceful novel into an artistic little drama bristling with pious certitudes, cathartic suffering and redemption. He also knew that Green was notoriously slow when it came to producing a finished play.[6] Houseman suggested that Wright do the dramatization himself, but Wright insisted that he did not feel competent. "My field is the novel; I know very little about the movies and still less about the stage," he told Houseman.[7] Under the circumstances, collaboration seemed the best solution.

Harper and Brothers wanted to publish the play, and offered an advance of $1,000. Wright's agent, Paul Reynolds, suggested a 60%–40% breakdown, with the greater share going to Wright, as author of the book. Green wanted fifty-fifty. Because the final contract gave "the author" (Wright) 55% and "the dramatist" (Green) 45%, it had an important symbolic significance: Wright was understood to be the dominant partner.[8]

Houseman arranged to meet Paul Green and Richard Wright in Chapel Hill for preliminary discussions. From June 20 to June 22, he and Wright stayed with Paul and Elizabeth Green on their farm.

John Houseman, like Paul Green, had good credentials in African-American theater. Born in Romania and sent to boarding school in Britain, he had come to the United States in the 1930s and discovered the theater. During 1935 and 1936, he had successfully co-directed the Federal Negro Theater in Harlem, as part of the Federal Theater of the Works Progress Administration.

While working there, he had invited Orson Welles to direct a production. He was taking a risk. Welles was twenty at the time (twelve years younger than Houseman), a mercurial young genius. Soon afterwards, Welles had phoned at two o'clock in the morning and suggested a nineteenth-century version of *Macbeth*, set in the jungle of Haiti, with voodoo priestesses as the witches. The production had aroused considerable controversy in Harlem. Many considered it a crazy white man's scheme to bring the theatre into disrepute. The play opened in mid-April 1936 at Harlem's old Lafayette Theatre—the first all-Negro production of Shakespeare in American theatrical history and the first time that Welles and Houseman collaborated. It proved a triumphant success—in Harlem, on Broadway, and on national tour.

In August 1937, Houseman and Welles established their own repertory theater, Mercury Theater, Inc. Their partnership proved both dazzling and explosive. Welles, both as an actor and a director, was frenetic, exhilarating and exhausting. Houseman, who managed the administration and budget, prided himself on his efficiency and practical sense as well as his skills as a scriptwriter and critical observer. Both men knew how to coax the best out of people they needed and were ruthless with those they didn't need. Houseman admits in his memoirs that he was "incapable of parity" in relationships, and this made him "a prey to competitiveness in its most virulent form."[9]

For a while now, the two men had been ready to go their own way. But then Welles had asked Houseman to help Herman Mankiewicz with the screenplay for *Citizen Kane*. And while he was doing that, Houseman read *Native Son*. Bowled over by its power, he told himself it would make a wonderful play. And he knew that there was only one man who could be relied upon to make it into an electrifying theatrical experience. Welles agreed to work on the play as soon as he had finished *Citizen Kane*. So Houseman had come to North Carolina to set things in motion.

> I was there when Wright arrived—a surprisingly mild-mannered, round-faced, brown-skinned young man with beautiful eyes. It was only later, when I came to know him better, that I began to sense the deep, almost morbid violence that lay skin-deep below that gentle surface. . . .
>
> I spent a day with him and Green, listening to Paul's ideas for the play. I watched Dick Wright for his reactions: I saw nothing. But my own apprehensions rose sharply. Paul Green was a man who sincerely believed himself free of racial prejudice. . . . Throughout his stay, according to Dick, he could not have been more courteous, thoughtful and hospitable in his treatment of his black guest. But, having granted him social equality, he stopped there. From the first hour of their 'discussions' it became clear

that he was incapable or unwilling to extend this equality into the professional or creative fields. Whether from his exalted position as veteran playwright and Pulitzer Prize-winner or from some innate sense of intellectual and moral superiority (aggravated by Wright's Communist connections), Paul Green's attitude in the collaboration was, first and last, insensitive, condescending and intransigent. (pp. 230–231)

Despite his misgivings, Houseman signed the dramatic rights. The three men told each other they had high hopes for a fine play and agreed that the script should be finished by October 1940.

Wright spent a couple of weeks in New York and Chicago and returned to Chapel Hill on July 8. He could not stay at the Carolina Inn, which was where visiting scholars mostly put up. He could not eat in the restaurants next to the university. Paul Green had found him a room in a boarding house in the black area between Chapel Hill and the white working-class cotton-mill district of Carrboro. Just a few streets away from the university, with its handsome old buildings and spreading live oaks, it was a different world. The streets were unpaved, the houses were shabby.

Paul Green was Professor of Dramatic Art at the University of North Carolina, and well known on that all-white Southern campus for his liberal views about race. In the past, his hospitality to black scholars had caused rumblings from the locals. When he organized a literary party at his house for the visiting writer James Weldon Johnson, he was reprimanded by the university administration. The year before Wright came to Chapel Hill, Zora Neale Hurston had spent the summer there, teaching drama at the North Carolina College for Negroes. Once or twice she came to the University of North Carolina to see Green.

> She wore a little red cap, and had a little red roadster; and she'd drive up to my office, and the boys would go 'whew' or whistle at her and make fun of her. She'd say, 'Good Morning, freshmen. How are you, freshmen?' And so they were about to drive her off.[10]

Green had sought official permission from the university president to have Wright work with him in an office on the university grounds. It was summer; the campus was quiet, and the president sincerely hoped that the presence of a black man would go almost unnoticed. Green and Wright were allotted space in Bynum Hall, an administrative building that was once the old gymnasium, on the town edge of the campus.

Chapel Hill was swelteringly hot that summer of 1940. For days on end, the temperature hovered between 100 and 106 in the shade, and scarcely dropped at night. The two men started out in a room on the southwest corner of Bynum Hall, and were driven out by the heat. For a few days they repaired to Green's log cabin, on his farm. But several miles out of town, that was less convenient and also hot. Eventually, they were given two rooms in the northeast corner of Bynum Hall, where at least they were not subjected to the afternoon sun. A friend lent them a fan. "So we were enabled to continue," Green wrote in his diary.[11]

Curious faces would look in at the window. Never had anyone in South seen such a sight. A white man and a black man were sitting across from each other at a long table. On the table was a large typewriter, a pair of horn-rimmed glasses that the white man would sometimes put on for reading (the black man wore steel rims), a book that looked like a novel with handwriting in the margin, a packet of Pall Mall cigarettes, an ashtray half full of stubs, and sundry notebooks and papers. Everywhere there was paper filled with type, crossings out and bold arrows in black ink. Sometimes the black man would sit at the typewriter and burst into composition, like a bird into song. The white man liked to pace the room, theatrically touching his forehead with the back of his hand as he pondered an idea.[12]

Thirty years later, in the 1970s, Paul Green gave several interviews in which he talked about those weeks with Wright. By then, the civil rights movement had fundamentally changed attitudes toward "blacks," as they were now called. Black students were now admitted to the University of North Carolina. A decade had passed since Wright's premature death. Paul Green now felt embarrassed about the way he treated Wright that summer of 1940.

> Something I regretted. I never understood it. He called me 'Mr. Green' and I called him 'Dick' or 'Richard.' What in the heck went on? But anyway that was the relationship, although we felt very close together.[13]
>
> Now when I look back on it—you know, when you have a friend who has died, you say 'Jesus, if I'd known he was going to die, I'd have done so different. I would have gone see him; I would have treated him so differently.' (Hall interview)

In the 1970s, Green claimed that before he agreed to dramatize *Native Son*, he had written several stipulations into the contract. The first was that he would have the right to "poke some fun" at communism. ("I didn't want to put something on the stage saying that I was behind this thing, communism" [NPR interview].) Another was that he would be allowed to make Bigger Thomas partially responsible for his own downfall. ("I didn't subscribe to the old familiar whine that 'the reason I'm a dead beat, or I'm mean, or I can't get anywhere in the world is that the world treats me wrong.' No. Every man has something to do with what he becomes.") [14]

In all of Green's meticulously kept contracts and correspondence at the University of North Carolina, there is no sign of any such clause. Wright would never have consented to such conditions. That was the point of the collaboration.

Green also claimed, after Wright had died, that he wrote the whole play himself, but that Wright was "so helpful" that Green insisted on using joint names. He says he once asked Wright "to try his hand at writing a scene." It did not work. "It was beautiful, but completely novelistic" (September 24, 1965).

Green's memory was flawed. In reality, it was understood from the beginning that the play would be published under joint names. And though Green, as a skilled playwright, almost certainly wrote more, the first draft was a mutual process—both in its conception and in the writing. In an interview in 1941, Wright explained that he and Green met each morning, discussed the content of a scene, then retired to write separately and came together again in the late afternoon to compare notes. "We would both work at a scene until we felt we had packed it with all the necessary action. Mr. Green would then compress it. After that, I would go over it, making sure that the dialogue and imagery were Negro and urban."[15] This picture of their collaboration is reinforced by Ouida Campbell, their secretary, who was often in the room with them, taking notes.

The collaboration was congenial, but Houseman was quite right; it was unequal. It was a play they were writing, and Green was the proven playwright. Green was forty-six; Wright was thirty-one. Green was a Pulitzer Prize winner, a university professor; they were on his territory; he was white, and he was stubborn. Years later, Paul Green was as adamant as ever about the "rightness" of his views:

> In the novel, as I read it, Bigger Thomas was practically completely a product of his environment: and I wouldn't subscribe to that. A human being has got some responsibility to his own career; and I don't care what Freud says or what the whining people say, you can't put it always on somebody else. (Hall interview)

What complicated the collaboration were the genuine—and major—problems associated with turning the novel into something appropriate for the stage. In the novel, the reader's sympathy with Bigger, such as it is, comes from seeing things through his consciousness. On stage, Bigger would be seen from the outside. The novel had already been described as "melodramatic"; the stage drama could all too easily become sensationalist. Violence that was just tolerable on the page would not be tolerable on stage. And then there was the interracial sex. If a black man fondling the breasts of a white woman was barely acceptable in a novel, a theatre audience would be stampeding up the aisles. The problem was how to solve these issues, given the two men's quite disparate personal philosophies. Paul Green was a dogged, do-good Southern gentleman. His speech, as well as his writing, had a stilted biblical ring to it. "The South is acquainted with sin, more than any other part of the country," he told an interviewer in 1960. "We are just full of the drip of human tears." In the same interview, he added: "The love between the Negro and the white is something wonderful to behold in the South."[16]

Green did not share Wright's focus on environmental forces; he thought entirely in terms of individual responsibility. It was the "human soul" that interested him—what he called "the god-like spirit in man."[17] He believed in self-reliance, courage, and righteousness—the founding principles of the American Constitution. His hero was Thomas Jefferson, a fellow Southerner, whom he liked to quote. ("A nation can only be as strong and healthy as its citizens are strong and healthy."[18])

Green's passion was Greek tragedy. He liked tragic heroes. Like the Greek playwrights, he believed in the benevolent effect of catharsis. "The urge to associate with, to help the suffering one, to lift him up, to ease him, brings with it . . . a gained fullness of personality," he once said. "The feeling is pleasurable."[19] His plays about Negroes were cathartic tragedies. His black characters were victims and martyrs. In the 1930s, communist critics had criticized him for his "tragic and defeatist attitude towards life."[20]

From the beginning, Green set out to soften the impact of *Native Son*. It was a story about hate; he believed in love. He vehemently disapproved of Wright's basic premise: that Bigger Thomas could transcend his circumstances only by an act of violence. He tried to make Bigger more likable. One of his strategies was to make the white woman, Mary Dalton, more dislikable. In Green's version, she no longer acts as she does toward Bigger out of leftwing idealism; it is more a question of brassy boredom. His stage directions have her "dressed in a flowing red robe, opened at the bosom."

Green proposed to replace the harsh realism of the murder scene with "the pale cast of dreaming."[21] Instead of killing Mary Dalton on stage, Bigger could be seen dreaming about the murder afterwards. And Green persuaded Wright that one murder was more than enough. "Bessie" (who in the play is called "Clara," since Green thought that too many of the characters had names beginning with "b") throws her arms around Bigger and is destroyed by police fire.

The final scene caused endless discussion. Green wanted Bigger to walk toward the execution chamber with straight shoulders and head high—"like a god." That way, Green insisted, Bigger would he a hero and the play would be a tragedy, rather than simply "pathetic."

Miss Ouida Campbell, who was employed to type up the work-in-progress, was a lively young radical from Carrboro. Mostly she sat at her typewriter in the small space outside the two office rooms. Some afternoons she would be invited behind the closed doors of Bynum 201. A space would be cleared for her at the table, and she would write down dialogue, in shorthand. Well aware that she was privileged to be witnessing literary history, several months later she described the scene for the *Carolina Magazine:*

> Mr. Green—big, tall, with his horn-rimmed glasses, his white suit and the old Panama hat he kept putting on and taking off—was a combination of a Southern Gentleman and a nervous artist as he walked around the little room. Richard Wright . . . sat by the window, smiling often as he talked, dressed in a pink sport shirt and maroon slacks. He had, as always, an air of quiet, assured, self-confidence.
>
> Bigger was their greatest problem. In the novel, Wright had Bigger hating violently, a hate caused by fear. He lived by this hate—it was his only creed. Mr. Green wanted to take some of this hate out of Bigger.[22]

The room, she writes, was filled with an excitement, "tense and suppressed." Mr. Green would walk up and down, smoking one cigarette after another and running his hand through his hair. Mr. Wright would tilt his chair back against the wall, swing his foot and smile. According to Campbell, the arguments were always affable. "They had an easy, joking, bantering relationship. They rubbed along very smoothly. If there were disagreements, they talked them out and compromised. Or did it Mr. Green's way."[23]

Ouida Campbell saw Bigger Thomas undergo a transformation. He started to say things like "I'm so hungry I could chew me a piece of the Lamb of God." At the end of that first draft, he said to his lawyer: "I wanted to be free, to walk wide and free with steps a mile long—over the fields, over the rivers, and straddling the mountains and on—like God." Miss Campbell wondered whether Bigger could survive this tug-of-war.

> At the time the first draft was finished and Wright went back to New York, Bigger Thomas was guilty not only of murder, but of the crime of inconsistency. He was about equally divided: one half Mr. Green's Bigger—sensitive, misguided, puzzled about life in general; and the other half Wright's Bigger—full of hate and fear, cunning, but at the same time looking for an answer to the questions that rise in his mind.

Among Wright's unpublished papers at Yale is a revealing seven-page drama called "The Problem of the Hero" written several months later, after the collaboration with Green ended. The two characters are called "white man" and "black man." At the top of the first page, Wright wrote: "The following is not a verbatim report of conversations that took place between Paul Green and me, but an attempt to re-construct the general sense of the central problem we faced in dramatizing my novel, *Native Son*". It opens with the white man talking:

> White Man: (graciously but seriously) I wasn't quite satisfied with your novel when I read it, but I liked it. I felt it was the best piece of fiction written by a Negro in America. Now, in dramatizing it, I would like to make your character, Bigger, a hero in the tragic sense. As he stands now, he seems a figure of pathos, more acted upon than acting.

The black man argues that Bigger is not able to determine his own destiny, which is what it takes to make a tragic hero. The white man says: "But there must be heroes!" The black man answers: "There shall be heroes, when men are *free!*" The white man does not like it that Bigger discovers the possibilities of life through "reprehensible deeds, through acts of murder, through evil." He sees Bigger as an "inverted Christ" figure. The black man worries that the play is no longer "true to Negro life." It has become a metaphysical drama. The white man sees Bigger "from the point of view of heroic tragedy." He is convinced that what they want is an "overreaching symbol that heals." "But he's got to be true, credible," the black man protests. [24]

Green and Wright managed to produce what they tentatively called "a first rough working draft." By mid-August, Wright had to return to New York. From now on, they agreed, Green would be mainly responsible for the re-writing and polishing, but they would continue their discussions from a distance and Green would make short trips to New York.

Paul Green had a reputation in theatrical circles for making constant changes to his scripts and never being able to stick to a schedule. "Directors had a lot of trouble with Paul," says a colleague, "and he with them. He was seldom satisfied with his writing or their staging. . . . In some cases, Paul was asked not to come back to rehearsals."[25] In between his other commitments, Green toyed endlessly with *Native Son*. He came to New York twice during the fall, staying at the Hotel Bristol, and he and Wright continued their discussions—until the hotel manager told Green there had been complaints about his black friend using the house elevator and forbade his visits.

The play was supposed to have been finished by October. It was not. Green had made major changes to the first draft, changes that left large gaps.

Wright continued to give way on important points. "The more I've thought of your idea of ending the play with Bigger killing himself, I like it," he wrote to Green in early October.[26]

John Houseman did not like it. He did not like the way Green had toned down the realism and toned down the impact. He did not want Bigger to be "godlike." He did not want dream sequences with Negro spirituals in the background. He did not want long reflective dialogues. It was his opinion, he told Paul Reynolds, that if Green did not like Wright's realism, he should not have undertaken this job in the first place. And he was heartily sick of Green's dillydallying. He wanted the script finished. By late October, Orson Welles had finished shooting *Citizen Kane* and in a matter of weeks could be ready to start work on *Native Son*. By late November, Green had still not finished the play. He was now suggesting that the play go into rehearsal while he fixed up the odds and ends. Houseman refused. "Years of bitter experience" had taught him where that led.[27]

Houseman writes in his memoirs that he lay in his raised red-velvet bed one morning and reflected that the situation was ridiculous. Paul Green had become an obstacle. On Christmas Eve 1940, Houseman sat down and wrote Green that he did not like the murder enacted as a dream scene in a blue haze. "In the novel the killing is a factual, tragic event." He thought Green's latest ending to the play "absurd." "I see no reason why anybody would reprieve Bigger, and having been reprieved, his killing of himself, if it proves anything at all, seems to me to prove something entirely different from Wright's conclusion in the novel. As I see it the point was that Bigger *did* find his personal truth (the truth which society had denied him) through violence."

He also told Green he wanted to start work on the play at the end of January 1941. He needed a finished script several weeks before that. "Wright, I believe, is also upset by the delays and feels that he has lost a great deal of time and does not want the matter to drag on much further. I know how terribly busy you are yourself. What do you think we should do about it?" (Houseman to Green).

Houseman was hoping that Green would opt "out of the picture."[28] Wright, who had gone along with Green's changes, felt like a traitor. But he was sandwiched between two strong-headed men. His agent, Paul Reynolds, who was strongly backing Houseman, tried to reassure Wright about their treatment of Paul Green:

> If he would pull out we could, of course, offer him the choice of having his name fixed to the final draft of the play or left off, as he preferred. The problem is probably going to be one of not offending his pride. . . .

Providing we can work out this headache I don't think you should regret that Green was the choice. I gather from what you have said that he has been valuable from the point of view of stage technique which is what was expected from him and that his defect is his liking for dreams and vagueness and fantasy and that we all of us knew beforehand. If that latter can be eliminated there ought to be a chance for a very successful play. (Reynolds to Wright)

In late January, Houseman decided to fix up the play himself—with the help of Richard Wright. They spent several mornings at Houseman's apartment on West Ninth Street, cutting what Houseman saw as sentimental and longwinded flab. (They crossed out large chunks of metaphysical dialogue between Bigger and his lawyer.) "It seems that the more we cut the more powerful the play becomes," Wright wrote to Green, as reassuringly as he could.[29]

A week later, Wright wrote again. This time, he was broaching a delicate subject; it was no longer a question of cutting. "I don't know just how you will like the last scene, but we recast it in terms of the book," he told Green. "It is short, effective, I think, and forms a good conclusion to the play."[30] Wright knew that Green wanted to make Bigger into a tragic hero, a kind of black god. Either he was to walk proudly to his death, or else he was to commit suicide. Now Houseman had the curtain dropping with Bigger Thomas awaiting his death, grasping the prison bars and looking straight at the audience, while the lights faded out. Wright knew that Green would hate it. He would see this scene as representing Bigger crucified by society. It was exactly the "pathetic" ending he had so adamantly fought against.

On February 11, Orson Welles arrived—a hurricane from the West. A giant of a man (six-feet three-inches tall and 220 pounds in weight) with a chubby boyish face, he was swaggering, domineering, exciting, and mesmerisingly intense. Welles was not particularly interested in the play's psychology or its moral message. He cared about dynamic theatre. He weighed in immediately on Houseman's side. Long passages of anguished dialogue did not make good theater. He wanted the action to sweep past the audience like a torrent.

In February, after a tortured visit to New York, Green wrote in his diary:

Struggle with Welles, Hauseman [sic] and Wright to make play come out with some sort of moral responsibility for the individual. . . . "No Negro singing" says Welles. "Too much spiritual stuff in all Negro plays." . . . Also took away dream murder interpretation. Left wing, left wing, propaganda complete. But since Wright was on their side I yielded. After all, his novel, his characters.[31]

Green could not stand up to this coalition, but he did not yield his rights to the printed play. Paul Reynolds now saw it as inevitable that there would be two different versions of the play—a printed and a stage version. (The first edition's title page would describe it as "A Play in Ten Scenes by Paul Green and Richard Wright" and "A Mercury Production by Orson Welles. Presented by Orson Welles and John Houseman.") It was an awkward compromise. Wright knew about it. So did Houseman. Nobody told Orson Welles. Nor was Edward Aswell of Harper & Brothers, the publisher of the printed version, informed. Aswell said later: "Had we been consulted about it at the time, we would have objected."[32] Paul Reynolds knew this, of course. Green's stubbornness now made Wright impatient. He himself had been making compromises all these months, and now Green was talking as if *he* owned Bigger Thomas.

Auditions for parts began on February 12. Five days later, rehearsals began. To create the atmosphere of the Chicago blackbelt, Orson Welles had the stage framed with dingy yellow brick. Within this outer brick wall, there was a different set for each scene. Welles wanted all scene changes to take place within one minute flat. During these blackouts, the audience would hear the roaring of the furnace or the sirens of police cars while thirty-five stagehands worked at high speed.[33]

In order to have no slackening of the tension, there was to be no interval. When the time came, Welles would instruct the ushers not to hand out programs until after the show. He did not want the audience lighting matches to study their programs and spoiling the blackouts at the end of each scene. "There were deep menacing shadows—a tension felt throughout," a member of the audience would recall later. "When Bigger was cornered—'Come out, you black bastard!'—he cowered, firing straight into the audience, and answering shots and searchlights came from the rear of the theatre. Sirens were turned on, increasing in pitch—and the curtain fell."[34] In the trial scene, the judge was separated from the audience by the railing across the apron of the stage, while the defense attorney, Bigger and his family sat below, in the pit. The staging was as inventive as the sound effects and lighting. This was theater at its most dynamic.

The much sought-after role of Bigger Thomas went to Canada Lee. A stocky, broad-shouldered former boxer with cauliflower ears and a broken nose, he had played Banquo in Welles and Houseman's production *Macbeth*. He was thirty-four, but looked much younger. "It isn't difficult for me to play Bigger Thomas," he told the *New York Herald Tribune*. "I've guys like Bigger Thomas all my life. . . . I saw some in school and I grew up with some pretty tough guys. Some of them are in jail now and some went to the electric chair."[35]

Doris Dudley was selected for the role of Mary Dalton. After a few days, she could not take the pressure from friends and acquaintances, and withdrew from the play. Twenty-two year old Anne Burr took over the part.

"You don't mind getting smothered every night?" the *Brooklyn Eagle* would ask her in June. Burr replied that Desdemona had been taking it for centuries, so she, Mary Dalton, could hardly complain. "It was a bit tough going at first, because Canada Lee makes it pretty realistic. There was one dress rehearsal when I thought I was really going to get it!"[36]

Native Son was Houseman and Welles's last Mercury production, and their last production ever as a team. They were more distant from each other these days, which meant that they quarreled less. During rehearsals, House-man found Welles "happy, overbearing and exciting to work with."[37] Their arguments, this time, were mostly about money. Welles refused to stint in any way; Houseman, as usual, was more down-to-earth.

They advised Wright to stay away from the theatre until the play took shape, but this was precisely the process that interested Wright. He went several times to watch rehearsals. He enjoyed the group's talent and spir-itedness. And he was both impressed and horrified by the bear-like Orson Welles, with his boundless energy and raging temper. Rehearsals would go on for hours. Welles was coaxing, encouraging and demanding. The actors were terrified of him, and worshipped him. Wright told *World-Telegram:* "One Orson Welles on earth is enough. Two of them would no doubt bring civilization itself to an end."[38]

Everyone associated with the play was conscious that *Native Son* was making history. It was a risk: *Native Son* could open up new opportunities for black actors, or it could cause a backlash. "The Negro has never been given the scope that I'm given in this play," Canada Lee said. "Now things are going to happen."[39] The play was breaking with the standard black caricatures: the primitive African savages, devoted Mammies, loyal Uncle Toms, and eye-rolling buffoons. Bigger, for once, was a rebel.

The interracial caste was breaking Broadway stage barriers. So was the interracial kissing. Welles and Houseman were well aware that a light-skinned black woman in the part of Mary Dalton would forestall criticism, but they were keen to set a precedent. Indeed, *Native Son* paved the way for Paul Robeson, just two years later, to kiss his white Desdemona on the Broadway stage.

Since Wright had re-written the final scene with Houseman, relations between Wright and Paul Green were tense. Wright no longer looked upon Green's role in the whole process with quite the same loyalty and gratitude. Until now, Wright had been anxious to keep any dissent between themselves; now he was prepared to make it public. On March 12, two weeks before the play was to open, Wright submitted his short play about the writing of the play, "The Problem of the Hero," to Brooks Atkinson, the drama editor of the *New York Times.*

He gave it four acts. The first two are set in Chapel Hill, six weeks apart. The white man and the black man are "laboring night and day through 105-degree heat." Act III is in a New York hotel three months later. Act IV in the same hotel one month later. Stage instructions indicate that the white man speaks "graciously but seriously," "impassioned," "with serious profundity," "his voice charged with faith." The black man speaks "skeptically but humbly," "earnestly" and "quickly and uneasily." The white man is at all times friendly, condescending, and he keeps reassuring black man that they share the "same vision."

In Act IV, the white man tells the black man: "The deletions which you have made helped the play enormously, but the heart has been cut out it. And the additions you have made constitute a message less optimistic than what I had hoped for."

Wright sent a telegram to Paul Green:

Wrote article for NY Times on our collaboration discussing problem of hero in US drama. Gave your views and mine. Tried desperately to be objective and fair. Maybe they wont use it then will publish elsewhere see you over weekend regards = Richard Wright.[40]

Green wired back the same afternoon. His words mirror the way he speaks in Wright's little play:

I am sure your article for the Times is a good one, but wonder whether it is wise to make public at this time any past difference of opinion between the authors. Since the published ending is so nearly in line with the stage version except for a little cutting here and there don't you think we had better stand or fall together on the production? . . . Affectionately, Paul Green.[41]

Whether Wright withdrew the piece, or Green prevailed upon Atkinson (who phoned him wanting to know whether there had been a major disagreement[42]), or Atkinson himself decided against it, "The Problem of the Hero" was never published.[43]

Early in March, Paul Green wired Paul Reynolds: "Since I am unable to be in New York at this time, and in order to help *Native Son* towards as complete presentation as possible, I wish Wright to take over the authority as author for the production of the final scene there, and likewise I will take the authority for the published script of the last scene, the rest of the play standing in joint responsibility as is."[44]

Green arrived in New York on Friday, March 7, after finishing his teaching for the week. He met with Wright and Paul Reynolds and signed the

Harper & Brothers contract. Then he made his way through heavy snow to the theatre. "Rehearsal continued for hours with Welles working terrifical-ly and somewhat playboyishly," he noted in his diary. "Air full of flashlight bulbs." He was interested in Welles's "intense close-up method." The next morning, Green handed in to Harpers' the complete proof of *Native Son,* with his final scene. Back in North Carolina on Monday he wrote to Reynolds: "After considering the method—a kind of fierce close-up intensity—which Welles is using in producing the show, I came to the conclusion that the script had best adhere somewhat to that, since the matter of a well-rounded, well-constructed play was already through the window. So I limped the end-ing across the goal line as best I could."[45]

Green had not yet seen the new ending to the stage play. He came back to New York to see the previews, planning to stay for the premiere. He sat in on a dress rehearsal. Houseman, with ill-concealed relish, recalls his reaction:

> He appeared in the theatre one evening, sat in silence and left without a word after the last scene. The next day, the day of our first preview, we held a meeting: Green, Wright, his agent, Welles and myself. Green insisted that we reinstate his version—particularly the final scene. I told him it was much too late for that and, besides, we had no intention of being parties to the distortion of a work we admired. Richard sat silent beside his agent, who informed us that Green's version (credited to Paul Green and Richard Wright) was already in his publisher's hands. I suggested he get it back and change it to conform to the acting version. Green was furious. When Orson began to howl at him, he got up and left and we never saw him again. (Houseman, pp. 233–234)[46]

Green's own story is more or less consistent with Houseman's:

> I finally gave up. Wright sided with Welles again. My contract would have protected me; I didn't have to yield, but I said, Richard, it's your book, and if you want to end it pathetic, all right. Orson spoke up. He said: 'Jesus, here I am beset by General Sherman from the North and they're driving up from the South. How can I do anything?' He had these figures of speech. And so I said, 'Well, all right.' And so I walked out. I said, 'It's yours. Go ahead.' So on opening night I didn't go. I just thought I'd let it be Richard's show. (Hall interview)

There were last minute problems. The technicians were not able to execute the scene changes fast enough to satisfy Welles. Opening night was
postponed twice, from March 17 to March 24. The troupe was beginning to
call the play "Native Grandson."

On opening night, the theatre was full. Middle-class Harlem residents
sat beside communists who sat beside Park Avenue glitterati. Orson Welles
was in the audience, with his glamorous actress girlfriend, Dolores Del Rio.
After every scene, there was vigorous applause. At the end there were cheers
and shouts and fifteen curtain calls. Finally, Richard Wright made an appearance and a short curtain speech.

Brooks Atkinson, in the *New York Times* called it "the biggest American
drama of the season."[47] This was "theatre that tingles with life." According to
the *New York World-Telegram:* "It proves . . . that Orson Welles, whether you
like to admit it or not, is no boy wonder but actually the greatest theatrical
director of the modern stage."[48] Canada Lee was unanimously hailed as a
brilliant new discovery. Eslanda Robeson said that even her husband, Paul
Robeson, could not have performed better than Lee did.[49] Several reviewers
billed *Native Son* the season's best play. There were murmurs about the Pulitzer prize for drama.

Paul Green was not overjoyed by the play's success. "Native Son, bastard
and mutilated as it is, doing well with the public," he wrote in his diary. "Can't
get much pleasure out of seeing it succeed since one edge of its truth has been
chiseled and blunted off."[50] But he was semi-gracious in reply to Paul Reynolds' congratulations: "I feel that in a great many places, Welles saw further
into the possibilities of the script than the authors did. The ending is, I think,
still weak, whereas it could have almost lifted the audience out its seat. Still, I
think we are all lucky—and we owe a lot to Welles."[51]

Aswell, at Harper & Brothers, had a nightmarish time with the last-
minute changes Paul Green made to the galleys. Nevertheless he managed
to rush the production through, so that the book came out a few days after
the premiere. When Orson Welles set eyes on the book, he bellowed that he
wanted his name and that of Mercury Theatre taken off the Jacket immediately. Paul Reynolds had some delicate negotiating to perform with Aswell.

For weeks *Native Son* was the talk of the town. During March and
April, box office sales' were less lively than Mercury Theater had hoped, but
still good—around $14,500 a week. Welles told the cast he was sure the play
would run for three years, and maybe for five. He had to return to Hollywood,
and was tied up with other commitments for at least a year, but he talked of
producing *Native Son* with RKO, filming it in Mexico. (It would be impossible to work with an interracial cast in Hollywood.) Fox and Metro also
expressed interest in the movie rights. The play's financial backers agreed the
picture rights should fetch $100,000.

Then, suddenly, after the initial clamor and controversy, interest dropped. The high-cost production depended on substantial box-office takings. The tickets were expensive; audiences dropped; profits dropped. By early June the weekly gross had slipped to $8,500. Only one definite bid came in for the picture rights: $25,000, and an all-white cast. Wright refused.

By early May, in order to keep the play going, the managers asked the cast to accept a reduction in salaries. Houseman and Welles agreed to work without pay for several weeks. Wright and Green took a 40% cut in their royalties. By late June, however, Welles and Houseman decided to close the season. The play had run for fifteen weeks—115 performances. It was a highly respectable tally, but the play nevertheless had a loss of some $36,000.

Native Son resumed in late summer, in a more economical version directed by Jack Berry. The set was far more modest, and the ticket prices were lower. Some of the actors—like Anne Burr—were not able to continue, and on the whole the acting on tour was less strong than in the New York version, but Canada Lee, all agreed, acted better than ever.

That summer, Houseman was back on the West Coast when a grateful note arrived from Richard Wright. "If it had not been for your willingness to give so generously of your time, I doubt gravely if *Native Son* would have ever seen the boards of Broadway," Wright told him. "It was a little shameful and ridiculous that you could not have gotten public credit for that help, but that would have meant dragging into the open those all-too-touchy relations between Paul Green and me, and I was seeking, above all, to keep any word of dissension out of the public press."[52] This, of course, was not entirely true. It was Paul Green, in the end, who had been so anxious to keep the dissension out of the press.

In April 1941 the New York Drama Critics Circle Award went to Lillian Hellman's *Watch on the Rhine,* a play about an American combating Nazism.[53] In May, Robert Sherwood won the Pulitzer Drama Prize a third time for his play *There Shall Be No Night,* about the Russian attack on Finland. The *New Masses* was disgusted by the bias of a committee that awarded the prize to this "war-mongering attack on the Soviet Union."[54]

A year later, when the play, back in New York, was once again in financial doldrums, Paul Green told Paul Reynolds: "Well, the chickens come home to roost crippled or not. The murder should have been played as Bigger's nightmare remembrance—as Wright and I first conceived it, and the final scene should have shown Bigger Thomas becoming more of a man. But it's all past now."[55]

Paul Green liked to have the last word. So did John Houseman. And both regularly spoke on behalf of Wright. The tragedy is that it was Bigger Thomas they were wrangling about. It was the man in the middle who should have had the last word.

Notes

1. Paul Green Papers, Southern Historical Collection, Perkins Library, University of North Carolina at Chapel Hill.

2. Richard Wright to John Houseman and Orson Welles, May 19, 1940. Orson Welles Papers, Lilly Library, Indiana University.

3. John Houseman to Richard Wright, May 25, 1940, Welles Papers.

4. Richard Wright to Paul Green, May 22, 1940, Green Papers.

5. Paul Green to Harper & Brothers, May 6, 1940, Green Papers.

6. Paul Reynolds relayed to Wright the doubts that Houseman told him over the phone. Paul Reynolds to Richard Wright, June 6, 1940, Richard Wright Papers, Beinecke Library, Yale University.

7. Richard Wright to John Houseman and Orson Welles, May 19, 1940, Welles Papers.

8. The contract was formally signed on July 22, 1940, but the terms would have been decided before the two scriptwriters began work.

9. John Houseman, *Unfinished Business, A Memoir* (London: Chatto & Windus, 1986), p. 4.

10. Jennie T. Hall interview with Paul Green, 1970. (I have slightly changed the punctuation of Hall's transcription from tape.) The interview is included as an appendix to her MA thesis from the North Carolina State University at Raleigh: "A Change in Philosophy—Richard Wright's *Native Son* to Paul Green and Richard Wright, Native Son, A Play in Ten Scenes, 1970."

11. Paul Green diary, August 12, 1940. (A retrospective entry.) Green Papers.

12. These observations are based on five photographs taken by the Raleigh *News & Observer,* held in the North Carolina Division of Archives and History.

13. National Public Radio interview with Paul Green, April 30, 1975 (interviewer unidentified), Green Papers.

14. Paul Green to Doris Abramson, September 24, 1965, Green Papers.

15. Unidentified interview with Mr. Bower, 1941, in *Conversations with Richard Wright,* Keneth Kinnamon and Michel Fabre (Jackson: University Press of Mississippi, 1993), pp. 40–42.

16. Interview with Paul Green in *The Rebel* (East Carolina College), 3 (Winter 1960), 4, Green Papers.

17. Paul Green, "Pleasure and Pain in Art," essay, Green Papers.

18. Paul Green quotes Jefferson in "Of Heroes and the Making of Nations," essay, Green Papers.

19. Paul Green, "What I Believe," April 21, 1947, Green Papers.

20. Laurence G. Avery, ed., *A Southern Life. Letters of Paul Green, 1916–1981* (Chapel Hill: University of North Carolina Press, 1994), p. 248.

21. Paul Green to Richard Wright, February 7, 1941, Wright Papers.

22. Ouida Campbell, "Bigger is Reborn," *Carolina Magazine,* October 1940, pp. 21–23.

23. Phone interview with Ouida Campbell Taylor, Colorado, September 19, 1998.

24. Richard Wright, "The Problem of the Hero," Richard Wright Papers, box 83, folder 946, Yale University.

25. John Ehle, "Reflections on Paul Green," in *Paul Green's Celebration of Man* (North Carolina: Human Technology Interface, 1994), Green Papers.

26. Richard Wright to Paul Green, October 3, 1940, Wright Papers.

27. John Houseman to Paul Green, December 24, 1940, Green Papers.

28. Paul Reynolds to Richard Wright, December 4, 1940, Wright Papers.

29. Richard Wright to Paul Green, February 3, 1941, Green Papers.

30. Richard Wright to Paul Green, February 12, 1941, Green Papers.

31. The entry is retrospective, written in February 1941.

32. Aswell to L. Arnold Weissberger, March 31, 1941, Harper Papers, Princeton University.

33. See Jean Rosenthal, "Native Son—Backstage," *Theatre Arts*, June 1941, pp. 467–470.

34. Harry Birdoff to Horace Cayton, May 9, 1960, Cayton Papers, Carter Woodson Library, Chicago.

35. *New York Herald Tribune,* March 30, 1941.

36. Robert Francis, *Brooklyn Daily Eagle,* June 8, 1941.

37. John Houseman, "*Native Son* on Stage," in *Richard Wright: Impressions and Perspectives,* ed. David Ray and Robert M. Farnsworth (Ann Arbor: University of Michigan Press, 1973), p. 97.

38. "Theatrical Folk Seem Queer to Author of Native Son," *New York World-Telegram,* March 22, 1941.

39. "Nothing Too Big for 'Bigger,'" *Negro Digest,* February 1945, pp. 77–80.

40. Western Union Telegram, March 12, 1941, Green Papers.

41. Paul Green to Richard Wright, March 12, 1941.

42. Paul Green mentions this phone call in several interviews.

43. It was aired on radio, WNYC, April 8, 1941. I owe this detail to Curtis R. Scott in "The Dramatization of *Native Son,"* *Journal of American Drama and Theatre,* 4 (Fall 1992).

44. Paul Green to Paul Reynolds, March 3, 1941, Green Papers.

45. Paul Green to Paul Reynolds, March 10, 1941, Green Papers.

46. Houseman uses his memoirs to demolish Paul Green, Orson Welles, and various others—in the most urbane possible manner.

47. Brooks Atkinson, *New York Times,* March 25, 1941.

48. Sidney B. Whipple, *New York World-Telegram,* March 25, 1941.

49. *New York Amsterdam-Star News,* March 22, 1941.

50. Entry marked "March 13 to April 16."

51. Paul Green to Paul Reynolds, April 4, 1941, Wright Papers.

52. Quoted by John Houseman in "*Native Son* On Stage," p. 100.

53. *Native Son* was the judges' third choice.

54. "The Pulitzer Prizes," *New Masses,* May 13, 1941, p. 21.

55. Paul Green to Paul Reynolds, December 13, 1942, Green Papers.

MARK DECKER

"A Lot Depends on What Judge We Have": Native Son *and the Legal Means for Social Justice*

In the final section of *Native Son*, Richard Wright introduces one of the more misunderstood supporting characters in American fiction. Lawyer Boris Max does an admirable job defending a foredoomed Bigger Thomas, arguing vigorously in an attempt to help his extremely unpopular client escape the electric chair. Yet beginning with the initial reviews, critics have rarely seen Max in an unreservedly positive light. An extensive but not exhaustive review of *Native Son*'s criticism reveals five common ways of reading Max: as a valuable social commentator,[1] as a naive white man who thinks he is a valuable social commentator,[2] as a sort of ideologue/therapist who is valuable because he triggers cognitive growth in Bigger,[3] as an ineffectual lawyer,[4] or as a competent lawyer engaged in a quixotic battle against a legal system predisposed to defeat him.[5] So while Max is clearly not universally reviled, a sizeable number of critics read him negatively. Furthermore, the friendliest assessments damn him with faint praise to the extent that they do not see him engaged in a project that could have immediate value. Instead, the more appreciative readings argue that Max makes an important statement while sacrificing more pragmatic legal concerns.

The inability of these assessments of Max's character and his professional skills to detect a pragmatic strategy that could see practical results likely depends on a widely held assumption that Max is a Communist, or at least

McNeese Review, Volume 41 (2003): pp. 52–75. Copyright © 2003 McNeese Review.

175

a thoroughly indoctrinated fellow traveler, and therefore places a commitment to Communist ideology above his professional responsibilities. And if Max were a Communist, the critical assumptions described above would be convincing. After all, why would Richard Wright portray a Communist as a pragmatic man with a workable plan? Those familiar with the complete text of Wright's 1944 biography *Black Boy* know that the author portrayed the Chicago Communist party as out of touch with the lives of the masses. In *Black Boy*, Wright also criticizes the communists for hating "intellectuals or anyone who tried to think for himself" and for being too ideologically rigid to provide any real leadership for the left.[6] Indeed, Wright argues that his time in the Communist party left him so frustrated that he could not write stories in which he could assign "a role of honor and glory to the Communist party."[7] Under these circumstances, portraying Max as an ultimately misled idealist who may or may not be a competent professional and who may or may not have something important to say would represent genuine even-handedness on Wright's part.

Yet a closer examination of Max within his historical context—both political and legal—suggests that the lawyer and his closing arguments should not be tagged with the still-pejorative label of Communist and dismissed, however gently and admiringly. Instead, a careful reading of Wright's text suggests that we should view Max as a skilled lawyer and as a representative of an important movement in progressive legal circles that embraced all lawyers and legal theorists working for social change. But in order to provide a clear evaluation of just what a character like Max is doing in a novel written by a committed leftist who nevertheless had many run-ins with the Communist party, this essay will examine two important issues that have been overlooked by most critical considerations of Max. First, it will investigate the realities of the legal left in the late 1930s. Then it will outline the progressive theory of jurisprudence Max employs to defend his client. This discussion will reveal that Max is best read as part of a larger call to use the law to bring about social justice that Wright participated in. After all, the author condemned the party, not its causes, and in *Black Boy* he often portrayed himself offering to mediate between Communist and non-Communist groups.[8] It should not surprise us, then, that Wright uses a figure with ties to the Party to showcase a pragmatic legal strategy that has the possibility of bringing a measure of social justice to all African Americans.

Wright, however, does not present Max and his pragmatic jurisprudence as a panacea. The author found the doctrinaire adherence of the Chicago communists to the party line an obstacle to improving the lives of actual human beings, and would not write a novel that advanced a theoretical construct without articulating the dangers of placing theoretical considerations over human realities. Consequently, this essay will also consider both

Bigger's reaction to Max's closing statement and Max's inability to truly connect with Bigger at novel's end, an important passage easily read as an implied critique of Max's jurisprudence. Indeed, this passage has probably led to the misunderstandings cataloged above, but when read in the context of the 1930s' legal left represents a healthy qualification, and not a condemnation, of Max's approach.

Let us first briefly address the issue of Max's supposed membership in the Communist Party. Others have already demonstrated that there is no clear textual evidence that the lawyer is a member of the Communist Party.[9] Of course, confusion about Max's politics is understandable since he is involved with a Party-sponsored group. When Max introduces himself to Bigger as "from the labor defenders,"[10] he refers to the Communist-sponsored International Labor Defense or ILD. But as we will see below, the ILD was a very pragmatic organization that did not pay attention to personal ideology when it hired legal talent. Additionally, we should keep in mind that, while there were members of the party who were lawyers and though the party hired non-Communist lawyers to defend its interests, in theoretical terms there is no Marxist jurisprudence. Obviously, there are judicial systems in Communist countries, but when *Native Son* was written American communists were still dreaming of the end of the bourgeois legal system.[11] When they went to court, however, the Communists were defended by both Communists-who-happened-to-be-lawyers and lawyers employed by Communists, all of whom used a widely accepted jurisprudence that allowed them to fight for the rights of workers, minorities, and other oppressed groups. But if Max is not himself a Communist, we nevertheless cannot fully understand Max's involvement with Bigger's case unless we investigate the ILD's place within the progressive legal movement of the late 1930s.

The brainchild of radical labor activists William "Big Bill" Haywood and James P. Cannon, the ILD was organized on June 28, 1925, in Chicago's Ashland Auditorium. Never envisioned as a Communist lawyers association, the ILD instead sought to aid people they saw as victims of the class war and members of oppressed minorities who had been imprisoned. The labor defenders also worked to obtain legal counsel for those prisoners, but did not base their aid on party membership. Instead the ILD provided mass protest and legal help, according to Charles Martin, a historian of the organization's relationships with African Americans, regardless of its recipient's "color, creed, nationality or political belief." Furthermore, while the Communists sponsored the ILD, its membership did not exclusively consist of Party members, and non-Communists always served on the ILD's executive committee.[12]

Additionally, the ILD did not serve as an employment bureau for Party members in the legal profession. In fact, most of the lawyers the ILD retained for publicly visible African-American clients were not Communists. When the ILD undertook the defense of the Scottsboro boys, they engaged George W. Chamlee and later Samuel Leibowitz, both not Communists. To assist Angelo Herndon, a young black Communist organizer charged with violating Georgia's anti-insurrection laws, the ILD first hired local lawyers Benjamin J. Davis, Jr., and John H. Geer not because of their political ideology but because Davis and Geer were black. After these lawyers were unable to win Herndon's freedom, the ILD assembled the high-powered, non-Communist team of Whitney North Seymour and Columbia Law School professors Walter Gellhorn and Herbert Wechsler to successfully defend the young organizer. And to defend Jess Hollins from charges of raping a white woman in Oklahoma, the ILD retained prominent local attorney J. J. Carney, also not a Communist. Consequently, association with, or employment by, the ILD did not automatically signal Party membership, but it did demonstrate a commitment to achieving social justice through legal means and probably indicated that the lawyer involved was one of the more progressive members of the bar.

Despite its pledge to ignore political ideology when defending clients of broad interest to those working for social change, the ILD often made enemies among other progressive and radical organizations during its first decade of existence. When the organization attempted to help blacks charged with crimes, it often ran afoul of the NAACP, which, according to Martin, frequently charged that the ILD's politics led to the "conviction of innocent victims."[13] Thus, the ILD engaged in a "vicious fight" with the NAACP for control of the Scottsboro case.[14] And after the ILD intervened in Jess Hollins' rape case, local NAACP leader Roscoe Dunjee became so angered by the labor defenders' tactics that he had the defendant sign "a declaration that repudiated the ILD and placed his case entirely in the NAACP's hands."[15] In part because of the damage that conflict with the NAACP and other organizations did to its cause, the ILD began to moderate its position in 1937. From this time, Martin notes, the labor defenders "accepted other organizations as reliable allies" and worked with groups like the NAACP when defending non-Party members whose ethnicity, race, or other affiliations would attract the attention of other radical or progressive groups.[16]

And finally, when discussing the ILD in an attempt to clarify the use of jurisprudence in *Native Son*, we should examine Richard Wright's personal experience with the labor defenders. According to biographers Addison Gayle and Michel Fabre, a run-in with South Side ILD representative, Communist party member, and attorney Oliver Law greatly influenced the author's decision to intellectually distance himself from the Communist

Party. In 1932, Law, described by Gayle as "abrasive and dictatorial"[17] and by Fabre as a "narrow-minded local official,"[18] disrupted an interview between Wright and black Communist activist David Pointdexter. Law instructed Pointdexter not to speak with Wright and was so abusive to the novelist that Wright abandoned plans for a pro-Communist book tentatively entitled *Heroes Red and Black*. Fabre points to this event as the beginning of Wright's long exodus from the Communist Party, with the author choosing to maintain his association with the Party because of its ability to work for social change but striving to think independently.[19]

When writing *Native Son* six years later, then, which face of the ILD would the author wish to portray? The second section of *Black Boy* suggests that Wright was still committed to much of the social change the labor defenders were promoting. If the ILD had by this time moderated its stance on working in coalition with groups like the NAACP—a strategy much like those the author urged when a party member—why would Wright recreate the same petty ideologue who silenced him and who represented everything that was wrong with the Party? Why would he hide the good that the party and other left organizations were trying to accomplish? Instead, wouldn't Wright invoke one of the dedicated and kindhearted progressive lawyers who shared the author's far-reaching desire for social reform and relative independence from the Party? Textual evidence that Max is not a narrow ideologue like Oliver Law comes at the very end of *Native Son*. While Law limited Wright's ability to participate in a critical examination of the world by dismissing him as an untrustworthy intellectual, Max liberates Bigger's ability to think critically about his life by asking "questions nobody ever asked" before and treating him "like a man."[20] Max does not represent the narrow Party member/ILD official who would have been part of the problem in Scottsboro and Oklahoma. Instead, he is the type of Lawyer the ILD would have engaged after it softened its tactics in 1937 and became an organization generally sympathetic to all progressive causes, an organization that employed talented, progressive lawyers to defend clients who would otherwise be at the mercy of a prejudiced and economically unjust society.

Yet while the above discussion of the ILD has helped us imagine a different relationship between Max and the labor defenders than that of ideological lackey to Communist overlords, it has not fully delineated the likely contours of the attorney's professional allegiances. To do this, it will be helpful to further examine progressive law in the late 1930s. In addition to the ILD, as the above discussion suggests, there were groups like the NAACP, which in the course of their activities routinely hired attorneys to litigate cases and defend clients. There were also groups like the ACLU, which were primarily involved in first-amendment issues. Yet at the beginning of the 1930s there was no professional association similar to the mainstream American Bar Association for liberal, radical, and progressive lawyers, let alone representatives of groups who hired those leftist lawyers.

To remedy this lack, in 1932 Maurice Sugar, a Marxist labor lawyer from Detroit, formulated a plan for such an association, envisioning it as a means both to advance progressive causes and to help its members advance professionally. Sugar promoted his idea in progressive circles over the next few years, and in February of 1937 several associates of Sugar founded the National Lawyers Guild or NLG. The Guild then grew rapidly, reaching a membership of 5,000 by the end of 1937. According to Victor Rabinowitz, NLG president in the late 1960s, those who founded the National Lawyers Guild came from two camps: established liberals and a "militant segment of the bar, mostly young and sometimes radical."[21] Not all of the founding members of the NLG, then, would have been comfortable with the Communist Party, even though they may have occasionally fought on the same side. Indeed, Rabinowitz reminds us that during the late 1930s the Guild engaged in bitter debates over Communism because, as Guild President Thomas Emerson reminisced in 1955, many of the issues the Guild dealt with in the 1930s "involved Communist Party problems or issues in which the Communist Party was interested."[22] Yet we should not downplay the radical/progressive wing of the Guild. Key ILD lawyer Joe Brodsky and Communist Party member Mortimer Riemer were two of the founding members of the NLG, and Riemer was the Guild's first Executive Secretary. And while there was no official NAACP representation at the Guild's founding, many of the NLG's initial members had already built impressive civil-rights credentials by attacking the Ku Klux Klan and fighting in the courts for racial equality and for an end to lynching.

If, keeping the lack of textual evidence in mind, we were to try to place Max in a radical or progressive organization, he seems a much likelier candidate for membership in the NLG than the Communist Party. Max's commitment to defending workers and minorities and his lack of overt and dogmatic support for the Party makes him much more like Maurice Sugar than Oliver Law. So while we cannot definitely assert membership, we can at least envision him as someone the Chicago chapter of the Guild would have recruited heavily. Yet after establishing where Max's affinities would probably lie, we still need to explore the labor lawyer's assumptions about the uses of the law to really see how he exemplifies progressive legal action. To do this, we must look at a movement in legal theory that was first known as Sociological Jurisprudence and then Legal Realism.

Before we discuss this progressive approach to the law, however, we should note that Legal Realism, as it became known in the 1930s, was popular in both NLG and Communist circles. According to NLG historians Ann Fagin Ginger and Eugene Tobin, many of the original members of the Guild were young lawyers who had recently "studied law under the direction" of the legal scholars involved in the movement then known as Legal Realism. When Maurice Sugar drafted the first proposal for what would become the NLG, he included a call to make prominent Legal Realists including Roscoe Pound and Frank Llewellyn active or honorary members of the Guild.[23] Additionally, several parallels exist between the Marxist critique of bourgeois conceptions of law and the Legal Realist's conception of law as a social construct judges constantly remade.[24] Legal Realism thus offered Communists a socially accepted praxis that loosely conformed to their own ideological critique of capitalist society. But in order to see just how this theory of jurisprudence would benefit progressive legal efforts—and would be appropriate to use in crafting Bigger Thomas' defense—we need to review the history and theoretical assumptions of Legal Realism.

Between the end of the nineteenth century and the middle of the twentieth, American legal philosophy underwent a "monumental change," primarily because of the ideas of United States Supreme Court Justice Oliver Wendell Holmes and Harvard Law School Dean Roscoe Pound. Writing in the last decades of the nineteenth century, Holmes attacked the then-prevalent formalism of American jurisprudence. He argued in works like *The Common Law*, "The Path of the Law," and "The Theory of Legal Interpretation" that the law was not some pseudoplatonic ideal but was instead a social construct. Holmes believed that instead of finding and then applying the eternal truths that the law consisted of, judges made the law through their decisions.[25] In *The Common Law*, for example, Holmes argues that in substance "the growth of the law is legislative. And this in a deeper sense than that what the courts declare to have always been the law is in fact new. It is legislative in its grounds."[26] Consequently, Holmes urged the legal profession to realize the legislative function of the courts and use them as an arena for social change. These views also led Holmes to urge legal educators to prepare students for careers as legislators and social engineers as well as jurists, to help them become social scientists with backgrounds in economics and statistics who could comprehend the interpenetration of law and society.[27]

Holmes's contentions were largely seconded in the works of Roscoe Pound, who began writing about ten years after the Justice put forth his ideas. Pound argued that "the task of a judge is to make a principle living" rather than apply dead principles to living situations.[28] Consequently, Pound believed, as did Holmes, that jurisprudence involved actively seeking to change the laws through ameliorative judicial legislation. According to Pound, the duty of a jurist included "the adjustment of principles and doctrines to the human conditions they are to govern rather than to assumed first principles." This meant that jurists should put "the human factor in the central place."[29]

Because of his position as the Dean of Harvard Law School, and because of his more activist stance, Pound obtained broad acceptance for a legal pedagogy and praxis that became widely known as Sociological Jurisprudence. Furthermore, Pound's conception of the role of the social sciences in legal education and legal practice went far beyond the acquaintance with economics that the more conservative Holmes had urged. In his essay "The Need for a Sociological Jurisprudence" Pound argued that

> the modern teacher of law should be a student of sociology, of economics, and politics as well. He should know not only what courts decide and the principles by which they decide, but quite as much the circumstances and conditions, social and economic, to which these principles are to be applied.[30]

For Pound, then, because jurists made law as they made their decisions, law represented a site for socially ameliorative intervention. Furthermore, that intervention should be carefully guided by a consideration of the social structure itself and by what social thinkers had to say about that social structure. We should emphasize here that the socioeconomic analysis required by Pound did not rely on the use of specifically Marxist theoretical assumptions, nor did it dismiss the use of critiques of capitalism. Therefore, this progressive legal praxis was open to a relatively wide variety of ideological positions.

Pound's Sociological Jurisprudence movement, which was at its strongest during the first two decades of the twentieth century, was continued in modified form by a group of jurists and academics led by Jerome Frank and Karl Llewellyn, who styled themselves as the Legal Realists. Pound's assumptions also influenced prominent jurists, like Holmes' successor on the Supreme Court, Benjamin Nathan Cardozo, although these jurists distanced themselves from Legal Realism.[31] We should note here that there are few substantive differences between the theoretical claims of Legal Realism and Sociological Jurisprudence. Like Pound and his school, the Legal Realists believed that sociological knowledge needed to inform judicial decision making. Indeed, Legal Realism borrowed so much from Sociological Jurisprudence that it may in fact represent a logical extension of the earlier movement.[32]

Though prominent in the 1920s and 1930s, after 1940, Legal Realism had a host of critics. These detractors called the philosophy dangerous and even totalitarian because it allegedly allowed social scientists and social science too much influence. Consequently, this theoretical movement largely disappeared in the early 1940s.[33] Working in 1938 and 1939, then, Richard Wright wrote *Native Son* at the high water mark of the Sociological Jurisprudence and/or Legal Realism movement, a time when the effort had become so powerful that it was beginning to generate a tremendous backlash.

Consequently, if the novelist had had access to the scholarly debate surrounding Legal Realism, he would have undoubtedly incorporated the social praxis advocated by the Legal Realists into a novel about the relationship between law, society, and crime.[34]

Of course, Wright left us no smoking gun, no letter discussing Pound's or Holmes's ideas. The author did, however, read extensively in the type of sociology that Pound or Holmes would have recommended to any young law student. And this reading was profoundly influential on the work of the young author. As Wright explains in *Black Boy*, reading canonical literary works began his development as a writer, but

> the most important discoveries came when I veered from fiction proper into the field of psychology and sociology. I ran through volumes that bore upon the causes of my conduct and the conduct of my family. I studied tables of figures relating population density to insanity, relating housing to disease, relating school and recreational opportunities to crime, relating various forms of neurotic behavior to environment, relating racial insecurities to the conflicts between blacks and whites. . . . [35]

This understanding of social forces would almost necessarily lead Wright to see a crime like Bigger Thomas's as socially constructed. Thus, it should not be hard to imagine that the author would pose a sociological solution to this social problem.

Wright was able to undertake this sociological self-education largely because he associated with people who would have been very aware of Sociological Jurisprudence. While the author worked on *Native Son* he received extensive tutorials in sociology and social theory from University of Chicago Sociology professor Louis Wirth and his African-American research assistant Horace Cayton.[36] In turn, Wright made a conscious attempt to incorporate that social theory into his novel: an attempt that was, at least according to one of his mentors, successful. Cayton wrote in a review of Wright's *12 Million Black Voices* that "a large research project which was carried on in Chicago's Black Belt for a period of four years substantiated the entire thesis of *Native Son*." Cayton also asserted that Wright's fictionalization performed a much-needed popularization of the concepts he and Wirth investigated. According to Cayton, his team "produced the material" and understood "the theory," but was indebted to Wright because they "could not state it in the power or form it needed."[37]

Wright's mentors, then, trained him well and helped him to translate their research into best-selling fiction. It would not be hard to imagine that they would have also urged an application of this sociology to jurisprudence.

Yet while Wirth, by this time a prominent sociologist, did not publish any material on Sociological Jurisprudence or Legal Realism per se, his work and his life both suggest an awareness that the legal profession was willing to listen to social scientists. Wirth himself practiced a form of Sociological Jurisprudence, testifying in 1948 before the United States Supreme Court in *Shelly v Kraemer*, a case involving restrictive housing covenants designed to block integration. He also testified in a Chicago courtroom in the 1951 urban renewal case *Land Clearance Commission of Chicago v Inez White et al.* In each case, Wirth testified as an expert in Urban Sociology, and in each case he was able to sway the court.

Wirth also dedicated his career to arguing for an activist Sociology that would address the problems of urban America. In his influential essay "Urbanism as a Way of Life," considered by many Urban Sociologists as the seminal work of their discipline and a favorite of Wright himself, Wirth enumerates many of the ills of urban life including segregation, "predatory" pecuniary relationships, and the danger of social disorder.[38] He then calls his fellow sociologist to action, noting that while "the sociologist cannot solve any of these practical problems—at least not by himself—he may, if he discovers his proper function, have an important contribution to make to their comprehension and solution."[39] We can easily infer from this passage that Wirth actively sought out ways to use his knowledge to better society. A sociologist of his stature would certainly know that Supreme Court Justices and prominent legal educators like the dean of Harvard Law School advocated the use of sociological data to decide individual cases and thus legislate from the bench. Consequently, it should not be too hard to imagine that he shared this knowledge with Richard Wright and that Wright, in turn, would somehow employ the theoretical approach of Sociological Jurisprudence in constructing *Native Son*.

Yet while Wright's relationship with Wirth strongly suggests that the author would have become familiar with Legal Realism, concrete proof of any familiarity with this theory would have to be found within *Native Son* itself. Cayton's assessment of the novel as the best possible fictive rendering of sociological data explains the work's first and second sections, Fear and Flight. The third section, Fate, however, is set largely in a courtroom and is dominated by Max's arguments. Structurally, then, Wright creates a strong set-up for his pragmatic and progressive counsel: hundreds of pages of sociological data followed by legal arguments that interpret that data in a way designed to encourage a judge to legislate from the bench and ameliorate the racism that data reveals. Wright also gives us a textual clue that reflects a more historical allusion. Just as for Holmes and Pound, Max's opponent is a legal formalist. In attacking Max's plea for mitigation, State's Attorney Buckley does label Max's summation "silly, alien, communistic, and dangerous."[40] But he does not limit himself to these dismissive comments. Instead, he also employs a formalist criticism of Max's use of Sociological Jurisprudence: "I say the law is holy because it makes us human. And woe to the men—and the civilization of those men!—who, in misguided sympathy or fear, weaken the stout structure of the law which insures the harmonious working of our lives on this earth."[41] Buckley thus presents law as a divinely created, and therefore preexisting, "stout structure" that creates a harmonious life. This conception of the law clearly represents how a formalist would respond to Max's contentions that the law was socially constructed, changeable, and designed to adjust itself to social conditions.

But we should not rely on Buckley to determine if Max is a Legal Realist. Instead, we must determine if Max attempts to create an atmosphere in which an application of Sociological Jurisprudence would work, something best done by a comparison of Max's methods with those prescribed by Pound. Then, we must decide if Max's arguments are in line with the key concepts of Legal Realism in the late 1930s. We will thus examine the texts of both *Native Son* and Roscoe Pound's *Social Control Through Law*, the work that perhaps best represents the theoretical contentions of Legal Realism at the time Wright wrote his novel.

When investigating whether the actual trial Wright creates for his readers represents an adequate forum within which to practice Sociological Jurisprudence, we must remember that Holmes was a Supreme Court Justice. Consequently, he did not have to interact with juries and could instead issue an opinion on the entire case, and not merely pass sentence after a jury decided guilt or innocence. Holmes' philosophy and the Sociological Jurisprudence that followed from it thus did not take into account the decisions of juries and assumed, ideally, a judge's—or a group of judges, in the case of a Supreme Court—freedom to act. Furthermore, in a capital case where the jury would decide the defendant's fate, one would have no hope of an activist judge making a ruling with social import. Max's decision to forgo a jury trial, then, offers further evidence that Wright attempts to put the novel's argument in the terms of Sociological Jurisprudence.

Of course, media attention to the case had created a great deal of public hatred for Bigger. Considering the very real possibility of a lynching, Max would naturally face an almost impossible job in impaneling an impartial jury—also a significant problem for the ILD lawyers who defended the Scottsboro boys, Jess Hollins, and others. Avoiding a jury trial could simply represent the only logical move given the situation. Yet when Max explains in his summation to the judge why he rejected a jury trial, his words suggest deeper motivations than this. Though Max does admit that a trial by jury would be less honest than an "outright lynching" under the circumstances, he also makes this curious explanation:

I could not have placed at the disposal of a jury the evidence, so general and yet so confoundingly specific, so impalpable and yet so disastrous in its terrible consequences—consequences which have affected my client and account for his being here today before the bar of judgment with his life at stake—I could not have done this and have been honest with myself or with this boy.[42]

Max's implications about the evidence he plans to bring forward only partially address the popular hatred of Bigger, and seem to suggest that a jury would not have been able to process the evidence because of a lack of intellectual perspective. Indeed, convincing a judge who sits in a courthouse surrounded by National Guardsmen holding back a lynch mob to forgo a jury trial would merely require a reference to the situation. Max's ruminations about a jury's inability to grasp the social import of his testimony make sense only if he were also offering the judge an opportunity to legislate from the bench.

Max intends, then, to present a summation designed to mitigate the penalty for Bigger's crimes based on the social forces that in part led him to murder. This will take place in a courtroom where an activist Judge could then rule in a way that would have significant social consequences. Yet State's Attorney Buckley seems deliberately to mistake Max's request as an insanity plea, suggesting that the prosecutor realizes what Max is up to and tries to make sure that any judgments will focus solely on Bigger and not on larger social forces. Buckley loudly insists that Bigger "be tried by jury, if the defense continues to say that he is insane" and then offers to give evidence and testimony showing Bigger "is sane and responsible." Max, however, carefully and successfully argues that Bigger is not insane.[43] By doing this, he not only avoids a dangerous jury trial and preserves the judge's ability to make a meaningful decision, but also escapes moving the grounds for mitigation away from the sociological and into the psychological. After all, if the discussion focused on whether or not Bigger was insane, and therefore different from the "normal" people who make up sane society, Max could not represent Bigger as a "tiny social symbol" that could shed light on "our whole sick social organism."[44] Thus, partially by necessities of plot and partially by design, Wright creates a situation that would allow a judge who accepted the grounds of Sociological Jurisprudence to use the case to address larger social ills. When Max attempts to reassure Bigger by telling him that "a lot depends on what judge we have," then, he is holding out the hope of social justice to his client that Legal Realism is designed to provide.[45]

To determine if the arguments employed in Max's summation fall in line with Sociological Jurisprudence, we will compare his reasoning with Roscoe Pound's *Social Control Through Law*. The work, originally given as a lecture at

Indiana University in 1941, represents the fullest articulation of Sociological Jurisprudence available, since it was the last major work published before the backlash of the mid-1940s. And while it did appear after *Native Son* and consequently could not have had a direct influence on Wright's novel, Pound's lecture nevertheless provides contemporary access to the theories Wright would have dealt with.

Social Control Through Law focuses on explaining the law's task and the means by which the law maintains its power and place in society. For Pound, who sees society as a constantly renegotiatied compromise between the various groups and classes within the social whole—a very unmarxist idea—these two projects are intertwined in an almost tautological way. Because this delicate social balance must be ameliorated slowly and carefully, the task of law entails "finding practical adjustments and reconciling and, if nothing more was possible, practical compromises, of conflicting and overlapping interests."[46] Law can perform this task because it has a great deal of socially granted power, and law keeps this power because it "performs, and performs well," the necessary adjustments and improvements to the social compromise.[47] For Pound, then, the law needs to work actively to improve social equilibrium or it will lose its power and, hence, its ability to provide an ordered society. Max employs this line of reasoning when after delineating how the conflicts between the interests of Black and White America have led Bigger to commit his crimes, he asks the judge

> to recognize the laws and processes flowing from such a condition, understand them, seek to change them. If we do none of these, we should not pretend horror or surprise when thwarted life expresses itself in fear and hate and crime.[48]

Here, Max presents the judge with an instance of social disequilibria leading to a lack of social control—the fear and hate and crime personified in Bigger. Thus, the judge must rule in a way that will ameliorate the situation, recognizing the conflict between Black and White America, and make a decision that will help renegotiate the social compromise in a way that recognizes the plight of Black America.

In *Social Control Through Law* Pound discusses the different social interests and values the law should seek to maintain. Pound describes the "interest in the individual life," the responsibility of society to offer a basic standard of living and a reasonable set of expectations to all of its members. As Pound reasons, there is

> the claim or demand asserted...in civilized society that each individual be secure in his freedom, have secured to him

opportunities, political, social, and economic, and be able to live
at least a reasonably minimum human life in society.[49]

If society cannot offer this, then law must seek ways to adjust the social
compromise.

Max makes a specific application of this argument when he describes the
social conditions obtaining in Chicago's Black Belt. Bigger thus emerges as a
representative of a race that constitutes "a separate nation, stunted, stripped,
and held captive within this nation, devoid of political, social, economic, and
property rights."[50] Consequently, Bigger's position as a member of a group
whose needs are not being met by society mitigates, but does not excuse his
actions. The judge, if accepting of the tenants of Sociological Jurisprudence,
could thus acknowledge these social disequilibria by giving Bigger a life sentence, legislating from the bench through a de facto modification of the definition of capital homicide. This would in turn set a precedent for other judges
to follow when faced with a similar situation.

Pound not only concerns himself with socially necessary minimum conditions, but also argues that it is in society's interest to allow individuals the
opportunity to make meaningful life choices and the freedom from a sort of
situational slavery in which those choices are made for the individual. Pound
calls this "the claim or want or demand of the individual human being to have
something or do something or, it may be, not to be coerced into doing what
he does not want to do."[51] Max also employs this argument. At one of the
points when he asks the judge to spare Bigger's life, he reasons that Bigger's
lack of individual choice placed him within an enclosed social horizon that
offered little hope and thus also led him to commit his crimes. By not taking
Bigger's life, however, the judge could acknowledge that fact in a significant
way since by

> making this concession, we uphold those two fundamental
> concepts of our civilization, those two basic concepts upon which
> we have built the mightiest nation in history—personality and
> security—the conviction that the person is inviolate and that
> which sustains him is equally so.[52]

Within Bigger's narrow social horizon, he could not fully actualize his personality and, thus, could only experience actualization through his crime.
For Max, the murder of Mary "was the first full act of [Bigger's] life; it
was the most meaningful, exciting, and stirring thing that had ever happened to him."[53] A life sentence, then, would acknowledge that African
Americans committed crimes in part because they did not have a right

to personal fulfillment. Once again, Max offers an argument in line with Pound's reasoning.

Max's summation does not focus solely on how society's faulty compromise affects Black America. Instead, it also examines how these same social conditions can adversely affect white America. An imperfect social compromise and its lack of social control, after all, eventually harm all members of society. In *Social Control Through Law*, Pound notes that the "most universal and fundamental" presupposition of the law is that in "civilized society men must be able to assume that others will commit no intentional aggression upon them."[54] To maintain social control, then, jurists must ensure conditions that do not breed aggression.

In *Native Son*, once again, Max employs this argument. He not only reasons that Bigger's social oppression should mitigate his crimes. He also argues that since Bigger's actions are largely socially constructed, someone else will surely repeat them. Whites cannot expect to ensure their own safety by electrocuting Bigger. Recognition of this inequality through a life sentence would thus offer a way to begin to create a generally more peaceful society. As Max observes

> This boy represents but a tiny aspect of a problem whose reality sprawls over a third of this nation. Kill him! Burn the life out of him! And still when the delicate and unconscious machinery of race relations slips, there will be murder again. How can law contradict the lives of millions of people and hope to be administered successfully?[55]

Max's concern here for the proper administration of the law reveals the Legal Realism behind his argument. He in effect tells the judge that the current state of race relations will eventually create conditions in which law cannot provide for social control. The judge should thus begin to take steps to renegotiate the social compromise and preserve the power of law.

We can see, then, that Max's summation follows the important points of *Social Control Through Law*. Sparing Bigger's life is not simply an act of individualized mercy but will benefit society by helping maintain social equilibrium and encouraging white America to provide blacks with the minimum conditions necessary to lead a productive life and perhaps advance. By diffusing social tensions, declining to execute Bigger will maintain safety for all. Clearly, then, Max employs Legal Realism, not merely a theory, but a legal praxis informed by theory, to argue Bigger's case. Max is a competent lawyer who makes the most effective choice he could in the situation he found himself in. Consequently, *Native Son* provides its readers with the legal and pragmatic means for a social justice that would ameliorate the racial injustices that Wright so aptly documents.

Of course, we need to remember that Max fails. The judge does not agree with his arguments, and Bigger is electrocuted. But we must also remember that both historically and theoretically the amelioration of society is not a zero-sum game. Arguments made in civil-rights cases that fail to convince a particular judge often convince more important judges or legislative bodies later on. In the Hollis case, for example, the Oklahoma courts refused to seat any black jurors, something that the ILD and NAACP lawyers attempted to use to their advantage. But while they were unsuccessful and Hollis died in prison, according to Martin, the Hollis case "brought some beneficial changes for Oklahoma blacks in the long run" including allowing blacks to serve on juries and seeing some convictions overturned because of all-white juries.[56]

We should also remember that Max ultimately fails to understand Bigger. Even though the lawyer helped Bigger to feel "like a man" for the first time,[57] *Native Son* ends with a pre-execution jailhouse interview that has led many critics to dismiss Max and his arguments. During his last meeting with Max, Bigger tries to connect on a basic level, as individuals and not as a client and his lawyer, but Max seems unable to reach out to the human being behind the ideal type. This inability is best captured when Max attempts an intimate gesture:

> Max reached over and placed a hand on his shoulder, and Bigger could tell by his touch that Max did not know, had no suspicion of what he wanted, of what he was trying to say. Max was upon another planet, far off in space. . . . And of all the men he had met, surely Max knew what he was trying to say.[58]

This passage and others like it have contributed to Max's bad reputation, and understandably so. Yet Bigger's musings do not critique the theory but the theoretician. In fact, Max's failure stems largely from his inability to act on his theoretical knowledge: because of his dedication to Sociological Jurisprudence, Max really could understand what Bigger is trying to say. But because Max hasn't really looked behind the sociological data that helped him craft his closing arguments, he cannot bring the logic of those arguments into his own life. Wright, then, uses Max's maladroit meeting with Bigger to give a warning that legal praxis, no matter what its potential, is not enough without a respect for the humanity behind the theory. This is no surprise coming from a writer who learned much from Marxism but who was greatly misunderstood by the inhuman ideologues of Chicago's Communist party.

Ultimately, however, Max's failures, both in the courtroom and in Bigger's cell, do not undercut Wright's argument for the validity of Sociological Jurisprudence as a legal praxis and as an explanatory tool. Wright gives us a fictive presentation of a strategy that worked in real courtrooms along with the fictive presentation of the sociological reality of Chicago's South Side noted by Cayton. Indeed, even Bigger himself validates the accuracy of Max's observations and the case he builds on them. While Bigger had not fully understood Max's arguments,[59] he nevertheless uses Max's urban sociology to come to terms with his actions. As Bigger tells Max at the close of their interview, he "hurt folks 'cause I felt I had to; that's all. They was crowding me too close."[60] He then reiterates this observation, saying that white society "wouldn't let me live and I killed."[61] While critics are right to point to Max's personal failure to connect with Bigger, then, they should not reject the legal praxis that Max creates simply because the lawyer cannot fully connect theory to reality. Though ultimately a flawed individual, Max creates a pragmatic defense grounded in contemporary legal theory that offers the best way to achieve a measure of social justice for Bigger Thomas.

Notes

1. Clifton Fadiman, reviewing the novel in *The New Republic* (18 March 1940), praises Max's closing arguments for helping readers understand the social import of Bigger's actions. Barbara Foley, in "Race and Class in Radical African-American Fiction of the Depression Years" (*Nature, Society, and Thought* 3.3 [1990]: pp. 305–324), argues that Max's speech does important rhetorical work by allowing readers to understand the social forces that lead Bigger to commit his crime. John M. Reilly's "Giving Bigger a Voice: The Politics of Narrative in *Native Son*" (Keneth Kinnamon, ed., *New Essays on* Native Son [New York: Cambridge University Press, 1990] praises Max's speech because it is an "articulation of Bigger's accurate story" (58). R.B.V. Larsen's "The Four Voices of Richard Wright's *Native Son*" (*Negro American Literature Forum* 6.4 [1972]: pp. 105–109) argues that "the long courtroom speech of Max is a measured and substantial critique of the position of blacks in America" (108).

2. In "Spectacle and Event in *Native Son*" (*American Literature* 70.4 [1998]: pp. 767–798), Jonathan Elmer claims that Max's "powerfully cogent and entirely futile" arguments are "an expression of the racial impasse it denounces" (791–792). Michael Berube's "Max, Media, and Mimesis: Bigger's Representation in *Native Son*," (*Approaches to Teaching Wright's "Native Son"* [New York: Modern Language Association, 1997]) sees in the labor lawyer a sympathetic white man who nevertheless "doesn't quite understand the widespread racial unrest of which he speaks" (113). Lale Demiturk's "Mastering the Master's Tongue: Bigger as Oppressor in Richard Wright's *Native Son*" (*Mississippi Quarterly* 50.2 [1997]: pp. 267–276) finds Max "humane but blind to the degree to which white proscriptions" influence Bigger's life (273). Craig Werner's "Bigger's Blues: *Native Son* and the Articulation of Afro-American Modernism" (Keneth Kinnamon, ed., *New Essays on* Native Son, [New York: Cambridge University Press, 1990] posits that an

excessive commitment to Marxism makes Max show "little sense of the complexity of Bigger's consciousness" (38). Caesar R. Blake's "On Richard Wright's *Native Son*" (M.L. Friedland, ed., *Rough Justice: Essays on Crime in Literature* [Toronto: Toronto University Press, 1991] also faults the putatively Communist lawyer and his "lengthy and doctrinaire speech" (192).

3. In "Invented by Horror: The Gothic and African American Literary Ideology in *Native Son*" (*African American Review* 35.1 [2001]: pp. 29–40), James Smethurst sees Max's 'Leninist' ideology as useful because it inspires Bigger to understand his world. In "From No-Man's Land to Mother-Land: Emasculation and Nationalism in Richard Wright's Depression Era Urban Novels" (*African American Review* 33.3 [1999]: pp. 451–466), Anthony Dawahare finds more to admire in the lawyer's character than ideological commitments when he suggests that the "nurturing Max teaches Bigger how to think about his feelings and actions" and "the hard lesson of the reality principle concerning the slow process of social change" (463). In Joko Sengova's "Native Identity and Alienation in Richard Wright's *Native Son* and Chinua Achebe's *Things Fall Apart*" (*Mississippi Quarterly* 50.2 [1997]: pp. 327–351), Max is seen as leading Bigger "on a path of self-vindication" (336), and in Joseph A. Brown's "I, John, Saw the Holy Number: Apocalyptic Visions in *Go Tell It on the Mountain* and *Native Son*" (*Religion and Literature* 27.1 [1995]: pp. 53–74), Max's humane treatment allows Bigger to understand the horror of his crime. In James A. Miller's "Bigger Thomas' Quest for Voice and Audience in Richard Wright's *Native Son*" (*Callaloo* 28 [1986]: pp. 501–506), Max becomes "an intermediary between Bigger Thomas and the white world" (504).

4. Malcom Cowley's review of the novel (cited in *Richard Wright: Critical Perspectives Past and Present*, edited by Henry Louis Gates and K. A. Appiah [New York: Amistad, 1993]: p. 10) posits that, while Max's summation persuasively describes the plight of "American Negroes in general," it does not work as a defense of Bigger. In *The Courtroom as Forum: Homicide Trials by Dreiser, Wright, Capote, and Mailer* (New York: Peter Lang, 1996), Ann M. Algeo notes that "as a defense attorney, Max is ineffective" while dismissively granting that he is "the perfect lawyer to support Wright's thematic agenda" (56). In "*Native Son*'s Guilty Man," (*CEA Critic* 54. 2 [1992]), Hilary Holladay portrays Max as a self-confessed "ideologue" more interested in defending the interests of the Party than in saving Bigger's life (30). Kalu Ogbaa's "Protest and the Individual Talents of Three Black Novelists" (*College Language Association Journal* 35.2 [1991]: pp. 159–184) dismisses Max as a clumsy representative of the communist party.

5. In "Slouching Toward Beastliness: Richard Wright's Anatomy of Thomas Dixon" (*African American Review* 35.3 [2001]: pp. 439–458), Clare Eby remarks on Max's "reasoned eloquence" that cannot prevail in an atmosphere of legal lynching (449). Similarly, Stephen Corey's "The Avengers in *Light in August* and *Native Son*" (*College Language Association Journal* 23 [1979]: pp. 200–212) argues that Max gives a "marvelous" argument in a futile case (208).

6. Richard Wright, *Black Boy* (1944; reprint, with introduction by Jerry W. Ward, Jr., and notes by Arnold Rampersad [New York: HarperCollins, 1993]) pp. 435, 422.

7. Ibid., p. 451.

8. Ibid., p. 402.

9. Paul N. Siegel's "The Conclusion of Richard Wright's *Native Son*" (*PMLA* 89 [1974]: pp. 517–523) documents that Max does not call himself a Communist,

nor does Wright's narrator call Max a Communist. Instead, as Siegel says, Max is called a communist only "by the red-baiting prosecuting attorney and newspapers" (517). Siegal's essay also notes that Max does not self-identify as a Communist when he logically should, if he were a member of the party:

> When he tells Bigger that others besides blacks are hated, he says (p. 402), "They hate trade unions. They hate folks who try to organize. They hate Jan."— not "Communists like me and Jan." Later he says, "I'm a Jew and they hate me" (p. 416)—not "I'm a Communist and a Jew and they hate me." (518)

In the original, Siegel's page numbers refer to the bowdlerized 1940 edition of *Native Son*. I have compared Siegel's quotations with Rampersad's more authoritative edition and used page numbers from Rampersad's edition. Dorothy S. Redden's "Richard Wright and *Native Son*: Not Guilty" (*Black American Literature Forum* 10.4 [1976]: pp. 111–116) seconds Siegel's observation by noting that Max "does not employ the orthodox phraseology, nor does he dwell on anything which might not also be noticed by any reasonably sensitive observer" of society (112).

10. Richard Wright, *Native Son* (1940; reprint, with introduction and notes by Arnold Rampersad (New York: HarperCollins, 1993), p. 335.

11. Generally speaking, there was no place for lawyers in the society the American Communists hoped to create in the 1930s and 40s. In the November 1935 article "Professionals in a Soviet America" (Bernard K. Johnpoll, ed., *Unite and Fight*, vol. 3 of *A Documentary History of the Communist Party of the United States* [Westport, Connecticut: Greenwood, 1994]), American Communist party member Edward Magnus wrote that lawyers "will be liquidated along with the bourgeoisie" when the party establishes a Soviet America. Yet lawyers were valuable nevertheless since they were "the group which can do the most to help the worker's cause right now, by defending them against the injustice of the capitalist courts" (824–825). This perception of the eventual uselessness of the bar finds further support in the lack of a formal Communist or Marxist jurisprudence. Instead of employing their own science or philosophy of law, most Marxists critiqued existing laws since those laws merely reflected the capitalist ideology that produced them. This theoretical position reflects Marx's view of the law in civil society as merely one of many bourgeois constructs that arise from the need to describe actual material conditions. As Marx argues in *The German Ideology* (*The Marx-Engles Reader*, ed. Robert C. Tucker. New York: Norton, 1972), "[c]onceiving, thinking, the mental intercourse of men [are] a direct efflux of their material behavior. The same applies to mental production as expressed in the language of politics, laws, morality, religion, metaphysics, etc., of a people" (118). Thus, bourgeois jurisprudence simply reflects the mode of production and, while problematic, is therefore a site for intervention.

12. Charles Martin, "The International Labor Defense and Black America," *Labor History* 26.2 (1985): pp. 167–168.

13. Charles Martin, "Communists and Blacks: The ILD and the Angelo Herndon Case," *Journal of Negro History* 64.2 (1979): p. 133.

14. Martin, "International," p. 171.

15. Charles Martin, "Oklahoma's 'Scottsboro' Affair: The Jess Hollins Rape Case, 1931–1936," *South Atlantic Quarterly* 79.2 (1980): p. 178.

16. Martin, "International," p. 180.

17. Addison Gayle, *Richard Wright: Ordeal of a* Native Son (New York: Anchor Press, 1980), p. 75.

18. Michel Fabre, *The Unfinished Quest of Richard Wright*, trans. Isabel Barzun (New York: William Morrow, 1973), p. 107.

19. Ibid. Though Wright used aliases, he describes much of the incident in *Black Boy*.

20. *Native Son*, pp. 494–495.

21. Victor Rabinowitz, "The National Lawyer's Guild: Thomas Emerson and the Struggle for Survival," *Case Western Reserve Law Review* 38 (1988): p. 609.

22. Qtd. in Rabinowitz, "National Lawyer's Guild," p. 616.

23. Maurice Sugar, "The Birth of the Guild," *The National Lawyers Guild: From Roosevelt Through Reagan*, ed. Ann Fagin Ginger and Eugene M Tobin, (Philadelphia: Temple University Press, 1988): pp. 6–7.

24. Raymond A. Belliotti, "Marxist Jurisprudence: Historical Necessity and Radical Contingency," in *Radical Philosophy of Law: Contemporary Challenges to Mainstream Legal Theory*, ed. David S. Caudill and Steven Jay Gold (Atlantic Highlands, New Jersey: Humanities Press, 1995), notes the similarities between Legal Realism and Marxism.

25. Morton White, *Social Thought in America: The Revolt Against Formalism* (1947; reprint, New York: Oxford University Press, 1976). See also Brian Z. Tamanaha, "Pragmatism in US Legal Theory: Its Application to Normative Jurisprudence, Sociolegal Studies, and the Fact-Value Distinction," *The American Journal of Jurisprudence* 41 (1996): pp. 315–355.

26. Oliver Wendell Holmes, *The Common Law* (Boston: Little, Brown, 1881), p. 35.

27. For further discussion, see Gary Minda, "One Hundred Years of Modern Legal Thought: From Langdell and Holmes to Posner and Schlag," *Indiana Law Review* 28 (1995): pp. 353–390.

28. Roscoe Pound, "Mechanical Jurisprudence," *Columbia Law Review* 8 (1908): p. 622.

29. Ibid., p. 610.

30. Roscoe Pound, "The Need of a Sociological Jurisprudence," *Green Bag* 19 (1907): p. 607.

31. Andrew L. Kaufman, in his biography *Cardozo* (Cambridge: Harvard University Press, 1998), notes that the Justice argued that "the method of sociology made the ultimate test of a rule its value for society" (208) when delivering the Storrs Lectures at Yale Law School in 1920. Richard Polenberg, however, asserts in *The World of Benjamin Cardozo: Personal Values and the Judicial Process* (Cambridge: Harvard University Press, 1997) that Cardozo did not push his conclusions as far as Holmes or Pound, drawing back from the "dizzying precipice" of an overly activist judiciary (248).

32. For more detailed discussions of the similarities between sociologic jurisprudence and legal realism, see Tamanaha, "Pragmatism," p. 318; Dragan Milovanovic, *A Primer in the Sociology of Law* (Albany, New York: Harrow and Heston, 1988), p. 93; and Marianne Constable, "Genealogy and Jurisprudence: Nietzsche, Nihilism, and the Social Stratification of Law," *Law and Social Inquiry* 19 (1994): pp. 1551–1638.

33. For a detailed discussion of the demise of Legal Realism, see Milovanovic, *Primer*, p. 95.

34. Since legal scholars have not clearly differentiated between Sociological Jurisprudence and Legal Realism, this essay will employ the terms interchangeably for stylistic purposes.

35. *Black Boy*, p. 327.

36. For a discussion of Wright's intellectual interaction with Wirth and Cayton, see Keneth Kinnamon, *The Emergence of Richard Wright: A Study in Literature and Society* (Urbana: Illinois University Press, 1972), p. 121, and Robert Bone, "Richard Wright and the Chicago Renaissance," *Callaloo* 28 (1986): pp. 446–468.

37. Horace R. Cayton, rev. of *Twelve Million Black Voices*, *Pittsburgh Courier*, 15 November 1941.

38. Louis Wirth, "Urbanism as a Way of Life," *The American Journal of Sociology* 44 (1938): pp. 1–24, esp. 11, 13, and 15.

39. Ibid., p. 24.

40. *Native Son*, p. 475.

41. Ibid., p. 476.

42. Ibid., p. 446.

43. Ibid., pp. 435–436.

44. Ibid., pp. 444–445.

45. Ibid., p. 415.

46. Roscoe Pound, *Social Control Through Law*, Powell Lectures on Philosophy at Indiana University 6 (New Haven: Yale University Press, 1942), p. 111.

47. Ibid., pp. 53–54.

48. *Native Son*, p. 451.

49. *Social Control*, p. 78.

50. *Native Son*, p. 463.

51. *Social Control*, p. 65.

52. *Native Son*, p. 472.

53. Ibid., p. 461.

54. *Social Control*, p. 81.

55. *Native Son*, p. 455.

56. "Oklahoma," p. 187.

57. *Native Son*, pp. 494–495.

58. Ibid., p. 493.

59. Ibid., pp. 488–489.

60. Ibid., p. 496.

61. Ibid., p. 500.

Chronology

1908	Richard Wright born to Ella and Nathan Wright on a farm outside Natchez, Mississippi.
1914	Nathan Wright deserts the family.
1916–1925	Attends, with interruptions, public and Seventh-Day Adventist schools.
1924	Publishes "The Voodoo of Hell's Half-Acre" in the black *Southern Register.*
1925	Graduates as valedictorian from Smith-Robinson Public School; moves to Memphis.
1927–1936	Works as a postal clerk in Chicago, where he becomes an active writer for leftist publications. He joins the John Reed Club and the Communist Party USA.
1937	Becomes Harlem editor of *Daily Worker.*
1938	*Uncle Tom's Children,* a collection of short stories, published.
1939	Receives Guggenheim Fellowship. Marries Dhimah Rose Meadman.
1940	Publishes *Native Son:* Wright and Dhima are divorced.

1941	Marries Ellen Poplar. Works with Paul Green toward a stage version of *Native Son. Twelve Million Black Voices* published.
1942	Julia Wright born.
1945	Publishes *Black Boy.* Meets James Baldwin.
1946	Visits France.
1947	Moves to France, his home for the rest of his life.
1949	Rachel Wright born.
1949–1950	Stays in Argentina, filming *Native Son.* Wright himself appears as Bigger.
1953	*The Outsiders* published. Visits the Gold Coast (now Ghana).
1954	*Black Power* and *Savage Holiday* published. Visits Spain.
1955	Attends the Bandung Conference in Indonesia.
1956	*The Color Curtain: A Report on the Bandung Conference* and *Pagan Spain* published.
1957	*White Man, Listen!* published.
1958	*The Long Dream,* to be the first of a trilogy, published.
1959	Dies suddenly of heart failure during a hospital stay for an unrelated complaint. At the time of his death Wright was selecting the best of some thousands of his haiku for publication.

Contributors

HAROLD BLOOM is Sterling Professor of the Humanities at Yale University. He is the author of 30 books, including *Shelley's Mythmaking* (1959), *The Visionary Company* (1961), *Blake's Apocalypse* (1963), *Yeats* (1970), *A Map of Misreading* (1975), *Kabbalah and Criticism* (1975), *Agon: Toward a Theory of Revisionism* (1982), *The American Religion* (1992), *The Western Canon* (1994), and *Omens of Millennium: The Gnosis of Angels, Dreams, and Resurrection* (1996). *The Anxiety of Influence* (1973) sets forth Professor Bloom's provocative theory of the literary relationships between the great writers and their predecessors. His most recent books include *Shakespeare: The Invention of the Human* (1998), a 1998 National Book Award finalist, *How to Read and Why* (2000), *Genius: A Mosaic of One Hundred Exemplary Creative Minds* (2002), *Hamlet: Poem Unlimited* (2003), *Where Shall Wisdom Be Found?* (2004), and *Jesus and Yahweh: The Names Divine* (2005). In 1999, Professor Bloom received the prestigious American Academy of Arts and Letters Gold Medal for Criticism. He has also received the International Prize of Catalonia, the Alfonso Reyes Prize of Mexico, and the Hans Christian Andersen Bicentennial Prize of Denmark.

KATHLEEN GALLAGHER is associate professor and Canada Research Chair in Urban School Research in Pedagogy and Policy in the Department of Curriculum, Teaching and Learning at the Ontario Institute for Studies in Education of the University of Toronto. She wrote *How Theatre Educates: Convergences and Counterpoints with Artists, Scholars and Advocates* (2003).

TONY MAGISTRALE is a professor of English at the University of Vermont. He wrote *Abject Terrors: Surveying the Modern and Postmodern Horror* (2005).

ALAN W. FRANCE was professor of English at West Chester University of Pennsylvania. With Karen Fitts he edited *Left Margins: Cultural Studies and Composition Pedagogy* (1995).

KIMBERLY W. BENSTON is the William R. Kennan, Jr., Professor of English at Haverford College. She wrote *Performing Blackness: Enactments of African-American Modernism* (2000).

ALESSANDRO PORTELLI is a professor of American Literature at the University of Rome. He wrote *The Battle of Valle Giulia: Oral History and the Art of Dialogue* (1997).

LALE DEMITURK is associate professor of American Culture and Literature at Bilkent University. She has published various articles on twentieth-century American novels and especially on Richard Wright.

DESMOND HARDING is an assistant professor of English at Central Michigan University. He wrote *Writing the City: Urban Visions & Literary Modernism* (2003).

DAMON MARCEL DeCOSTE is an associate professor of English at the University of Regina.

JONATHAN ELMER is an associate professor of English at Indiana University, Bloomington. He wrote *Reading at the Social Limit: Affect, Mass Culture, and Edgar Allan Poe* (1995).

HAZEL ROWLEY is an independent scholar living in New York City. She wrote *Tête-à-Tête: The Tumultous Lives & Loves of Simone de Beauvoir and Jean-Paul Sartre* (2005).

MARK DECKER is an assistant professor of English at The University of Wisconsin-Stout.

Bibliography

Adams, Timothy Dow. *Telling Lies in Modern American Autobiography*. Chapel Hill: University of North Carolina Press, 1990.

Algeo, Ann M. *The Courtroom as Forum: Homicide Trials by Dreiser, Wright, Capote, and Mailer. Modern American Literature: New Approaches 1*. New York: Peter Lang, 1996.

Avery, Evelyn Gross. *Rebels and Victims: The Fiction of Richard Wright and Bernard Malamud*. Port Washington, New York: Kennikat, 1979.

Bakish, David. *Richard Wright. Modern Literature Monographs*. New York: Ungar, 1973.

Bell, Michael Davitt. *Culture, Genre, and Literary Vocation: Selected Essays on American Literature*. Chicago, Illinois: University of Chicago Press, 2001.

Berry, Faith. *Pagan Spain*. Jackson, Mississippi: University Press of Mississippi, 2002.

Bone, Robert A. *Richard Wright*. University of Minnesota Pamphlets on American Writers 74. Minneapolis: University of Minnesota Press, 1969.

Brignano, Russell C. *Richard Wright: An Introduction to the Man and His Works*. Pittsburgh: University of Pittsburgh Press, 1970.

Cappetti, Carla. *Writing Chicago: Modernism, Ethnography, and the Novel. The Social Foundations of Aesthetic Forms*. New York: Columbia University Press, 1993.

Davis, Charles T.; Fabre, Michel. *Richard Wright: A Primary Bibliography*. Boston: Hall, 1982.

Fabre, Michel. *Richard Wright: Books & Writers*. Jackson: University Press of Mississippi, 1990.

————, and Barzun, Isabel. *The Unfinished Quest of Richard Wright*. New York: William Morrow, 1973.

Felgar, Robert. *Student Companion to Richard Wright*. *Student Companions to Classic Writers*. Westport, Connecticut: Greenwood, 2000.

Felgar, Robert. *Richard Wright*. Twayne's United States Authors Series 386. Boston: Twayne, 1980.

Fishburn, Katherine. *Richard Wright's Hero: The Faces of a Rebel-Victim*. Metuchen, New Jersey: Scarecrow, 1977.

Franzbecker, Rolf; Bruck, Peter; Real, Willi. *Der moderne Roman des amerikanischen Negers: Richard Wright, Ralph Ellison, James Baldwin*. Ertrage der Forschung 108. Darmstadt: Wissenschaftliche, 1979.

Gibson, Donald B. *Five Black Writers: Essays on Wright, Ellison, Baldwin, Hughes, and LeRoi Jones*. New York: New York University Press, 1970.

Gysin, Fritz. *The Grotesque in American Negro Fiction: Jean Toomer, Richard Wright, and Ralph Ellison*. Cooper Monographs on English and American Language and Literature 22. Bern: Francke, 1975.

JanMohamed, Abdul R. *The Death-Bound-Subject: Richard Wright's Archaeology of Death*. *Post-Contemporary Interventions*. Durham, North Carolina: Duke University Press, 2005.

Joyce, Joyce Ann. *Richard Wright's Art of Tragedy*. Iowa City: University of Iowa Press, 1986.

Kinnamon, Keneth; Benson, Joseph; Fabre, Michel; Werner, Craig. *A Richard Wright Bibliography: Fifty Years of Criticism and Commentary, 1933-1982*. Bibliogs. & Indexes in Afro-Amer. & Afr. Studies 19. Westport, Connecticut: Greenwood, 1988.

————. *The Emergence of Richard Wright: A Study in Literature and Society*. Urbana: University of Illinois P., 1972.

Knipp, Thomas, ed. & introd. *Richard Wright: Letters to Joe C. Brown*. Kent: Kent State University Library Occasional Papers, 1968.

Kostelanetz, Richard. *Politics in the African-American Novel: James Weldon Johnson, W. E. B. Du Bois, Richard Wright, and Ralph Ellison*. Contributions in Afro-American & African Studies 143. New York: Greenwood, 1991.

Lackey, Michael. *African American Atheists and Political Liberation: A Study of the Sociocultural Dynamics of Faith*. History of African American Religions. Gainesville, Florida: University Press of Florida, 2007.

Lamming, George; Wright, Richard. *In the Castle of My Skin*. New York: Collier, 1970.

Lynch, Michael F. *Creative Revolt: A Study of Wright, Ellison, and Dostoevsky*. American University Studies XXIV: American Literature 12. New York: Peter Lang, 1990.

Margolies, Edward; Moore, Harry T., pref. *The Art of Richard Wright*. Crosscurrents: Modern Critiques. Carbondale: Southern Illinois University Press, 1969.

McCall, Dan. *The Example of Richard Wright*. New York: Harcourt, Brace & World, 1969.

Miller, Eugene E. *Voice of a Native Son: The Poetics of Richard Wright*. Jackson: University Press of Mississippi, 1990.

Ouchi, Giichi; Suzuki, Mikio. *Richard Wright no Sekai*. Tokyo: Hyoronsha, 1981.

Rajiv, Sudhi, Dr. *Forms of Black Consciousness*. New York: Advent, 1992.

Rampersad, Arnold. *Later Works: Black Boy (American Hunger), The Outsider*. Library of America 56. New York, New York: Library of America, 1991.

———. *Early Works: Lawd Today!; Uncle Tom's Children; Native Son*. Library of America 55. New York, New York: Library of America, 1991.

Ray, David; Farnsworth, Robert M.; Davis, Charles T. *Richard Wright: Impressions and Perspectives*. Ann Arbor: University of Michigan Press, 1973.

Reid-Pharr, Robert. *Once You Go Black: Choice, Desire, and the Black American Intellectual. Sexual Cultures: New Directions from the Center for Lesbian and Gay Studies*. New York, New York: New York University Press, 2007.

Reilly, John M. *Richard Wright: The Critical Reception*. American Critical Tradition 6. New York: Franklin, 1978.

Relyea, Sarah. *Outsider Citizens: The Remaking of Postwar Identity in Wright, Beauvoir, and Baldwin. Literary Criticism and Cultural Theory: The Interaction of Text and Society*. New York, New York: Routledge, 2006.

Rowley, Hazel. *Richard Wright: The Life and Times*. Chicago, Illinois: University of Chicago Press, 2001.

Schmidt, Klaus. *'The Outsider's Vision': Die Marginalitätsthematik in ausgewählten Prosatexten der afro-amerikanischen Erzähltradition: Richard Wright's Native Son, Toni Morrison's Sula und John Edgar Wideman's Reuben. Mainzer Studien zur Amerikanistik 28*. Frankfurt: Peter Lang, 1993.

Stepto, Robert B. *From behind the Veil: A Study of Afro-American Narrative*. Urbana: University of Illinois P, 1979.

Van Antwerp, Margaret A. *Dictionary of Literary Biography: Documentary Series: An Illustrated Chronicle*, Volume 1. Detroit: Gale, 1982.

Warnes, Andrew. *Hunger Overcome?: Food and Resistance in Twentieth-Century African American Literature*. Athens, Georgia: University of Georgia Press, 2004.

Webb, Constance. *Richard Wright: A Biography*. New York: Putnam, 1968.

Weiss, M. Lynn. *Gertrude Stein and Richard Wright: The Poetics and Politics of Modernism*. Jackson, Mississippi: University Press of Mississippi, 1998.

Williams, John A. *The Most Native of Sons: A Biography of Richard Wright*. Garden City, New York: Doubleday, 1970.

Wright, Richard. *Native Son*. New York, New York: Harper, 1957.

Acknowledgments

Gallagher, Kathleen. "Bigger's Great Leap to the Figurative." *College Language Association Journal*, Volume 27, Number 3 (March 1984): 293–314. © 1984 College Language Association. Reprinted by permission of the publisher.

Magistrale, Tony, "Petersburg to Chicago: Wright's *Crime and Punishment.*" *Comparative Literature Studies*, Volume 23, Number 1, Spring 1986. Copyright © 1986 by The Pennsylvania State University. Reproduced by permission of the publisher.

France, Alan W. "Misogyny and Appropriation in Wright's *Native Son.*" *Modern Fiction Studies*, Volume 34, Number 3 (1988): 413–423. © Purdue Research Foundation. Reprinted with permission of The Johns Hopkins University Press.

Benston, Kimberly W. "The Veil of Black: (Un)Masking the Subject of African-American Modernism's 'Native Son.'" *Human Studies: A Journal for Philosophy and the Social Sciences*, Volume 16, Numbers 1–2 (April 1993): 69–99. © 1993 Springer Publishing. Reprinted by permission of the copyright holder.

Portelli, Alessandro. "Everybody's Healing Novel: *Native Son* and Its Contemporary Critical Context." *Mississippi Quarterly: The Journal of Southern Cultures*, Volume 50, Number 2 (Spring 1997): 255–265. © 1999 Mississippi Quarterly. Reprinted by permission.

Demiturk, Lale. "Mastering the Master's Tongue: Bigger as Oppressor in Richard Wright's *Native Son.*" *Mississippi Quarterly: The Journal of Southern Cultures,* Volume 50, Number 2 (Spring 1997): 267–276. © 1999 Mississippi Quarterly. Reprinted by permission.

Harding, Desmond. "The Power of Place: Richard Wright's *Native Son.*" *College Language Association Journal,* Volume 40, Number 3 (March 1997): pp. 367–379. © 1997 College Language Association. Reprinted by permission of the publisher.

DeCoste, Damon Marcel. "To Blot It All Out: The Politics of Realism in Richard Wright's *Native Son.*" *Style,* Volume 32, Number 1 (Spring 1998): 127–147. © 1998 *Style Journal,* Northern Illinois University. Reprinted by permission.

Elmer, Jonathan. "Spectacle and Event in *Native Son.*" *American Literature,* Volume 70, Number 4 (December 1998): pp. 767–798. Copyright, 1998, Duke University Press. All rights reserved. Used by permission of the publisher.

Rowley, Hazel. "Backstage and Onstage: The Drama of *Native Son.*" *Mississippi Quarterly: The Journal of Southern Cultures,* Volume 52, Number 2 (Spring 1999): 215–237. © 1999 Mississippi Quarterly. Reprinted by permission.

Decker, Mark. "'A Lot Depends on What Judge We Have': *Native Son* and the Legal Means for Social Justice." *McNeese Review,* Volume 41 (2003): 52–75. © McNeese Review. Reprinted by permission.

Index